Manhood and the Duel

EARLY MODERN CULTURAL SERIES

Ivo Kamps, Series Editor

PUBLISHED BY PALGRAVE MACMILLAN

Idols of the Marketplace: Idolatry and Commodity Fetishism in English Literature, 1580 – 1680
   by David Hawkes

Shakespeare among the Animals: Nature and Society in the Drama of Early Modern England
   by Bruce Boehrer

Burning Women: Widows, Witches, and Early Modern European Travelers in India
   by Pompa Banerjee

Manhood and the Duel: Masculinity in Early Modern Drama and Culture

Jennifer Low

MANHOOD AND THE DUEL
© Jennifer Low, 2003

All rights reserved. No part of this book may be used or reproduced in any manner whatsoever without written permission except in the case of brief quotations embodied in critical articles or reviews.

First published 2003 by
PALGRAVE MACMILLAN™
175 Fifth Avenue, New York, N.Y. 10010 and
Houndmills, Basingstoke, Hampshire, England RG21 6XS
Companies and representatives throughout the world.

PALGRAVE MACMILLAN is the global academic imprint of the Palgrave Macmillan division of St. Martin's Press, LLC and of Palgrave Macmillan Ltd. Macmillan® is a registered trademark in the United States, United Kingdom and other countries. Palgrave is a registered trademark in the European Union and other countries.

ISBN 1-4039-6130-1 hardback

Library of Congress Cataloging-in-Publication Data
Low, Jennifer A., 1962–
   Manhood and the duel: masculinity in early modern drama and culture / by Jennifer A. Low.
     p. cm.—(Early modern cultural studies)
   Includes bibliographical references and index.
   ISBN 1-40396-130-1
     1. English drama—Early modern and Elizabethan, 1500–1600—History and criticism. 2. Dueling in literature. 3. English drama—17th century—History and critism. 4. Dueling—England—History—16th century. 5. Dueling England—History—17th century. 6. Masculinity in literature. 7. Men in literature. I. Title. II. Series.

PR658.D84 L69 2003
822'.309355—dc21   2002072831

A catalogue record for this book is available from the British Library.

Design by Newgen Imaging Systems (P) Ltd., Chennai, India.

First edition: January, 2003
10 9 8 7 6 5 4 3 2 1

Printed in the United States of America.

Contents

Permissions vi
Series Editor's Foreword vii
List of Illustrations x
A Note on Texts xi
Dedication xiii
Acknowledgments xv

Introduction 1
1 The Duellist as Hero 11
2 The Art of Fence and the Sense of Masculine Space 41
3 Sexual Status and the Combat 71
4 Misperceiving Masculinity, Misreading the Duel 93
5 When Women Fight 135
Conclusion 169

Notes 171
Bibliography 213
Index 231

PERMISSIONS

Extracts from *Swetnam The Woman-Hater: The Controversy and The Play*
© 1969 Purdue University Press/Reprinted by Permission.
Unauthorized duplication not permitted.

Extracts from the Nottingham Drama Texts edition of Beaumont and
Fletcher's *Love's Cure* (1992), edited by Marea Mitchell. By permission
of Nottingham Drama Texts.

Excerpts reprinted from *A FAIR QUARREL* by Thomas Midleton and
William Rowley, edited by George R. Price, by permission of the
University of Nebraska Press. Copyright © 1976 by the University of
Nebraska Press.

A portion of this work originally appeared in *Centennial Review*, Vol. 43,
No. 3, 19[ ], published by Michigan State University Press.

Excerpts by permission of *Comparative Drama*.

Engraving "Man Holding a Sword" from Lo schermo: nel quale si discorre
intorno al'eccellenza dellarmi, & delle lettere by Angelo Viggiani, 1575.
Reference (shelfmark) Douce V 213. Courtesy of Bodleian Library,
University of Oxford.

Saviolo, Vincentio, *Vincentio Saviolo his Practise*. London, 1595. Leaf 16 r,
woodcut only. This item is reproduced by permission of The
Huntington Library, San Marino, California.

G. F., *Duell-Ease. London*, 1635. Title page. This item is reproduced by
permission of The Huntington Library, San Marino, California.

Excerpts reprinted from Evans, G. Blackmore (Editor), *The Riverside
Shakespeare*. Copyright © 1974 by Houghton Mifflin Company. Used
with permission.

Series Editor's Foreword

It is one of the defining insights of historical criticism of the last two decades that the literary text and history (or culture) stand in what Louis Montrose called a "reciprocal relationship." The insight has been routinely associated with new historicism or cultural poetics, but it seems to animate virtually all types of historical scholarship today. And rightly so, because the recognition of reciprocity has liberated us from a kind of hierarchical thinking that made us privilege one over the other: history over literature or literature over history. What is more, it allows us to see that one does not merely determine the other, but rather, that each influences, shapes, contends with the other in ways that do not conform to any single or generic formula of interaction. Hence, the study of literary artifact in their cultural context becomes a study of the particular and, often, of the unique. All the titles in the Early Modern Cultural Studies series have embraced this "reciprocal relationship" between literature and culture to one degree or another, and Jennifer Low's *Manhood and the Duel: Masculinity in Early Modern Drama and Culture* is no exception.

Under ideal circumstances, a duel was a violent but formalized encounter between two gentlemen that, again, ideally, was believed to clarify a number of important issues. In the context of trial by combat, it clarified who was on the side of God and truth and who was not. It could also reveal who was loyal to the crown and who had betrayed his monarch. In the context of the extralegal duel, it ideally confirmed who was "gentle" because commoners were not allowed to participate in the practice. It bestowed much-coveted honor on some, and it withheld that honor from others. Partly because it required a certain amount of bravery, it also figured into definitions of masculinity. In short, the duel played an active and constructive role in upholding and validating the social as well as the cosmic order of the early modern world. But things are of course rarely ideal. What happens to God's justice in trial by combat, for instance, in Shakespeare's *Richard II* when both participants, Bolingbroke and Mowbray, have engaged in illicit dealings? Or what happens to ideas of honor and courage when Sir John Falstaff pronounces discretion the better part of valor, or when the king's substitutes march about the battlefield shielding the real king from harm? Or what happens to the duel's role in definitions of masculinity when *Twelfth Night*'s Viola, disguised as Cesario, is forced to engage in a duel with the silly Sir Andrew Aguecheek, or when Middleton's roaring girl dons breeches and sword and exposes weak and effeminate males such as Laxton? It is in these and many other instances that Jennifer Low finds the rich and highly complex meaning of the duel in early modern England.

Setting out to examine an "old" subject and renew our understanding of it in light of new theoretical, social, and political concerns, Jennifer Low puts into play a variety of texts—fencing manuals, courtesy books, antiduelling tracts, proclamations, and stage plays—to show us just how deeply the practice of duelling, and people's feelings about that practice, were embedded in early modern English culture. She shows duelling to be simultaneously a reflection of gender roles and class distinctions as well as a practice that defines and transgresses those roles and distinctions. As such, duelling turns out to be not merely a way to settle disputes or gain honor but an activity indispensable to the shaping of manhood. Although aristocratic men generally viewed nobility and masculinity as prerequisites for engaging in a duel, Low argues that aristocratic men as a group had only a vague sense of masculinity as something *inherent* in their identity. Masculinity, for them, more typically was something that could be derived from brave meritorious *behavior* in a variety of activities including the duel. Low therefore draws on Judith Butler's idea of gender as a performative act which, while lacking an identity or meaning of its own, nonetheless constitutes a (masculine) reality. Such things as the duellist's body language and the assumptions about spatial divisions in fencing, together with other shapers of ideas of masculinity such as family, state, church, and so forth, engaged with standard conventions of the drama such as staged combat, cross-dressed heroines, and mimetic representations of verbal power.

But just as texts like Castiglione's *Book of the Courtier* had the unintended consequence of giving social aspirants a wealth of guidance on how to imitate and impersonate their social "betters," so the celebrated practice of duelling was represented and reinterpreted by playwrights on the public stage. As the practice of duelling spread, it acquired a broad range of meanings, some of which were negative. She reveals, for instance, that stage plays that catered to the proto-bourgeois "middling sort" generally viewed the aristocratic duel with suspicion, criticized the practice, and represented it on the stage in ways that compelled a rethinking of concepts of masculinity. In Low's *Manhood and the Duel,* the duel becomes a kind of microcosm of the early modern world in transition, finding in the appropriations, representations, and adaptations of this once narrowly-defined practice a highly compressed account of the evolution of gender roles and class distinctions.

Ivo Kamps

List of Illustrations

Figure 2.1   Illustration from Viggiani's Italian fencing manual. 43
Figure 2.2   Woodcut from *Vincentio Saviolo, his Practise* (London: 1595). 52
Figure 4.1   Frontispiece of *Duell-Ease* [detail] (London: 1633). 104

A Note on Texts

Most original spellings have been preserved, but I have expanded occasional contractions and modernized i/j and u/v.

For Richard Low, Stephanie Low, and Barbara Bonn

Acknowledgments

From inception to completion, this book has benefited from many generous godparents, and it gives me great pleasure to thank them.
 I want to begin by acknowledging those who helped bring the first version of this book to birth: J. Daniel Kinney and Katharine Eisaman Maus, who read each chapter of my dissertation repeatedly. Both Dan and Katharine have continued to nurture me in numerous ways; their support has greatly contributed to my intellectual growth. Thanks are also due to other professors at the University of Virginia, including Stephen D. Arata, Mark Wright Edmundson, and Martin J. Havran. David Scott Kastan and James V. Mirollo helped make Columbia University a home away from home at a critical time, aiding me in obtaining the use of an excellent library and membership in a valuable intellectual community that continues to support me today. Members of that community include Jean Howard, Edward Tayler, James Emmanuel Berg, Douglas A. Brooks, Pamela A. Brown, Ian Frederick Moulton, and Jill Niemczyk Smith.
 My life has been greatly enriched by intellectual friendships of the sort that makes eager readers into discriminating scholars. Most valuable of all has been the support of more senior scholars and their generous welcome into the academic community. Joan Ozark Holmer generously shared her knowledge of fencing and duelling. Linda Woodbridge was a marvelous reader of the manuscript; her global suggestions improved the entire shape of the book. Paul Yachnin's comments also illuminated dark areas of the manuscript; they helped substantially in reaching this final version. Jon Bloch helped me navigate my research in proxemics. I have also benefited from uncounted conversations with a number of people including Ursula Appelt, Alexandra G. Bennett, Mark Thornton Burnett, Anne Coldiron, Mary Thomas Crane, Kevin Gustafson, Nicholas Pullin, Marjorie Raley, Alan Shepard, Mihoko Suzuki, and Dan Vitkus. Longstanding friendships with Elizabeth Hollander, Lisa Berglund, Jim Berger,

Jennifer Klein, Jonathan Bumas, Martha Hollander, Dean Dietrich, Rita Gelb, Dave Stein, Jimmy Johnston, Mark Palius, Miriam Payne, and Jai R. Zion have helped me to sustain the determination necessary to finish this project. Finally, with many warm feelings, I acknowledge the enduring influence of Wayne Adamson, Jeremiah Evarts, Carol Farbar, Dorothy Pixley-Rothchild, Cornelia Reid, Stanley Rosenberg, and Hortense Tyroler.

This book could not have been written without library support. I wish to thank the staffs of Alderman Library at the University of Virginia, Butler Library at Columbia University, Wimberly Library at Florida Atlantic University, and The Folger Library. Certain people associated with these libraries deserve particular thanks: Bryson Clevenger at Alderman Library, Georgianna Ziegler and Lena Cowen Orlin at the Folger, William Clyde Armstrong III at Wimberly.

My colleagues at Florida Atlantic University have done all they could to support this endeavor. I am particularly grateful to William Covino, who instituted a policy of release time for junior faculty and enabled me to complete this manuscript. Teresa Brennan arranged a forum for me to present part of Chapter Two to the Faculty of Arts and Letters. Ben Lowe helped me to define this project and tracked down several sources for me. Michael Harrawood has been a wonderful sounding board for several parts of this work. Anna Hutcheson, who recently completed her M.A. at Florida Atlantic University, provided invaluable aid during the copyediting process; her humor made the task much more pleasant. Oliver Buckton, Tom Sheehan, Mark Scroggins, Johnny and Miriam Payne, and Jeff and Karen Galin have offered attention and encouragement. The community here has been the richer for their presence. I am fortunate in having had students like Roman Kazmin, David LoSchiavo, Laurie Tanner, and Anna Hutcheson, whose engagement with my ideas has stimulated my scholarly efforts. A more general thanks is owed to the students of Florida Atlantic University, who have been eager to learn about this project as it developed.

I have presented parts of this book to helpful readers and audiences at various forums. I thank the Group for Early Modern Studies for the opportunity to present part of this book in the fall of 1999. The Shakespeare Association of America has provided support for the development of my ideas over the course of several years. I wish to thank Skiles Howard and the members of the "Dancing and Dumb-Show" seminar at the 1997 SAA meeting; Lauren Shohet, Julian Yates, and the members of the "Epistemology of Place" seminar at the 1998 SAA meeting; Joel Altman and the members of the "Early Modern

Subject as Actor" seminar at the 1999 meeting; and Frank Whigham and the members of the "Manuals and the Scripting of Behavior" seminar at the 2001 meeting. Chapter One and Chapter Three contain material that appeared originally in *Comparative Drama* Vol. 34, No. 3 (2000): 269–90. A portion of Chapter Four originally appeared in *The Centennial Review* Vol. 43, No. 3 (1999): 501–12. A version of Chapter Five will appear in the Woodbridge and Beehler collection *Women, Violence, and the English Renaissance: Essays Honoring Paul Jorgenson* (Medieval and Renaissance Texts and Studies, 2003). Thanks are due to both journals and to MRTS for permission to reprint this material.

My deepest gratitude is owed to my family. Stephanie Low, Richard Low, and Barbara Bonn, to whom this book is dedicated, had faith in my critical and scholarly abilities long before any notable success occurred; their support has been beyond price. My grandmothers, Regina Low and Grace Taubman, each supported my endeavors through their accomplishments and their peculiar examples. My dear husband, Mark Walker Scroggins, has inspired me as a scholar by his own example. He forced my attention to details and, as *il miglior fabbro*, made me a better stylist. This book is the better for his discerning eye; he read each chapter more often than anyone else besides me. Finally, I wish to express my gratitude to someone who was *not* present during the writing of this book. I am deeply grateful to Philippa Scroggins for delaying her arrival until two days after the book was finished—and for being the best reward that anyone could ever desire for completing a lengthy project.

Introduction

Although James I declared duelling illegal in 1613, his edict failed to lessen the popularity of the custom. The English duel of honor had arisen in the 1580s, when Italian weaponry and customs had reshaped the single combat. Unlike the more traditionally "English" broadsword, the rapier gave no advantage to superior strength but, on the contrary, rewarded superior expertise. Its lightness made the rapier popular; ease and popularity altered the nature of its use.

A plethora of references in fencing manuals, courtesy books, playscripts, and anti-duelling tracts indicates how deeply embedded the duel was in the culture of the English Renaissance and, more broadly, in that of the early modern period.[1] For example, when G. F., the anonymous author of *Duell-Ease* (1635), creates a mythic origin for the duel, he follows a well-established humanistic tradition, and the myth he invents indicates how greatly English popular culture had been influenced by the humanist emphasis on self-fashioning.[2] G. F. describes Lucifer using the duel to make good his attempt at personal transformation, and the author smugly explains the inevitable result:

> Duells and Devils begun together. *Lucifer* conceited himselfe the better creature, and would not give wall to man made of a mould-hill: hee worded the matter, with the master, stept to his face, *Ascendam*, and told him to his teeth, he was as good as God: *Similis ero altissimo*: upon this quarrell, *Lucifer* and *Michael* met, with their seconds: the valiant Archangell (with leave) came to close fight: and the lawlesse challenger *Lucifer*, with his seconds fell. (2)[3]

G. F.'s work vulgarizes the ideals of human aspiration and transformation found in humanists from Pico to Erasmus.[4] As Thomas Greene has suggested, the failure of many humanists to distinguish between "formation" (training) and "transformation" led to the unique character of much Renaissance thinking:

> "Transformation" means...the surpassing of natural human limitations, undoing the constraints of the incomplete, the contingent, and the mortal. Once the Humanist mind discovered...the receptivity of the mind to fashioning, it was very difficult to determine where the upper limits of the fashioning process intervened. It was difficult to know when the ideal of individual development approached the superhuman, the impossible, the divine. ("Self" 250–1)

In G. F.'s amusing attempt literally to demonize a popular fad, we also see him condemning Satan's almost classical hubris, the conviction that he is not only as good as man, he is even "as good as God." This anecdote dramatizes on a grand scale the typical cause for a quarrel and challenge: a dispute over social precedence. Significantly, G. F. places the quarrel in the context of these new beliefs about human potential.

G. F.'s myth also suggests that the mechanisms of the challenge actually derive from the humanist valorization of language and public performance. Note the emphasis on the verbal aspect, the challenge itself: "he *worded* the matter." To word something is to name it, to give it utterance, and to bring it into the abstraction of speech. When Lucifer words God, he challenges him by the threat of knowledge that the naming expresses: I know you and I will proclaim you. The act of naming that God had used repeatedly to create the world is here turned back on him as a strategy of limiting his powers. G. F. characterizes this as a direct challenge to the ineffable deity whose limitlessness depends in part on remaining unbounded by language. Lucifer's effrontery is expressed as well in his naming of difference by not-difference: his analogy between himself and God challenges God's uniqueness. His wording of God is a definition of both self and Other by way of similitude: *similis ero altissimo*.

This account of the wording of God also implies a theatricality on Lucifer's part that cries out for an audience. In wording God, he defines him for others, plays to the gallery. Lucifer's actions call for a third party, an audience with the power to assess the relative claims of God and Lucifer. G. F.'s use of the verb "to word" indicates the magnitude of the challenge by alluding implicitly to the naming power of God's Word.

Although G. F.'s story is of course an original embroidery, his sense of what the quarreler was trying to do is in many ways apt and appropriate. The duel was, however, less a derogation of opponents than a valorization of individual challengers and of a whole social group. As a social phenomenon, the duel in early modern England became an overdetermined sign of masculine identity that helped to stabilize significantly volatile notions of both rank and gender. Perhaps because it rested on the assumption of an unproblematic link between essence and self-representation, the practice helped to define appropriate manners among a number of different social groups.

Although the success of Italian fencing schools in London could be considered the proximate cause of the craze for duelling in late-sixteenth-century England, most social historians more broadly attribute the popularity of the duel of honor to the instability of the social institution of the aristocracy. Lawrence Stone's "crisis of the aristocracy" could in fact be called a crisis of noble masculinity: while the disintegration of certain patriarchal institutions and the alteration of others affected aristocratic women comparatively little, aristocratic males as a group lost a previously well-defined sense of identity. When the aristocracy ceased to be defined as a military elite, male aristocrats lost the warlike tradition that had structured their way of proving themselves, their way of serving their sovereign, and their way of employing their time.[5] In the wake of that change, they developed new traditions derived from Continental manners or revised older traditions initially revived by Tudor monarchs for political reasons.[6] The institution of the duel became popular because, in the face of the changing social structure, it drew on both Continental and older English traditions. The duel became a nexus for several different notions of masculinity; in fact, as a cultural practice, it both indicated and shaped the gender assumptions of wealthy young men. Although comparatively few aristocrats actually fought duels, a great deal of romantic attention was brought to the practice, enhanced further by the stature of the noblemen who often seemed to be the combatants. Examination of the duel in society and in dramatic representation enables us to gain a sense of how masculinity was understood by a specific segment of the early modern population and how that construction was reinterpreted for a larger community in the popular theater of the day.

As we examine the construction of masculinity in the early modern period, however, it is important to recognize that manliness was defined differently by those of different ranks. Although duelling is primarily a gentle phenomenon (ironically), the easy intercourse between gentlemen and other types in London disseminated once-exclusive cultural practices. (Consider the widespread interest in the underworld practice of canting, evidenced by the number of cony-catching pamphlets published at this time.) The duel of honor, strongly associated with the aristocracy, was not practiced by aristocrats alone. But the rising protobourgeoisie regarded such forms of self-assertion much more negatively, and their views of duelling indicate a very different system of values linked to such basic assumptions as gender identity. While historical study of the duel and related forms of conduct allows us to track the shifts in how masculinity was proved, analyzing different kinds of response to duelling across lines of social rank during a single period offers a nuanced understanding of gender assumptions. Consideration of the duel is particularly useful because it can lay bare assumptions about masculinity that were seldom elaborated as such.

This book focuses on fencing and duelling with some reference to single combats and judicial duels, considering these acts first as social practice and second as practices represented on the early modern stage. It is essential that we acknowledge the gap between the social rank of the playwright and that of the aristocrats most frequently represented as duellists—not because the drama elides the distinction, but precisely because it does not. While Richard Helgerson and Arthur F. Marotti have considered the role played by social rank in the work of coterie poets, and Paul Yachnin has suggested that the playwrights' artisanal status was reflected in their work, few New Historicist critics have considered how the social rank of a playwright might inflect the portrayal of a practice not his own.[7] Laura Levine, for example, asks, " 'Why is it that it is only masculinity in these texts that needs to be enacted?' " (8). I suggest that there is no single unitary masculinity; that different social ranks manifest different kinds of masculinity; and that we may recognize these varied ideas of masculinity in the dramatic depiction of different aspects of the duel. Insofar as gender assumptions are represented onstage, that representation is mediated by a given writer's alienation from assumptions that he did not hold. Playwrights were often skeptical about the ideal of aristocratic masculinity that underlay the duel, and this skepticism is evident in several different aspects of the duel performed onstage. The staged duel involves not only physical enactment but historical and social significance complicated by the mimetic reification of dramatic representation in the theater. Because the ideas underlying the duel seem to have held sway primarily over one sex, one age group, and one or two segments of the population, my reading of this subject is heavily historicized, making use of both gender studies and cultural materialist approaches. These modes of thinking seem to me the ones best able to help make the kinds of distinctions that will illuminate this aspect of early modern masculinity.[8]

This project draws on the work of Judith Butler specifically because of her helpful distinction between biological sex and socially determined gender. The distinction is useful, first of all, because it opens up the consideration of physical experience itself as an element that constitutes gender identity.[9] Although the physical experiences of each sex may differ according to communal notions of propriety, the sense of identity derived from fleshly embodiment merits examination, particularly in the context of a historical analysis of theatrical elements.[10] Butler's approach also suggests that gender interpretations and gender assumptions may be considered separately. That is, a phenomenological approach enables us to consider the gap between abstract notions of masculinity and ideas of gender developed in response to the behavior of others. Notions of masculinity per se were, for the majority of the early modern population, exactly that: vague thoughts, unexamined assumptions. Such assumptions simply bypassed the theories of gender developed at that time by those educated in medicine. Most men of the early modern period indicated the contesting conceptions of manhood that underlay their actions not when writing about the concept of gender identity but when they wrote about appropriate or admirable behavior.

By focusing on the duel, a form of ritualized violence, we learn a great deal about English society between 1580 and 1620. Derived from the legal realm and the realm of cultural entertainment, restructured by Italian and French influences, the duel captured the popular imagination. As the duel of honor, it embodied a masculine code that shored up the faltering sense of masculinity among young male aristocrats and members of the gentry. For a Tudor or Stuart courtier, the term "honor" represented a substantially different concept than for his grandfather. There had been a time when "knight" and "warrior" were synonymous expressions that denominated a single segment of patriarchal society indispensable to the state. But by the early seventeenth century, the two terms meant very different things.[11]

The extralegal duel was an echo of lost dignities. Its ties to the past were strengthened by its direct historical precursors, the trial by combat (or judicial duel) and the joust, which linked it to the chivalry of the time of Ramon Llull. During the reign of Elizabeth I, ludic battles, heavy with allegory and nostalgic for chivalric single combat, replaced real battles for most of the rising generation of gentle and aristocratic young men. The cultural connotations of the duel were structured by the aristocratic perception of the heroic ideal, deriving from jousts, from late medieval romances, and from classical antecedents. These elements were modified in the duel of honor, which still bore much of the cultural semiotics of these phenomena. Many duellists liked to believe that they were enacting a heroic role when they undertook to send or accept a challenge, even though the duel had in fact lost any connection with legal justice.

The romantic nature of the ritual gave the nobleman a mirror that reflected and idealized his reality. It offered him a way of asserting his elite status by linking essentially transgressive violence with more culturally acceptable forms. As I explain in Chapter One, although the custom of duelling was taken up by sophisticated young gallants of the gentry and merchant class (and even helped create the character of the "roaring boys" as urbane young men quick to quarrel and to fight), duelling itself remained aristocratic in the popular mind. The amount of publicity about the threat that duelling posed to society shows how much the culture's values were changing. Part of that publicity occurred onstage: the connections between duelling, masculinity, and heroism were reexamined and revised in the drama for a period roughly coterminous with the craze for the duel itself. An example of a certain slippage among the three occurs in Shakespeare's *Much Ado about Nothing*, when Benedick challenges Claudio to the duel. The terms of the challenge (which set up a duel that never occurs) place personal heroism in an anachronistic chivalric context. The play then shifts its focus from Claudio to Benedick and revises its definition of heroism. At the point when Benedick's ethos of masculinity reshapes the generic imperatives of the play, this comedy of wit is transformed into a dramatic version of a chivalric romance—and the threat inherent in violent aristocratic masculinity is erased.

Not only did the duel link masculinity with older historical and literary traditions, it also helped to develop the physical sense of masculinity. In Chapter Two, I examine the spatial assumptions inherent in the art of fence and consider how that discipline enabled young men to develop a sense of bodily control denied to the swordfighters of the past. Fencers were distinguished from other swordfighters by their use of the rapier, or epée, a weapon developed in Spain or Italy in the late fifteenth century as the result of improved techniques of steel-forging (Turner and Soper 5–8). The rapier blade is much thinner than that of the sword, "a weapon intended for cutting or slashing, and heavy enough to cut off an arm or a leg" (Turner and Soper xvi, xxii).[12] With the advent of the rapier, which first came to England early in Elizabeth's reign, the combat became an entirely different undertaking.[13] Although, as the Elizabethan swordsman George Silver points out, the rapier is useless against heavier weapons (30–3), in a fight between two rapier-fencers the victory is no longer decided by physical strength or stamina.[14] Footwork and warding protect the fencer rather than a buckler or shield, and the fencer is taught to strategize according to the strength he can wield by using different sections of his sword's length (di Grassi B1r, E1r). Thus, skill and nimbleness can override brute force. This new kind of fighting increased in popularity until the older weapons passed out of fashion—first among the aristocracy, then among the middling sort.

A gentleman's understanding of spatiality derived in part from training in the use of the rapier, which influenced him to develop a sense of extended personal space that eventually became a visible sign of gentle birth. Such elements as the positive value of flexibility and the broadening of one's personal space distinguish the gentleman's sense of space from that of lower-ranked men. This spatial understanding is particularly significant to the development of the concept of noble masculinity. It structured the understanding of masculinity in ways that its practitioners were hardly even aware of, although the bodily carriage that resulted was recognized as provocative and challenging, particularly to those who were similarly trained. Such elements of masculinity could enable actors to stage differences of rank with greater sophistication, particularly in works like *The Alchemist* that thematized the transgression of social boundaries.

The extended sense of personal space also differentiated gentlemen from gentlewomen, who were trained specifically to limit their personal space to their actual bodies and even to endure male intrusion into that space. But the fencer's sense of space was severely compromised when his ward was breached and his body penetrated by a rapier-thrust. As I discuss in Chapter Three, such penetration could lessen his sense of masculinity, creating a correspondence between his physical experience and that of the permeable body of the female or the vulnerable body of the unseasoned youth. Penetration and the bleeding that resulted carried suggestions of sexual emasculation, further associating the wounded man with women or boys (whose sexuality was perceived as more aligned with that of women than with that of men). The evident dichotomy that develops, distinguishing between mature masculinity and immature boyhood, is highlighted in the father/son duel in Massinger's *The Unnatural Combat* and in the thematics of Shakespeare's *1 Henry IV*, particularly in the combat that Shakespeare stages between Hal and Hotspur.

Within the groups that practiced it, duelling reinforced the patriarchy through its validation of the duellist's status as a principal representative of his family or social group. In Chapter Four, I consider different ideas of honor, their degree of acceptance in different segments of early modern society, and their defining power for gentry and members of the aristocracy. These ideas were not always compatible with sturdy bourgeois ideas of the duel; as I show, most of the tracts written against duelling failed to reach their audience because the authors refused to acknowledge the warrants held by those who engaged in duelling. Social status influenced the perception of the duel, as we see not only in anti-duelling tracts but also in plays that presented duels onstage. Those playwrights who mistrusted the ideology of violent masculinity could use the staged combat in a way that only intermittently or partially achieved the ends that the duel did in real life and in written narrative. Shakespeare's show-stopping climax in *Hamlet* is oddly inconclusive. The duel in Chapman's sequel, *The Revenge of Bussy D'Ambois*, undermines the stance on heroic masculinity offered in the original *Bussy D'Ambois* play.

As Chapter Four considers factors that challenged the association between duelling and masculinity, Chapter Five continues this project with an examination of female duellists onstage. When cross-dressed figures enact the duel in early modern dramas, they pose a challenge less to traditional ideas of femininity than to concepts of manhood. After discussing classical models for the man-woman including the androgyne, the hermaphrodite, and the Amazon, I consider the early modern understanding of these categories in literary and cultural contexts. I then analyze several theatrical portrayals of duelling cross-dressers and duelling women. In all the plays considered, the authors attempt to juxtapose *eros* and *virtus*, either opposing them or bringing them into congruence by using the figure of the female duellist. Feminine power is repeatedly undermined in the supposedly protofeminist play *Swetnam the Woman-Hater* but enlarged and expanded even in such submissive figures as Aspatia in Beaumont and Fletcher's *The Maid's Tragedy*. In this play, as in Heywood's *The Fair Maid of the West*, Middleton and Dekker's *The Roaring Girl*, and Beaumont and Fletcher's *Love's Cure, Or, The Martial Maid*, women's willingness to accept certain patriarchal assumptions gains for them the opportunity to expand the definition of woman's role. Women's duels in these plays differ from men's in that they enact an almost purely didactic function; by contrast, men's duels are almost invariably prompted by the desire for revenge or for glory, both of which motives derive from the values of heroic self-assertion. Plays in which women fight define a broader range of acceptable behavior for women; however, as they do so, they challenge the link between masculinity and violence by suggesting that motive can redefine the practice of duelling—almost to the extent of changing the name of the act when the duel no longer engages the corpus of social practices with which it had seemed indissolubly linked.

The staged duel did not mirror the duel in society unproblematically: each worked on the other, bringing varied elements to bear on the cultural meaning of the practice. The association of the duel with heroic self-assertion, for example, an association largely derived from literary presentation, was severely compromised by the satiric or cynical portrayals of the duel in Jacobean dramas. On the other hand, the culture's connection between duelling and high social status was one that playwrights could exploit in their subtle shaping of audience sympathies.

The duel's affiliation with masculinity, though undercut by the very idea of female duellists, remains a notable and complex cultural phenomenon. Although the duel was enacted by a relatively small number of men, the practice was so central to the notion of the courtier that its meaning helped to define the aristocracy of the period as a whole. The construct of the duel enabled male aristocrats and members of the gentry to figure themselves in ways consistent with both the old military ideal and that of the courtier. While it had little reference to the new modes of government and civil administration, it helped to restructure gender relations for the gentry and aristocracy in ways made necessary by class mobility and the modern state that the Tudors had ushered in. Through analysis of the duel we recognize manhood as an element whose demonized opposite could be represented as the feminine but also as clownishness (a distinction based on social status), youthfulness (a distinction based on maturity), unaffiliated individualism (a distinction derived from longstanding notions of honor), or even as didacticism (a confused and faulty distinction that permitted the possibility of the female duellist). Such a diversity of Others indicates the variety of contexts in which manhood and masculinity were, on some level, understood; they provide us with salutary notice not to assume that any single axis of difference can adequately represent the early modern understanding of gender.

Chapter 1

The Duellist as Hero

A duel of honor consists of the following elements: a challenge, oral or written; a challenger; a defendant; and a combat. The proper duel results from the lie, as fencing-master Vincentio Saviolo specifies: "hee unto whome the lie is wrongfullie given, ought to challenge him that offereth that dishonour, and by the swoorde to prove himselfe no lyer" (*His Practise,* sig. R4r). Saviolo offers hypothetical examples: "Caius sayth to Seius that hee is a traitour: unto which Seius aunswereth by giving the lie: whereuppon ensueth, that the charge of the Combat falleth on Caius, because hee is to maintain what hee sayd, and therefore to challenge Seius" (sigs. R3v–R4r). The one who gives the lie is the defendant, who is "both accused and constrained to fight"; the one who proves his assertion (or accusation) is the challenger, who is "to overcome, unles hee will altogither loose the quarrell … to the one it appertaineth to proove, and to the other it is sufficient onely to defend" (Saviolo, sig. BB2v). The two meet on a chosen day between sunrise and sunset, and "after that the Combatters are entered the lists, if they have no further agreement betwixt them … the fight is to continue to the death or flight, or til it be forbidden" (Saviolo, sig. BB4v).

Combats were more often forbidden, however, before they began.[1] Institutional sanction against the early modern duel is one significant element that distinguishes it from its predecessors. Another is the form of combat—fencing, not swordfighting, a new fighting style that resulted from the development of the lightweight rapier in the 1580s. Unlike the more traditionally "English" broadsword, the rapier gave no advantage to superior strength. But even after we redefine the early modern duel by its legal status (interdicted), its weaponry (rapiers), and its purpose (to settle quarrels over honor), we have yet to explain its significance for the population that both feared and admired it. Why did so many men choose to engage in this extra-legal proceeding instead of more established and socially acceptable forms of ritual violence? To understand the attraction, we must become familiar with the relationship between the extra-legal duel and earlier forms of ritualized combat. As we shall see, the peculiar status of the early modern duel depends on changes in ideas about gentility and indicates a shift in the self-conception of well-born males.

The judicial duel was formalized as an adjunct to civil law in the middle ages. While not as universal as the trial by ordeal, it gained wide acceptance throughout Western Europe.[2] It was entered into the annals of English law shortly after 1066, presumably brought to England from Normandy by William the Conqueror.[3] By 1086, it had been integrated into English law (Neilson 31–2).[4] The alternative term for the judicial duel—trial by combat—derived from the duel's position within the law as a supplement to criminal trial and judgment. It served as a part of due process to distinguish between two disputants when inadequate evidence could not determine the case. As the social historian Robert Bartlett explains, "The components, in the fifth century as in the thirteenth, are clear: the absence of other means of proof, divine judgement, single combat, a means of proof" (115).

Another type of ritual fight, the single combat, should not be confused with either the judicial duel or the extra-legal duel, although early modern writers sometimes used the terms interchangeably (as, for example, in John Selden's title *The Duello; or, Single Combat*). The term "single combat" can refer specifically to the medieval practice of concluding a war through a public fight between the two opposed leaders (usually princes but occasionally generals). Geoffrey of Monmouth recounts that King Arthur conquered Paris by single combat against Flollo, Roman tribune of Gaul; some versions of Anglo-Saxon history say that England was partitioned between Cnut of Denmark and Edmund of England as the result of a single combat between the two (cf. Neilson 25–8). One can easily cite instances from literature (the elder Hamlet's victory over the elder Fortinbras, the challenge Hal wants to send to Hotspur in *1 Henry IV*). But historical accounts of such combats actually occurring are generally judged unreliable and, after discussing them, Neilson discounts most of the evidence he cites. However, in certain countries, this kind of fight was probably used to settle vendettas between great families, as Philippe de Beaumanoir's *Coutumes de Beauvasis* indicates (II:417; qtd. in Bartlett 113). Precise categorizing is confounded by the political structures in force prior to the rise of the nation-state.

The judicial duel was used for a long time on the Continent as an optional means of settling any dispute. Aristocrats used this method to decide issues of insult, descent, and inheritance. Glanvill's *Tractatus de Legibus Angliae* (c. 1187) tells us that in England the duel was almost entirely reserved for appeals in cases of treason and felony, and in property disputes involving the writ of right.[5] Although many regulations governed the relative equality of challenger and challenged, Bartlett cautions us against allowing that fact to structure our assumptions about the status of those involved: "The apparent exclusivity should not delude us. The principle was that one could only challenge one's peers, not that challenges were in any way aristocratic. In the early and high Middle Ages the judicial duel was not a distinctive habit of the upper classes" (110). The customary procedure that led to the trial by combat in thirteenth-century England began when the accuser charged the defendant with a crime, stated the details of the offence, and offered to prove it upon his body if the Court would permit it (Lea 110). If the defender denied the charge and elected to prove his innocence by his body, it remained for the judge to assess whether or not a combat was appropriate. Before the actual combat, according to Bracton, the accuser first swore "to his own personal knowledge ... of the crime alleged, *visu et auditu*" and the accused also swore an oath (Lea 166). The loser of the fight was fined and, if he lived, was often considered a convicted perjurer.

Throughout its practice, the trial by combat was generally understood as a test in which God's hand would intervene to settle the dispute on the side of the right.[6] Ritual elements had been invested in the duel quite early on because of its connection with the civil oath (Lea 118). Because of the religious and moral implications of the oath, and because of the religious assumptions on which the rite of the duel was based, the rite itself was invested with ceremony of a gravity associated with Church rites. Asad cites Gaudemet as saying that the judicial duel was an improvement on the sacred oath because the outcome of a duel cannot serve as a potential occasion for blasphemy, as a false oath could through its contempt for God (Asad 93, Gaudemet 105). Yet the outcome of the duel was qualified by the circumstances surrounding the case. Shakespeare simplifies the significance of the judicial duel in

Richard II considerably when the king aborts the process because he believes that the outcome will indicate his own complicity in Woodstock's murder.[7] One could also regard the ritual with cynical skepticism: as Bartlett comments, "The idea of 'letting them fight it out' is at least as strong as the sentiment 'may the best man win' (even given that 'best' means 'with the best case')" (114).

Moreover, the results of the outcome generally were modified by judicial assessment of the case:

> A man whose reputation is completely besmirched and who has been accused on very powerful grounds, must go to the ordeal. Failure means mutilation or death. But success at the ordeal does not enable him to leave the court without a stain on his character.... Careful provision has to be made for him.... Other factors—the nature of the accusation, the man's status—would be weighed alongside the verdict of the ordeal. (Bartlett 68)

Thus, the judicial duel combined elements of both civil trial and execution. Legally, it was a trial proceeding containing investigation, judgment, and, if a combatant was killed outright, summary execution.[8]

The combatants' relation to the civil authorities was curious: the duel simultaneously added to the power of civil authorities and took power away from them. One could read the victor of the combat as an arm of the authorities or of God, or one could consider him a person who took upon himself the government's privilege of carrying out its own sentences. While establishing truth in eighteenth-century France was the "exclusive power of the sovereign and his judges," as Foucault writes (35), in the English trial by combat as early as the thirteenth century, the establishment of truth was the prerogative of the accuser and the accused.

It was not long before disputants recognized that the combat's connection with divine justice could be turned to advantage. People began to request the trial by combat because they could manipulate its outcome by, for example, the use of a champion.[9] As English civil law was improved, and as instances of such corrupt practices mounted, the judicial duel fell into disuse (although the custom took some time to die out entirely). Trial by combat persisted for as long as it did for many reasons. Conveniently, it made state-chartered violence legal. The judicial combat could even function as state-sponsored revenge, providing a legal outlet for conflicts among the gentry. Moreover, it dissipated the violent energies of the gentry, preventing the spread of discontent and incitement to rebellion.

As the prevalence of the judicial duel waned, another form of state-sanctioned single combat enjoyed renewed popularity: the joust. The joust had begun as a performance that could precede a tournament. Early tournaments were war games on a grand scale, initially intended as military training for knights, especially those preparing for the Crusades. Tournaments were part of the chivalric tradition—an ethos, as Keen says, "in which martial, aristocratic, and Christian elements were fused together" (16).[10] Initially, tournaments and jousts enabled young swordsmen of gentle birth to display their prowess, thereby giving them a chance to gain a place at court or in wealthier households. Since paired fighting "proved less dangerous and more demonstrative of individual prowess," the joust superseded the tournament over time (Wickham I:17).

Originally focused on the military aspects of aristocratic culture, the code of chivalry was reconceived more broadly during the sixteenth century (Bornstein 20). Both Henry VIII and Elizabeth I found chivalric pageantry an important tool to help create an often illusory "sense of national and social unity," idealizing the past to conceal political conflicts (Bornstein 110).[11] Chivalry also served the needs of the aristocracy: it promoted what Bornstein calls "a sense of social identity and social cohesion" (90). Both the romanticism and the symbolism of chivalry brought together old and new families, helping the two orders to perceive themselves as one group united against outsiders (Bornstein 90). Moreover, the chivalric code provided opportunities to create a personal definition: "For the aristocracy the image [of the knight] affirmed their position. For members of the gentry and the middle class, it served as a symbol of aspiration" (Bornstein 105). For monarchs, emblematic aspects of chivalry could aid in the construction of their public definition.[12] While tournaments had originally "signified the private web of responsibilities and rights between lords and vassals.... [b]y the sixteenth century, they had come to serve a nationalistic purpose" (Bornstein 124). Tournaments also provided a safe outlet for domestic unrest. Although such war games might seem to promote aristocratic violence, these festivities actually served to contain aristocratic aggression and to offer aristocrats an alternative to extravagant escapades in war. The custom diffused the energy of the nobility in courtly combat, hindering them from creating factions or fomenting discontent over the monarch's policies.[13]

As the ties between the joust and martial training became looser, the emphasis of the combat shifted from skill to art. Keen posits a connection between "the expansion of the element of theatre in the *pas d'armes* and the growing divorce between skill in joust and tourney and true military skill" (206).[14] Although the elitist aspect of chivalry excluded all but a small segment of the population, the Tudor revival ensured that this small segment was very much in the public eye. Elizabeth's favorites were well known to the people of London, and not just because of their military triumphs. They were seen engaged in tournaments, some of the largest-scale productions that the sovereign had ever created for her people. Although the monarchs paid for these tributes to their greatness, the performances were enacted by knights who, for this purpose, continued to train in and to practice increasingly anachronistic feats of war. Such performances should be understood as evidence of the courtier's preoccupation with form, ritual, and precedence.[15] As Frank Whigham points out,

> courtesy theory was precisely a tool for "making places" in the social order and was used for this purpose by Elizabethans on both sides of the struggle. First promulgated by the elite in a gesture of exclusion, the theory was then read, rewritten, and reemployed by mobile base readers to serve their own social aggressions. (5–6)[16]

At the same time, the romance of the chivalric code could carry away even those who attempted consciously to manipulate it—consider, for example, Henry VIII, Sir Walter Ralegh, or Sir Philip Sidney. As Bornstein observes, "The chivalric code was more than a set of gestures and ceremonies.... Boundaries between play, ritual, and everyday life were not firmly drawn" (126). While many statesmen of the period demonstrated an awareness of the effects that chivalric performance could achieve, they also seem to have internalized the ideology of chivalry.

The extralegal duel should be recognized as an outgrowth less of the joust, a combat in itself, than of the chivalric revival of which the sixteenth-century joust was itself a product. Certainly the chivalric tradition provided early modern noblemen with a stronger connection to the masculine identity of the medieval aristocrat than did the judicial duel, not least because the code of chivalry promoted individualism (Bornstein 116). While the trial by combat obviously influenced the development of the duel of honor, the assumptions that had enabled the judicial duel to function effectively had disappeared by the early modern period. The seriousness of the judicial duel was in some sense mocked by the casual violence of the duel of honor; the two types of duel manifested different beliefs about the place of the combat in social life. Most significantly, the judicial duel was a legal practice with a religious component. Its justification was the faith that God would intervene to indicate the more righteous cause. In the late 1580s, however, combatants generally recognized that victory in a duel depended more on skill in rapier fight than on God's intervention.

In contrast to the trial by combat, the duel of honor defended one's overall reputation as much as it defended the actual value of any given statement. While the popular understanding was that the test of truth was essentially a test of character, in practice the result was more ambiguous. Many quarrels of extraordinary triviality led to the duel. Combatants intended not to prove another man wrong but to prove themselves the "better" man—a broadly ambiguous concept that involved honesty, rank, and fencing skill.[17] Neither righteousness nor fact was of much concern to the duellist; what mattered was public opinion. Among the aristocracy, losing a duel was said to lead to moral censure, to being widely known as a rascal, to being publicly ignored by acquaintances. In practice, such results were highly unlikely.[18] The loser, while he lost status among men, was still accepted by his community. Occasionally, remnants of the old view were mingled with the popular understanding of the duel of honor, but most anti-duelling tracts interpret the duel as different in kind from the trial by combat, perceiving it as a form of lawlessness rather than as an appeal to God for judgment. The judicial duel settled legal questions but it did not serve to settle matters of precedence, and the aura of manhood surrounding the victorious early modern duellist was no part of the outcome of the judicial duel.

The same impulse to performative violence does seem to have inspired both the duel and the joust. In both, the courtier's ideal of self-presentation involves conscious consideration of his identity and the best way to present it. Although both combine ritual and playful elements, the joust differs from the duel: not only was the first endorsed by the sovereign while the second was frowned upon, the first was primarily ludic, while the second was deadly play.[19] Residual elements of the joust, however, persist in the duel of honor.[20] The duel of honor retained the joust's ludic quality in the rituals surrounding the fight. The challenge to the duel, its acceptance, and the practical arrangements of the combat were all meant to impress a small elite community with one's style. The revival of chivalry elevated reputation to the status of personal worth: what once was defined by one's accomplishments on the battlefield became defined by one's skill at social performance, one's personal style. Just as the jouster expects to gain renown through his participation in the event, the duellist hopes to raise his status within his community. In both events, the grace with which the rituals are performed contributes to the final impression of the combatant. The sense of play—of performance—was also evident in the combatants' cool estimation of their honor as more valuable than their lives. Many challenges to the duel were sent with amazing nonchalance. Sir Charles Blount challenged Essex to the duel upon hearing that Essex had obliquely referred to him as a fool (Naunton 76). Lord Bruce of Kinloss's challenge to Edward Sackville is phrased with amazing sangfroid: "Be master of your owne weapons and tyme; the place wheresoever I will waite on you, by doeinge this you shall shorten revenge and clere the idle opinion the world hath of both our Worthes" (Folger MS. 1054.4, qtd. in Akrigg, *Pageant* 254).

This sense of sport is part of a larger element: the performative nature of the ritual, something the duel of honor shared with both the judicial duel and the joust. Although the duel of honor was not a public occasion, the presence of seconds guaranteed that the event would become public knowledge. To participate in the duel was to become known for one's courage, and even the losers seem to have gained renown for having fought. In this practice, performance itself was translated to another level. The performance of the duel was necessarily transmitted by the few observers (seconds, surgeons, and such). The actual performance was discussed rather than seen—transmitted further as it was imagined by those who heard it recounted.

Such comparisons explain the relation of these two contemporaneous phenomena; however, these analyses are more useful for establishing the duel's genealogy than for explaining the questions that logically follow. Why did the duel develop when the joust was already firmly established? What purpose did the duel serve? More specifically, what explains the timing of its rise in England?

In practical terms, the extralegal duel could not have developed without the widespread acceptance of the rapier, which made such casual violence possible. The rapier (and rapier fencing) had been popular on the Continent for most of the sixteenth century, and the increasing English interest in fencing and duelling arose largely from increased travel on the Continent—corresponding, in fact, to the rise of the English Renaissance.[21] Humanist interest in classical antiquity flowered as an aristocratic fascination with both ancient and contemporary Italy: although the primary reasons for travel changed, the number of peers and heirs of peers who visited the Continent increased throughout the sixteenth century and finally peaked around 1620 (Stone, *CA* 701–2). Many of these aristocrats "desired to acquire polite accomplishments, to fence and ride and dance, or to gain book-learning or an exact knowledge of the language of Petrarch and Tasso" (Stoye 93).[22]

Fencing—practice in the use of the rapier—functioned primarily as training for the eventuality of the duel. Unlike jousting, fencing served no performative function.[23] Fencing was a sport in which men engaged primarily in pedagogical settings—that is, in fencing schools or private lessons.[24] Those who studied the use of the rapier fenced primarily as pupils to their teachers, either with their teachers or paired with other pupils. The purpose of fencing was to train for the possibility that a quarrel might get out of hand.[25] Although the public was welcome to visit the fencing schools in London, there were no formal rapier exhibitions on the parts of gentlemen. While the English Masters of Defence engaged in public displays of skill to advertise their expertise and to entice potential pupils, their exhibitions were eventually perceived as a sign of the Masters' lowly social status (Castle 264–6),[26] and it is likely that concern for their social status often prevented members of the gentry and aristocracy from fencing in public. The English swordsman George Silver recounts that he himself, as well as many Masters, challenged the Italian fencing masters in London to public fights that the resident aliens fairly consistently refused. Such refusals seem to have turned on the issue of social rank: the Masters saw themselves as skilled men, almost an unofficial guild; they were happy to give public performances at the Palace of Greenwich at the king's request in 1606 and 1614 (Aylward 78). But the Italians were gentlemen—Rocco Bonetti, indeed, was affiliated with the French court—and they regarded such displays on their own part as demeaning.

Most of the extant fencing manuals also reveal a bias against fencing exhibitions. Indeed, Italian fencers seemed to regard their skill as the sign of a secret brotherhood: Marozzo, a Bolognese master whose Italian manual went through numerous editions, says that he bound his new students to secrecy upon a cross-hilt "as if it were God's Holy Cross ... never to teach any other person without his permission the secrets he is about to impart" (qtd. in Castle 60). Marozzo also discouraged his students from practicing with each other—he allowed his pupils to fence only with skilled swordsmen "of pleasant dispositions" (Castle 59–60). Vincentio Saviolo enjoins his students from accepting the offer of a "friendly" match:

> although hee were your freend or kinseman, take him for an enemye, and trust him not... for the inconvenience that may grow therby, is seene in many histories both ancient and moderne. ... and therefore if he be your freend that will needs fight with you, you maye tell him that you have given him no cause, nor offred any wrong. (Sig. E2v)

Referring in his manual to the pupil's opponent, Saviolo alternates between the term "maister or teacher" and "your enemie"; fencing is not a game but an opportunity for learning and for exercise (Sig. L3v); the goal is never mere recreation so much as it is physical fitness and a readiness to respond to insults with confidence in one's duelling ability.

Yet fencing, like dancing and riding, was perceived as a gentlemanly accomplishment. Along with the repeated waves of nostalgia that increasingly idealized chivalric practices, the duels that fencing made possible revised the medieval tradition of the warrior elite. As older practices were adulterated with elements of artistry during the Tudor era, those practices' original aims were reinterpreted. Chivalric values were problematic, if not absolute anathema, for sixteenth-century humanists, but aristocratic pastimes were blended with humanistic goals, as courtly accomplishments came to include skill in reading and writing in classical languages. Castiglione's Courtier blends many elements of both European traditions. But the response in England to such Italianate customs was mixed. Some Englishmen—for the most part gentry and aristocrats—perceived the Continental influence as a modernization of manhood that rendered the sixteenth-century nobleman more useful. Others—mostly of the middling sort—responded to it xenophobically, perceiving it as an attenuation of English sturdiness. The plurality of acceptable masculine behaviors in England gradually became more polarized: the semiotics of aristocratic masculinity became literally foreign to the middling sort. The very pastimes that seemed unmanly to the middling sort appeared refined to the courtier who wished to avoid an antiquated or coarse self-presentation. The very term "fashion," which suggested fads and vogues, was positive for most noblemen and negative for much of the rest of society. Display, too, viewed with suspicion by many commoners, was an unqualified positive for gentry and nobility of both sexes. The sartorial display that seemed effeminate to merchants seemed masculine to courtiers.[27] The melancholic pose that seemed unmanly to city folk was attractive in aristocratic circles (Schiesari 243–67).

Composing poetry, a task scorned by those who considered themselves plain men, was a popular courtly pastime. Hence, what was elitist, exclusive, and Italian was coded as weak and womanish by the middling sort but appropriate and manly by the gentry and aristocracy.[28]

Like fencing itself, the duel broadened the notion of masculinity through its ties to the Continent. But even among the gentry and aristocracy, the duel did not possess a unitary meaning. Its practice enabled young males of good family to define themselves both within the chivalric model and against it. Given the competing models of masculinity, one attraction of the duel was probably that enacting it flouted the wishes of the sovereign.[29] Even as the monarchs regulated duels ever more strictly, the popularity of the custom increased. François Billacois reads the rise in duelling at this time as a two-pronged response on the part of the nobles:

> The upsurge [in duelling ... is linked to the political and religious crisis that the country was going through at the time. When a king's authority is no longer unanimously respected, knights revert to aristocratic values. ... However, those who opposed the royal prerogative were certainly also tempted by the duel, for it was a way of proclaiming and realising equality between the gentry of the Commons and the Lords of the Upper House. (29–30)

In both these ways, the practice of the extra-judicial duel helped define the idea of the aristocrat and the idea of the gentleman.[30] Duelling manuals suggest that the codification of duelling customs increased over time, a change that Stone perceives as beneficial to society as a whole. The duel, unlike the brawl or the feud, was intended to be fought in cold blood and to conclude the matter in question (Stone, *CA* 245). Yet, while violence overall may have lessened, the duel itself became more common. Members of the aristocracy, acutely concerned with their changing status under the Tudors, were constantly jostling for precedence in both figurative and literal ways. In contrast to Billacois, Brian Parker argues that during the Jacobean period, the duel functioned as one of many elements of a courtly code of conduct used to identify and close ranks against parvenus; duelling, he says, was used to define what a courtier's "personal place should be in the hierarchy of the elite" (56). Either way, it is clear that anxiety over place did prompt an increasing number of combats among members of the gentry and nobility.

From the perspective of the monarch, duels threatened social stability. James's 1613 proclamation forbidding the duel, for instance, was prompted by the half-dozen that occurred that year among some he king's closest associates (Stone, *CA* 247). Aristocratic duellists ropriated royal authority, demonstrated the monarch's inability to restrain them by law, and encouraged the imitation of the gentry, the middling sort, and even the underclass. One of the most frequent criticisms of the duel was that its practitioners appropriated the role of judge from the king, who rightfully held that position. (The perception of the duellist as judge derives, of course, from the duel's association with the trial by combat.) By engaging in extra-legal duels, the aristocracy not only reclaimed the power that the monarch was trying to centralize, they also arrogated to themselves a state-sponsored institution—the trial—that had been perceived as lawful, ceremonial, and just.[31] The balance of power between monarchy and aristocracy was clearly weighted in favor of the ruler, but the appearance that the situation was reversed had a popular effect, increasing admiration for the nobility in some circles and increasing fear of their lawlessness in others. Perhaps even more important, a small number of aristocratic men were able to present this image to the English aristocracy as a whole, offering themselves as a mirror that defined aristocracy both for themselves and for parvenus eager to join their ranks.

Perhaps most important to Englishmen looking across the Channel for a new mode of self-definition was an element specific to the Italian Renaissance: a positive view of self-determination, self-shaping. This view was most baldly stated in Pico's retelling of a fable in which God describes man as "the maker and molder of [him]self, [who] mayest fashion [him]self in whatever shape [he] shalt prefer" (225). Thomas Greene points out (as I mentioned earlier) that this notion of fashioning bore other meanings as well:

> many men of the Renaissance, particularly the Italian Renaissance, tended to confuse "formation"...with "transformation." "Transformation" means here the surpassing of natural human limitations, undoing the constraints of the incomplete, the contingent, and the mortal. ("Flexibility" 250)

The duellist's ethos depends, I would argue, on this desire both to shape oneself and to transcend human limitations. These desires were heightened by the aristocrat's frequent confusion between reputation and essential being and by the educated man's awareness of Classical heroic models, although the sense of self-determination was available to men without either of these resources.

Numerous critics have stressed the importance of chivalric romances in the development of chivalry.[32] In fact, however, as contemporary writers were well aware, the ethos of the duel was informed by both the romance and the texts of classical antiquity. William Wiseman, condemning the practice of the duel in 1619, suggests that it originated in

> a multitude of idle bookes and ingenious devises as I said, but much naughtinesse in them, to invegle the minde of man, and wrie our understanding quite on t'one side. Such as *Amades,* and *Ariosto*... that are full of these challenges, and bravadoes.... Every one will have one of these, or a play booke in his hand, and what men delight in, they are made like unto (57).

Despite Wiseman's censure, however, the ethos of the duellist related only indirectly to that of the Christian knight, which was in many ways antiheroic. As John M. Steadman asserts,

> Epic tradition had placed emphasis on military valour. Ethical and theological traditions, on the other hand, had usually condemned this ideal.... In place of the warrior-hero, they had identified the hero with the just man, the *honnêtte, homme,* and the saint. (6)

The concept of the hero was subsequently modified in different contexts.[33] For those attracted to duelling, heroism reverted to the military ideal and, most crucially, to classical models. Aristotle defines the classical hero as godlike; from this term and from Homer's epics, many critics have postulated a special relationship between the hero and the gods. As Victor Brombert suggests, the hero provides "a transcendental link between the contingencies of the finite and the imagined realm of the supernatural" (11). Most classical heroes are generals or free agents who consent on occasion to aid nearby rulers. Not only is the task of ruling distinguished from the performance of glorious deeds, the king and the hero may be independent of one another. A hero's career does not necessarily depend on serving the king; his heroism may serve the larger community instead, without any implication of servitude or significant fealty to another. The hero stands apart from governing institutions, and on another plane.

In Renaissance literary and philosophical circles, the reconciliation of classical and heroic values—what Braden calls the alteration or disappearance of content—was quite controversial.[34] In England, both Davenant and Dryden condemned Homer's Achilles as vicious (Spingarn II:10, 61); only Hobbes asserted that ambition "has somewhat Heroick in it, and therefore must have place in an Heroick Poem" (Spingarn II:51). Yet the same philosophy that promoted the idea of the governor also promoted the notion of an aspiring self whose individualism might violate cultural norms. The word "hero," as Morton W. Bloomfield points out, was seldom used in England before the sixteenth century, but by the seventeenth century the term could be applied to "any notable or great human being," although the more specific meaning could also be intended (28).[35] Because the maverick was hard for the Renaissance mind to conceive, the warrior-courtier developed instead. Fulke Greville's *Life of Sidney* crystallized a popular view of the courtier-as-hero based on Sidney's gallantry, appearance, and mastery of the social arts. Bolgar calls Sidney a *miles christianus* in the aristocratic mode, meaning that his type of heroism came to the modern world through literary notions of chivalry.

Over time, Renaissance authors revised classical myths to bring them into consonance with Christian values. Eugene Waith has convincingly documented the ubiquity of the Hercules figure in Renaissance culture: well-known representations and parallels include Salutati's *De Laboribus Herculis,* Ripa's *Iconologia,* Landino's *De vita activa et contemplativa,* and even the biblical Samson, to whom Hercules was often compared (39–43). As classical education became a more standard part of a male aristocrat's training, these images of heroism offered an attractive model. They endorsed an active heroism resembling the feats of arms that had been the staple of the aristocratic elite; however, young Renaissance men, heavily influenced by the valorization of individualism, were equally drawn by the magnitude, the sheer scale of the Hercules figure. We find the same way of measuring excellence in both *The Iliad* and the masculine competition frequently discussed in Castiglione's *The Courtier.*

Waith convincingly argues that Chapman's Bussy D'Ambois is an early modern development of the classical hero. This hero remains entirely aloof from court hierarchies:

> When I am wrong'd, and that law fails to right me,
> Let me be king myself (as man was made)
> And do a justice that exceeds the law. (II.i.197–9)

As well as redefining "justice" as "revenge," Chapman offers a surprising assumption quite parenthetically: that the individual was created by God to be king over himself. For the early modern subject, transcending the finite often involved transcending the one institutional power that inhered in a single individual: the monarchy. But the magnitude of the hero often promoted a conception of the self as, in Chapman's phrase, a king oneself, as man was made. The sense that unaccommodated man possessed an inherent element of divinity fit easily into a social hierarchy in which the individual's virtue, intellectual ability, or (more commonly) his lineage brought him certain privileges, whether these were recognized by the community or not.

In Homer, as Gordon Braden points out, the hero must demons[?] his right to be free from common constraint by continually surp[ass]ing others.[36] Lacking a group ethos with which to identify, early modern gentry and aristocracy also perceived that one gains status only at the expense of another. Once the solidarity of rank was replaced by competition for largely symbolic honors, the Homeric notion of honor resurfaced in the pages of Castiglione, the plays of Shakespeare, and the practice of the duel of honor.

In the classical tradition, as Brombert comments, the hero's "uniqueness helps define or condemn social conventions; his violence challenges or confirms the rules of order. Behind the noble and irate figures...loom many questions. Where does morality lie? Who is or should be its repository?" (12–13). The phenomenon of the duel, while hardly heroic in itself, answered many of the same questions. The motivation for duelling becomes easier to define once we recognize that the early modern duellist redefined the public sphere or commonweal to suit himself. As the hero's acts shaped a private self, so the duellist's combat shaped *his* sense of self. The corpus of beliefs underlying the Greek hero constitutes an internal heroics equally applicable to the duellist.[37] Like that of the Homeric hero, the braggadocio of the early modern duellist seems to derive from a decision to risk all for the sake of glory. The stories of men like Drake, Sidney, and Ralegh, the mythic courtiers of Elizabeth's reign, frequently indicate this desire to exceed past triumphs. Telling the story of the combat between Essex and Blount, Naunton speculates on the motives of the two:

> [M]y Lord of Essex in a kind of emulation, and as though he would have limited [the Queen's] favour, said, "I perceive every fool must have a favor." This bitter and public affront came to Sir Charles Blount's ear, who sent him the challenge, which was accepted by my Lord of Essex. (76)

The story manifests not only Essex's desire to be recognized as the Queen's preeminent favorite but also his faith in the glory of fighting over the most trivial expressions of the Queen's favor. The sense of excess so obvious in his behavior was one of the chief criticisms made of duellists in general: that they often fought over trivial matters. But their behavior can be understood as an attempt to magnify the scale of the courtier's life. By acting as heroes, duellists brought a momentousness to the minutiae of court conduct.

This ethos could not have come into being without the development of what Stone calls the humanists' "cult of heroes"

(*CA* 35–6).[38] We can trace the development of the concept of the hero from the medieval knight through the protagonists of rediscovered classical texts to the aristocratic males who shaped the ethos of the duellist. Many duellists saw the duel as an alternative system of justice and a way of gaining glory. Their behavior suggests that they perceived themselves as engaged in forming their own world in which aggression was a form of self-realization. The duellist created the meaning of his name through contest with others. Combat tests one's excellence, revealing it by one's victory over another.

In the culture of the English court, those who could conform served ably as counselors. But many others felt that their integrity would be diminished by enacting such politic behavior. Naunton's *Fragmenta Regalia* reveals such a bias in favor of the active life in the author's comment on Lord Willoughby: "it was his saying (and it did him no good) that he was none of the *reptilia*. ... Neither was the court his element, for indeed as he was a great soldier, so was he of a suitable magnanimity and could not brook the obsequiousness and assiduity of the court" (61–2). Naunton's obvious admiration of such "suitable magnanimity" reveals that, for him, enacting the role of the politic courtier reduced a man's stature. In a community that stressed behavior, ritual, and appearance, the matters that prompted challenges must have been perceived as far more significant than they are today. Though duellists both defied monarchic displeasure and dispensed their own justice, there is no evidence that they perceived their actions as antisocial. They were selecting one of several competing values; they could dismiss others all the more easily because this one endorsed the urges of pride and egotism.

The craze for duelling actually may be perceived as a triumph of personal style over (though inflected by) courtly mores. Certainly, the practice was taken up by many who had no contact with the court per se; yet duellists evidently took pleasure in the courtly nature of this accomplishment. Its practice must not be perceived as an assertion of personal pride so much as of status definition. Yet, although duels could raise obscure aspirants by their engagement with better-known men, the ritual did not necessarily convey a sense of fraternity among the combatants. Whereas the historian François Billacois points out that French duellists honored their opponents "to honour themselves. ... For it was the worth of the loser that gave the greatest proof of the worth of the victor" (213), English duels were frequently prompted by rude comments that suggest the opposite factor at work. Richard Brathwait, in *The English Gentleman* (1630), builds up a careful portrait of the young, urbane city-gallant as a duellist "who many times upon a tavern quarrel [is] brought to shed [his] dearest blood" and a "raw and unseasoned youth [who glories] much to be esteemed one of the *fraternity*" (40–1). In other words, the French system is one of inclusion in a clearly defined group. But the English system is one of aspiration, in which victory is understood to mark the victor as an insider and the loser as a pretender. The duellist's sense of self is legitimated by his proven skill with the weapon.

In the drama, the duel frequently became a touchstone; how it was performed indicated the stature of the protagonist and, often, how the playwright conceived the place of the heroic ideal in contemporary culture. Although combat is rarely staged, the verbal presentation of the duel often clarifies both the parameters of the metafiction and the subtleties of the dramatic genre. The attitude that the play presents toward the duel, whether romantic, ironic, or farcical, offers implicit judgment of the modern construction of honor, reputation, and the man's role in society.

As the Renaissance playwright decided how to structure the generic boundaries of his plot, the physical carriage of fencers was a theatrical boon. This bodily expression of spatial assumptions could be reproduced by actors, and the very stance of the expert fencer could serve as the mark of a hero. As playwrights reconsidered standard plot elements taken from epics and romances, actors could indicate a given character's stature through his physical carriage long before his centrality to the plot became evident. The ideal represented by heroism could be subverted or mocked by corporeal characterization.

The duel that Benedick proposes in Shakespeare's *Much Ado about Nothing* diverges from the standard contest enacted in late-sixteenth-century England: it reverts to trial by combat, the contest that decided between competing truth-claims. The duel Shakespeare depicts is not the contest over insult, the fight over personal preference or etiquette that was fought by gallants in that period. On the contrary, its stated purpose is to indicate truth—as if it were a late medieval trial by combat.[39] Yet, if it is constructed as trial by combat, its occasion recalls the romances produced by the Renaissance chivalric revival: it is prompted by the need to prove a woman's virtue. By making a challenge in defense of Hero's honor, Benedick consciously undertakes the role of the Christian knight—what we may read generically as the romance hero. Benedick's challenge to Claudio reframes masculine values and demonstrates the shortcomings of

Claudio as the play's romantic lead. As a result, the principal roles shift: Beatrice and Benedick replace Hero and Claudio as the primary love-interest, forcing the audience to reconsider the notions of young love that the play initially presents as ideal. Even after the play's comic denouement, Benedick retains center stage; generically, the witty figure proves more flexible than the more traditional hero.

In a thematic context, Benedick's challenge reframes masculine values, redefining the role of both the soldier and the knight. Benedick's decision to accept Hero's innocence without proof (that is, making his combat the proof) is a reversion to the ideal of Christian faith, a version of chivalry that privileges interiority and the private realm. These qualifying factors enable Benedick to accept the breach of fraternal bonds that seems concomitant upon performing this role. His challenge to Claudio brings acts and words into consonance for Messina, a society so involved in ceremonial discourse that words no longer necessarily correspond to reality. This potential gap between appearance and truth undermines the accepted early modern notion of aristocratic manhood. While the play ultimately presents court society positively, it implies that manhood may not be defined best by outward manifestations such as success in war or rhetorical ability. Benedick's challenge refigures knighthood not as a set of behaviors but as a set of beliefs, countering the early modern valorization of courtliness. It is faith and instinct (Benedick and Dogberry), valorized in late medieval romances, that restore the courtly society of Messina, which, despite the disquieting undercurrents of the final cuckold jokes, appears recovered in the end.[40]

The questions that we have been considering run through all of *Much Ado*. From the first, characters query the role of the young aristocrat under cover of jocose quips. Inquiring about Benedick, Beatrice poses the question central to the play: "[A] good soldier to a lady, but what is he to a lord?" (I.i.54–5). By the time the play was written, soldier and lord had become two distinct roles; many of even the most competent military commanders were finding it difficult to navigate court society.[41] As Elizabeth replaced soldiers drawn from the followers of the gentry and nobility with impressed men, the relation of the English aristocracy to military service altered radically. Moreover, as Stone explains, with the advent of new military technology, "[a] military commander had now to be an expert in logistics, in transport and victualling, in engineering and administration. The nobility were ill-adapted to such a change, which in any case deprived war of most of its aristocratic glamour" (*CA* 265). Fewer peers chose to receive training for the new warfare; instead, they went to court, although their eager desire to prove themselves on the battlefield was generally gratified whenever England went to war. Military opportunities for the nobility were limited, however, by several long periods of peace during the Tudor and Stuart reigns. These changes in the army affected the domestic life of the nobility. The nobleman's band of retainers generally diminished in size and the gentleman servant became relatively rare by the seventeenth century (Stone, *CA* 213).[42] With the custom of impressing vagrants and other men into the army, landlords had less need for their tenants' services and the mutual dependence of landlord and tenant diminished.

In this play, Shakespeare initially implies that all soldiers are courtiers. Despite various differences in character and temperament, all the men returning from war are acceptable in Messinian society. But, as the play continues, individual crotchets become more pronounced and the characters' abilities to interpret and communicate in court society are sharply differentiated. Difficulties ensue.

The play opens as if there were one set of stable values defining the role of the noble male. With the arrival of the messenger with news of the recent victory, every line of dialogue further clarifies these masculine values. Before Beatrice speaks, introducing her concern with wit and Cupid, the messenger and his hearty reception have already shown the importance of battles, victory, and honors for this community. The news is joyous enough that Leonato shrewdly judges that Claudio's uncle must have "[broken] out into tears" upon hearing it. Despite the ensuing festivities, the wars—and warlike concerns—are a serious business. As Janet Adelman comments of *Macbeth* (in which Shakespeare similarly uses a messenger as a device to fill in background), "[t]he opening scenes strikingly construct male and female as realms apart" (*Suffocating Mothers* 141). Although the play's concern is with love, we should not undervalue the information that both Claudio and Benedick "[f]or shape, for bearing, argument, and valor, / [Go] foremost in report through Italy" (III.i.96–7).[43]

That a military career offered minor gentry a way to earn favor and advancement is hinted at when Leonato comments, "I find here that Don Pedro hath bestow'd much honor on a young Florentine call'd Claudio" (I.i.9–11). Even Castiglione speaks at length about the aristocrat as a soldier. For Castiglione, war was a noble pursuit for display of talent and finesse, like dancing or poetic composition. The emphasis on dance and music in this play suggests that Messinian society might well resemble Castiglione's; certainly critics have long noted the charm of this community and its inhabitants' "easy charm, their wit and conviviality" (Cook 189). Yet the young noblemen, the Florentine called Claudio and the Paduan Signior Benedick, do not find themselves altogether adequate to the demands of this courtly society.

For a soldier living before the widespread diffusion of Humanist ideals, words—and skill with words—were almost supererogatory. The word of a gentleman (at a time when "gentleman" was synonymous with both "soldier" and "knight") was understood to be as good as his bond because it could be backed by physical things—*verba* and *res* were indivisible. If a man signed a contract saying that he would pay another man a sum of money, his signature was backed by real estate and movables. Similarly, if a man swore to the truth, he would be ready to back his words with his sword. Mervyn James argues that this attitude derived from

> a long-established military and chivalric tradition ... it assumes a state of affairs in which resort to violence is natural and justifiable; the recurrence of personal and political situations in which conflict cannot be otherwise resolved than violently. Honour could both legitimize and provide moral reinforcement for a politics of violence. (308–9)

Such an attitude obviously privileges *res* over *verba*, as well as creating a false closure of the gap between them. Claudio's and Benedick's concern with *res* and *verba* can be understood if we recognize its origin in the disintegration of the warrior ethic and the increasingly complex relation between words and things.

While Leonato and Don Pedro demonstrate their ease with the language of ceremony in greeting each other, the younger soldiers have no such skill at address. Although they have performed conspicuous feats of arms (conforming to Castiglione's model in that regard), they are unfamiliar with the skills of social intercourse that courtesy-book authors deem equally fundamental. The scene begins with Leonato's welcome:

> *Leonato*: Never came trouble to my house in the likeness of your Grace ...
> *Don Pedro*: You embrace your charge too willingly. I think this is your daughter.
> *Leonato*: Her mother hath many times told me so.
> *Benedick*: Were you in doubt, sir, that you ask'd her?
> *Leonato*: Signior Benedick, no, for then were you a child. (I.i.99–108)

Benedick resists constructing the world in ceremonial terms. His suspicion of ceremony conforms to proverbial ideas of the soldier during the Renaissance: the blunt but honest soldier was a mainstay of literature, evidenced by such works as Greene's *Tullies Love,* Barnaby Rich's *Farewell to Militarie Profession,* and even (in parody) Castiglione's *The Courtier.*[44] Benedick later refers to this type when he asks Claudio, "Do you question me, as an honest man should do, for my simple true judgment?" (I.i.166–7). He considers his tactlessness a positive trait. But in the context of this courtly exchange, Benedick's flippancy challenges conventional courtesies. His remark, following hard on the heels of Don Pedro's formal presentation of himself to Hero, seems particularly forward, since it is his opening address to an older man. But Leonato's compliment to Benedick saves the occasion, and Don Pedro follows his host's lead by pointing out that Benedick has been bested. He proceeds to offer formal compliment to Hero, and again Benedick chimes in with a flippant comment. At this point, Beatrice's mordant response seems most appropriate: "I wonder that you will still be talking, Signior Benedick, nobody marks you" (I.i.116–17). This reproof is well-merited, for Benedick's pert comments disrupt the tone of the occasion.

Initially the romantic lead, Claudio appears to be a more able manipulator of courtly conventions. He speaks as a conventional courtly lover, referring to jewels, desires, and love's ministers: "How sweetly you do minister to love, / That know love's grief by his complexion!" he says to the sympathetic Don Pedro (I.i.312–13). But several critics have noted Claudio's concern with dowry and inheritance (I.i.294).[45] In fact, he seems unable to tailor his discourse to his addressee. When he speaks of Hero to the cynical Benedick, he sighs, "Can the world buy such a jewel?" (I.i.181). But when Don Pedro and Leonato tell him that he has won his Hero, Beatrice's pert "Speak, Count, 'tis your cue" implies that he can find no words (II.i.305). Claudio's ability to speak love only through conventional compliment suggests his character's literary derivation from traditional epic romances of the chivalric revival, works such as *Rosalynde, Amadis of Gaul,* and *The Mirror of Knighthood.* Despite some recent comments on the subtext of his compliments,[46] this derivation from epic romance seems clear. But the very association also indicates the shortcoming of Claudio's rhetorical mode. As Bakhtin comments disparagingly, the epic "excludes any possibility of activity and change" (*DI* 17). Its monochrony renders it impervious to adaptation to the present; in fact, Bakhtin perceives it as being "as closed as a circle; inside it everything is finished, already over. There is no place in the epic world for any openendedness, indecision, indeterminacy" (*DI* 16). In Bakhtinian terms, Benedick's wit, his irony and, most of all, his willingness to accept paradox and confusion, render him a novelistic character, a figure with a capacity for multivoicedness and for a linguistic improvisation not so different from that of Pico's "maker and molder of himself."

Claudio's epical self-concept structures his behavior as a set of rhetorical gestures. His self-conscious, elaborate language suggests a deliberate attempt to enact his role properly. Claudio's incomplete understanding of chivalry, based on outward forms, not only perpetuates his naivete but also lays him open to Don John's manipulation.[47] By playing on Claudio's sense of himself, Don John can manipulate the younger man by changing the story in which the hero appears. Claudio's naivete is first evident when Don John attempts to provoke a quarrel between Claudio and his military commander by saying that Don Pedro has courted Hero for himself. The young man's failure to question his informant's veracity indicates the danger of this society for him.

Initially, Beatrice's repeated sallies against Benedick seem to indicate his ordinary stature. Their mutual antagonism makes him seem amusing but trivial. That Beatrice characterizes "the Benedick" as a disease suggests that the man is changeable in his sudden friendships (a woman's trait); that it will cost Claudio "a thousand pound ere 'a be cur'd" (I.i.90) suggests that Benedick is a wastrel, a contemporary English roaring boy who comes to town, spends his substance, and becomes known for disorderly ways. Moreover, Benedick's investment in verbal conquest makes us wonder whether he can attain anything larger. His flowing words lay him open to the charge of immaturity. In Act II, Beatrice compares Don John's silence to Benedick's verbosity, "too like my lady's eldest son, evermore tattling" (II.i.9–10). Note the implication of immaturity in loquacity, of hobbledehoydom.

The duality between words and action was often expressed in gendered terms, as in a proverb from Thomas Howell's *Devises* (1581): "Women are wordes, Men are deedes" (Sig. D2r).[48] This general belief neatly divided *res* and *verba,* sharing the pair equally between the sexes (although, as Patricia Parker points out, such gendered oppositions were quite unstable).[49] The idea that language was the province of women, that it represented a sphere inferior to that of action, probably derived partly from the military values of the old warrior elite. Such a view, however, was becoming outdated. When the play was written, skill in language was an acceptable, even a desirable trait in a nobleman, in part because of its very association with the humanist ideal. The elaborate courtesies of Leonato and Don Pedro provide a form to express the positive feeling among ruling patriarchs, soldier and administrator alike.

But as Stephen Greenblatt and Katherine Eisaman Maus have pointed out, these forms may easily be perverted by any machiavel.[50] The taciturn Don John seems at first to demonstrate an old ideal: "I am not of many words, but I thank you," he says to Leonato (I.i.157–8). But when he begins to speak at length, he forces wide the division between speech and action: "The word [disloyalty] is too good to paint out her wickedness. I could say she were worse; think you of a worse title, and I will fit her to it" (III.ii.109–11). What Don John offers to do is to construct a plausible story in which Hero serves as the exemplar of some given trait. In the world of epic romance, such deceptions as the supposed disloyalty of Hero are common; Don John uses Claudio's aspirations to courtly ideals to undermine Claudio's confidence in visible reality (Cook 192–3). By convincing Claudio that he is reenacting the story of Arthur and Guenevere (or any other one of many tales of traduction), Don John destroys Hero's less rhetorically able plausibility. His language shows the negative side of Benedick's apparently trivial skill with words; he can turn words into stories—into interpretations. While Benedick intends his banter to be understood merely as light words, Don John presents his stories as *more* significant than they are (Dawson 214). His framing devices take the fact—a woman at the window conversing with a man—and present it to give the impression that a specific woman is unchaste. Control of language becomes the purview of the villain (who has already failed at the use of force), and the gracious exchanges between courtiers prove ripe for his exploitation.

Words not grounded in action become dangerously open to malicious misinterpretation. Ceremonies need stronger, more definite ties to the things they represent; otherwise, even such men as Leonato and Don Pedro lose their authority. As the denouement approaches, the two elder statesmen no longer trust each other, presenting perhaps the bleakest scene of the play as Leonato implies that Don Pedro has taken advantage of his hospitality, while Don Pedro responds as if his host were a superannuated dotard.

Few have seen in Don John a mirror of Benedick, but I read Don John as a negative image of the considerable power of rhetoric.

His skill with language complicates that easy gender dichotomy from Howell's proverbs because he is a man who uses words, that flimsy commodity, to compel change in the physical world. Although he initially insists that he will be "a plain-dealing villain," he follows Conrade's advice and conceals his malignity, his discontent fuelling his mischievous, antisocial plots, compounding his malignity with interest. His opportunities arise from the recognition of accepted gaps between appearance and reality:

> *Borachio*: I ... heard it agreed upon that the Prince should woo Hero for himself, and having obtain'd her, give her to Count Claudio.
> *Don John*: Come, come, let us thither, this may prove food to my displeasure. (I.iii.60–6)

Clearly he sees the opportunity to "fashion" a scheme—to reframe to others the actions of his brother from a skewed perspective.

Don Pedro's little deception of Hero is the first opportunity offered to Don John, but as the play proceeds we see that both words and actions may easily be distorted.[51] Characters expect their meaning to be transparent, but subsequent dialogue indicates how much is left to the viewers' perceptions. Disjunction between *res* and *verba* recurs in Don John's more serious scheme, not least in Shakespeare's decision not to present the Borachio–Margaret scene onstage. The playwright's choice prevents the audience members from assessing the impersonation ourselves. Instead, we hear the confession of the morally muddled Borachio.[52] Borachio's indiscreet conversation with Conrade both gives him away and fills us in, even giving us a moral framework within which to view his actions. The taste for fashion in clothing that Margaret evinces and for fashion in show that motivates Borachio are desires that this henchman repudiates as tawdry even as he recounts his enslavement to them. The show that we watch (his confession) substitutes for the show we desire to see (his masquerade with Margaret as Hero's lover and Hero herself); his resulting shame as he confesses may evoke our sense that our desire for titillation, our desire to be deceived, is as tawdry as these characters' desire to impress others by means of show.

Wholesale distortion results from Don John's ambiguous "show"; in response to it, Claudio stages another:

> There, Leonato, take her back again.
> Give not this rotten orange to your friend,
> She's but the sign and semblance of her honor. (IV.i.31–3)

To the watchers, this outbreak is incomprehensible. Like that of the two lovers whom Claudio has watched from a distance, Claudio's performance needs to be framed by information if it is to be meaningful. His violence opposes his prior gentility; his harshness contrasts with his earlier affection; his rudeness denies his hitherto respectful manner.[53]

As a result of his performance, Beatrice learns a hard lesson about the gendered nature of performative speech. Claudio's impressions, based on Margaret and Borachio's masquerade are, of course, false, and his term for Hero, "an approved wanton" (IV.i.44), a misrepresentation of her. Yet Beatrice finds that the alternative terms she offers (which the audience knows are true) are not accepted as truth. Even though she may insist that her cousin is belied, her words do not have the rhetorical force of Claudio's accusation. She learns, to her dismay, not that words have no effect, but that some words are privileged over others. Despite her desire to champion her cousin, she cannot find an illocutionary utterance that can refute Claudio's charge effectively. Claudio's ritualistic rejection of Hero—his anti-wedding ceremony—has demonstrated the devastating effect of performative speech, which seems to unite word and world. When Beatrice utters a challenge to Claudio's words, insisting that Hero is belied, her gender invalidates the significance of her speech. As the result of her sex, her threats are empty, for they must be backed by the possibility of fulfillment in order to have illocutionary force.

Unsurprisingly, when Benedick confesses his love for Beatrice, she hesitates to believe that his speech unites word and meaning. She repeatedly reminds Benedick that his promise of love conjoins three elements—his promise, his sword, and his honor. He in turn insists that he will not need to retract (eat his words), thereby losing his honor (his sword).

Yet Beatrice still hesitates. "Men are only turn'd into tongue," she says (IV.i.320). What kind of evidence can Benedick provide as proof? Her request, "Kill Claudio," which at first sounds like a reversion to a revenge tragedy plot, gradually becomes clarified. Once we see that Beatrice is asking her lover to challenge Claudio to the duel, the generic conventions of the play shift again, and we recognize that Shakespeare is blending contemporary romantic comedy with the somewhat older traditions of the Continental romance. Beatrice's request that Benedick act as Hero's champion, which at first outrages him, soon seems to both characters an appropriate proof of manhood, now understood as the ability to provide physical proof of sincerity. At first Benedick hesitates, but he resolves to show that he *can* back his aration with concrete proof:

> *Benedick*: By this hand, I love thee.
> *Beatrice*: Use it for my love some other way than swearing by it. ...
> *Benedick*: Enough, I am engag'd. ... By this hand, Claudio shall render me a dear account. (IV.i.324–33)

Although Beatrice initially sees Benedick's challenge as a means of revenge on Claudio, it becomes a promise to reunite virtuous reputation with virtue embodied. After Don John's reticence, which conceals his animosity, is mistakenly coded as manly, the duel appears in response to the need for an unambiguous sign of truth. In the discourse of the duel, the challenge—"You lie"—is made good by the duel itself, for staking one's life on it is the ultimate proof of one's word. As Susan Frye explains, "an oath is a form of language that promises action—indeed, guarantees that the word and the deed are one and the same" (4). The challenge to the combat is a powerful speech-act because it constitutes an oath backed by physical action. Once it is made, the question at stake (no matter what the accusation) becomes that of honor: to issue or to accept a formal challenge is to back one's word with one's sword and one's life. The challenge serves both as a promise to fight and a pledge of one's words. Such speech is consonant with the life of action that belongs to a soldier.

Benedick's pledge echoes the promise of knights in much earlier romances. But his enactment of the heroic role, unlike Claudio's, is based upon faith—if not faith in Hero herself, then faith in Beatrice's belief in her cousin's innocence. Whereas Claudio structures his behavior according to the forms approved by his elders and by tradition, Benedick takes an unpopular stance because his feelings prompt him to see it as morally correct. This choice carries him beyond the *fortezza* formula that many Renaissance writers found inadequate (Steadman 6–10). Shakespeare resolves the incompatibility of the epic hero with the Christian knight by linking Benedick's valor with faith and magnanimity. This noble spirit raises his eminence beyond Claudio's. True manhood does not belong to the braggart but to the man who, as Don Pedro says of Benedick, either "avoids [quarrels] with great discretion, or undertakes them with a most Christian-like fear" (II.iii.191–2). With the revelation of the false ideals represented by the failure of Hero and Claudio to wed, Benedick steps into the role of hero that Claudio has vacated. This scene alters both the nature of Beatrice and Benedick's interaction and the play's implied definition of the code of courtly conduct. Benedick's notion of heroism is the performance of deeds rather than ceremonial forms. He undertakes not to speak as a chivalric knight but to act as one. The hand on which he swears is the hand that will execute his intentions.

The duel might provide decisive closure to the play if Shakespeare had chosen to write a tragedy. But, rather than enacting the physical attack, Shakespeare resorts to interruptive mechanisms that highlight Benedick's integrity in issuing the challenge. Before Benedick can challenge Claudio, Don Pedro's protégé is approached from another quarter. Leonato's grief at his daughter's disgrace erupts in an outburst that turns into a farcical challenge. As governor of Messina, one of Leonato's chief duties is to keep the peace; yet now this reverend signior actually proposes a duel. His challenge to Claudio seems almost an emblematic inversion of authority, authority transformed into disorder. It demonstrates, moreover, the degree to which the play's moral center has been lost; in contrast, Benedick's challenge functions as an attempt to rediscover that center. The older man's vacillation between support for and condemnation of his daughter leaves a gap in the moral structure of Messina that Benedick, inspired by Beatrice, helps to fill.

Benedick speaks directly and responsibly about consequences as the other male characters appear increasingly irrational, immature, and volatile. His words promise that those accountable for the wedding fiasco and Hero's humiliation will pay for what they have done. He presents himself as a character who recognizes when lightness is no longer appropriate. Quite measured for an avenger, he neither rants nor storms but guarantees to bring together his word and his deeds. Such thoughtful behavior contrasts not only with Leonato's and Antonio's wild words but also with the dismissiveness of his friends. Despite Claudio's and Don Pedro's response to Benedick's challenge, it is clear that Benedick has come into his own. By refusing to let his companions divert his purpose, Benedick gains a stature beyond that previously possessed by the more uncertain Claudio. His desire to serve Beatrice and to champion her cousin shows his engagement with the world of the elders, Don Pedro and Leonato, whose decisions structure the Messinian community. When Benedick accepts the need to turn against his comrade, he becomes one of the men who shapes society.

The promised contest, however, strains at the confines of comedy. In Shakespeare's Messina, the proposed combat carries neither the subversive overtones of the Elizabethan duel of honor nor the legal validity of the judicial duel. The combat that Benedick proposes actually conflates the purpose of the trial by combat with the results of the duel of honor. Historically, the judicial combat was accepted as a part of due process; in such a fight, Benedick's victory would prove that Hero was chaste. But in the duel of honor, the key issue was reputation; the presumption in this case would be that the winner's view of Hero would become, *ipso facto*, the accepted one. While Benedick undertakes to prove Hero's innocence through the duel, the lack of a legal context for the combat ensures only that he can defend her reputation, as in a duel of honor. Perhaps for this reason, or perhaps to maintain *Much Ado* within the bounds of romantic comedy, Shakespeare gives us the discovery of the Watch rather than Benedick and Claudio's combat. Despite Benedick's efforts, the restoration of Messina's moral order cannot be accomplished entirely by a duel. Benedick's faith in Hero's innocence is reinforced by the staging of Borachio's confession to Claudio and Don Pedro, and by Dogberry's intuitive recognition of criminal behavior.[54]

The word grounded in action, the antidote to uncontrolled rhetoric is represented by the binding of Borachio and Conrade, indicated in the playscript by Dogberry's malapropism: "Come let them be opinion'd" (IV.ii.67). As soon as Dogberry has spoken, Don John's henchmen are, presumably, bound (Conrade immediately shouts, "Off, coxcomb!"). Dogberry's phrase offers a verbal representation of staged action; it is an order prompting an unmistakable constraint of the physical body of another. Once the two men are "opinion'd," they are bound both physically and emblematically, in the sense that they are put under legal constraint. Opinions, interpretations, and personal perspectives have been the chief threat to the comedy and to the social stability underlying Messina's festivity; opinions, finally, must yield to pinions, to rough and constraining ties. These ties suggest both the world of objects that exist with or without names and the ties of meaningful action that connect names and things. With this binding, the drama indicates a movement toward closure. The pinions guarantee the confinement and forced submission of wandering signifiers. As the Watch recite Borachio's confession and the Sexton records it, the danger that comedy will be overturned is reduced and brought under control.

At the very least, Benedick's challenge to the duel offers a pragmatic solution to the problem by backing his interpretation with the threat of force. Read more positively, his challenge, by its moral courage, restores the community's inner vision and makes possible the happy results of the legal investigation. Like the duel of honor, legal inquiry can only promise settlement, not truth: both result in the victor's control of the narrative. But the traditions from which the duel derives both stage the conflict here and offer a tool to resolve them. Shakespeare seems seduced to some extent by the very medium of romantic comedy: at certain moments he colludes with the genre's conventions to envision a world in which true nobility can be demonstrated by a man's swordsmanship. Such simple equivalences themselves are a sign of nostalgia; they enable both author and audience to avoid the anxieties concomitant on considering the true complexity of masculinity and its relation to social status in early modern England.

From examining this use of the duel, we can recognize that Shakespeare found only certain aspects of combat dramatically useful. In *Much Ado*, Shakespeare uses the challenge to develop the lightweight Benedick into a figure of at least arguably heroic stature. In doing so, Shakespeare reconceives the nature of the hero (or at least of the gentleman) as more human, more fallible, and more psychologically rounded than he was traditionally conceived.[55] Yet, in doing so, Shakespeare must also borrow from older traditions of the combat, as if the duel of honor itself could not adequately represent the heroic. Certainly, the symbolic freight of Benedick's proposed duel is its uniting of word and world, an ability by no means guaranteed by an extra-legal duel. Shakespeare's use of this ritual here, I would argue, manifests in mimetic form both the desire of the duellist and the frustration of that desire. In *Much Ado*, despite disturbing overtones of chauvinism and fraternal strife, the conservative return to older traditions appears as a viable response to a complex and potentially mendacious world. But the duel of honor itself did not seem adequate as a sign of manliness without the adumbration of other, significantly dissimilar, traditions.

CHAPTER 2

THE ART OF FENCE AND THE SENSE OF MASCULINE SPACE

This chapter analyzes late-sixteenth-century fencing manuals in order to articulate the assumptions about spatiality derived from early modern fencing and duelling; the analysis both defines the sense of gender implicit in these spatial assumptions and enables us to consider how these spatial assumptions may enter into the drama. Our focus shall be what Gail Kern Paster calls "the subjective experience of being-in-the-body" (3). Although fencing manuals only give information about a specific social group, they may be contextualized through comparison with more general directives in courtesy manuals and, as we shall see in Chapter Three, through contrast with directives addressed to well-born women.

Since the translation into English of Norbert Elias's groundbreaking work, substantial numbers of scholars have accepted the idea that the semiotics of early modern body language affected social definition. (We have, for example, Elias's own discussion of a discipline of shame in young men, cultivated during the early modern period at the urging of such educators as Erasmus through social strictures urging against "boorish" or "rustic" behavior.) But evidence of body language seldom indicates exactly what assumptions about the self that body language manifests. Like Erasmus's directives, fencing manuals were addressed to a specific readership, so their directives about body language may be assumed to relate to the behavior of men of higher rank. However, as with Erasmus's writings, we cannot immediately assume that we understand how those engaged in specific behaviors perceived themselves—only how others wished to shape that behavior.

Those engaged in sociohistorical interpretation today who attempt to decipher the codes of gesture and behavior have had difficulty making sense of conflicting data. On the one hand, as Elias points out, Erasmus condemns drawing attention to oneself; on the other hand, Castiglione's Gasparo Pallavicino defends straightforward boasting, a verbal behavior that David Quint interprets in spatial terms as "the spontaneous, natural extension of the personal magnificence...of the aristocrat" (400). Quint's spatial metaphor is literalized in Book Two, Chapter 29 of William Vaughan's *The Golden Grove* (1600), in which noblemen are described as spreading out physically or as already too large: their "properties...are to flaunt like Pea Cockes...and to trust most impudently in the hugeness of their lims and in their drunken gates" (qtd. in Anna Bryson 152). Their behavior seems to manifest the same assumptions that Quint defines. The art historian Joaneath Spicer examines painters' representations of what she calls "the Renaissance elbow," arguing that sixteenth-century painters conveyed "the manly virtues...through both attributes and body language, such as the arm akimbo, most frequently showing one hand on the hip by a sword or rapier" (93). Such gestures, she says, indicate confidence that one's physical boundaries will be respected.[1]

But in "The Rhetoric of Gesture," Anna Bryson examines the many negative comments written in response to these behaviors. She asks why young noblemen frequently assumed physically expansive postures seemingly expressive of incontinence or arrogance. Based on uniform class-based condemnations of swaggerers, Bryson regards this behavior as a reversal of class—an assumption of the privilege (or license) granted to rank. She sensibly observes that, based on the evidence, "the response of the elite to ideals of gracefully controlled carriage and modesty of demeanour was less than complete. Status could be associated with deliberate license" (152).[2]

While this view seems to offer the most comprehensive explanation of an overdetermined phenomenon, Georges Vigarello's study "The Upward Training of the Body from the Age of Chivalry to Courtly Civility" looks at different kinds of evidence and offers yet another interpretation, one quite opposed to Bryson's. In research derived from that of Philipe Aries, Roger Chartier, and Norbert Elias, Vigarello uses early modern French conduct-books, fencing manuals, tracts about dancing, anatomical treatises, and medical texts to

Figure 2.1 Illustration from Viggiani's Italian fencing manual. A fencer in fencing clothers, carrying a rapier and swaggering as he walks.

support his Foucauldian thesis that as deportment became more rigorous, increased attention was brought to bear on the body, which was physically constricted by clothing, training, and verbal directives.[3] He argues convincingly that social prescriptions concerning posture became increasingly constricting and oriented toward performance throughout the seventeenth century.

Bryson's and Vigarello's differing interpretations of the aristocratic masculine demeanor derive in part from the fact that they work with different data, but there are meaningful conflicts between the two scholars that should be addressed. I attempt to gain a more inclusive view by using one to read the other—and applying both to the evidence offered in the fencing manuals of Saviolo, di Grassi, and Silver. In my view, the phenomena Bryson discusses would be better understood as a development of the physical demeanor taught to men in courtly arts such as fencing. The fencer develops extended corporeal parameters that structure his behavior in relation both to the opposite sex and to men lower on the social scale. The provocatively aggressive hand-on-hip posture that Spicer examines is an indication of something far more fundamental than a conscious assertion of superiority to the need for good manners: the sense of physical superiority derived from an expansion of one's personal boundaries.

When the techniques of rapier-fighting developed, the absolute standards of strength and endurance in swordfighting were replaced by a much more slippery and relational standard: skill. Such shifts as this one adumbrated the sense of flux brought about by the many large changes during this period. Mark Franko has pointed out Montaigne's use of a certain vocabulary of dance to suggest "both a shifting and unstable universe and a dance floor on which a shifting dance is performed to acknowledge and compensate for cosmic instability" (60). The relational standards—relational particularly because no measure other than victory was reliable—offered courtiers a new vision of themselves. While David Quint suggests that the aristocracy underwent "the gradual exchange of an openly expressed and aggressive egotism for the manners and style of indirection" (429), I would argue that in fact fencing offered its practitioners a more complex way of conceiving themselves. The frequency with which fencing manuals conflate the body and the defensive ward suggests that the penetration of the ward was interpreted as penetration of the body. In fencing, a combatant gains a psychological advantage from invading his opponent's space, though a more successful practice was to press one's opponent through a gradual incursion into his space. On the basis of this training, the fencer manifested a physical expansiveness denied to women and to men untaught in fencing—essentially making this proxemic behavior a class marker. Over time, I would argue, the extended proxemic sense gained from fencing became part of how men of a certain rank conceived of their masculinity. Yet the art of fence, as practiced by the English, also renewed the upper-class

Englishman's perception of himself as one linked to the yeoman class, or even to the soil of England.

The fencing manuals that I draw on were written principally by fencing-masters known throughout Elizabethan London, and they explicate the practice that the authors taught to numerous courtiers and wealthy commoners.[4] Written to school men in fencing techniques, these manuals reveal the proprioceptive experiences of swordfighters trained in different traditions of violence or in aggressive and competitive forms of play. By analyzing the language in these texts, we can see how training in rapier-fencing taught spatial assumptions that helped structure a corporeal sense of masculinity that eventually spread beyond those communities defined by devotion to the art of fence.[5]

Subjectivity is intimately related to the awareness of being embodied, enfleshed: it is not derived merely from the recognition of possessing a unique consciousness but, as importantly, from the awareness and acknowledgment of one's tactile relationship to the physical world.[6] Insofar as subjectivity is the knowledge of one's own individuation, that experience is related to sensory experience as much as to thought. Judith Butler's discussion of phenomenology emphasizes "bodily gestures, movements, and enactments of various kinds" and further alludes to "the tacit conventions that structure the way the body is culturally perceived" ("Performative Acts" 270, 275). Early modern texts of rhetoric or courtesy theory often reveal a self-consciousness about presentation, including a concern with body language. The sense of the semiotics of the body revealed in these texts was sophisticated. For example, in *The Art of Rhetoric* (1560), Thomas Wilson quotes Cicero: "The gesture of man is the speech of his body, and therefore reason it is that like as the speech must agree to the matter, so must also the gesture agree to the mind" (244). In *Of Education, Especially of Young Gentlemen* (1673), Obadiah Walker urges his readers to conform to "a certain mine [sic] and motion of the body, and its parts, both in acting and speaking, which is very graceful and pleasing" (217). Walker suggests that body and manner should be in harmony "as for a young man to be active and sprightly ... a grave man slow and deliberate" (217). Such directives suggest that one's carriage could communicate a recognizable message, and Walker's specifics demonstrate that early modern society endorsed an assertive, vigorous stance for young noblemen.[7]

My own focus, however, will be on inner experience, the physical sensations that shaped the way individuals conceived of or presented themselves. Critics such as Gail Kern Paster have resorted to Mauss's conception of *habitus,* theorizing a "connection between outer and inner" (3). In a consideration of the skills learned in fencing, both are important: the physical perceptions of the subject, experiencing sensually the movement of the torso and limbs, the air-flow, air-temperature, and other external stimuli; and the educated inferences of the outside observer, assessing the subject semiotically in order to interpret the information provided by stance and gesture.[8] In analyzing one aspect of physical subjectivity, the anthropologist Edward T. Hall has asserted that "[t]he boundaries of the self extend beyond the body" (11). Hall alludes to what we have come to call "personal space" or "personal distance." The latter term, developed by the anthropologist H. Hediger, refers to "the normal spacing that non-contact animals maintain between themselves and their fellows. This distance acts as an invisible bubble that surrounds the organism" (Hall 12). Hall's work, which examines populations of animals, mental patients, and members of different ethnic groups and nationalities, analyzes the structure and parameters of personal distance. As Hall and his followers have shown, human beings' "bubbles" of comfortable distance alter, depending on the activity in which they are engaged and the relation between them and the persons nearby. Other factors that influence the extension of personal space include tactile information, visual information, and one's perception of body temperature. Yet another factor is one's cultural group, probably because most members of a cultural group have certain experiences of comfort and discomfort in common.

The uniqueness of the fencer's perception of his body resulted from the development of the rapier—the new, lightweight weapon that could be extensively used for defense as well as offense (Aylward 39, 57–8; Stone, *CA* 242–50). The rapier also changed the form of attack: because of its thin blade, it was used much less for slashing, as a sword was, than for thrusting (Turner and Soper xxii). The introduction to *Vincentio Saviolo, His Practice* (1595) emphasizes that the chief art of rapier-fencing is the art of defense:[9] "I will shewe you the wardes which I myself use, the which if you well marke and observe, you cannot but understand the art, and withall keepe your bodye safe from hurte and danger" (*His Practice* D2v). By the term "ward," Saviolo means the stance of readiness, "on guard," in which a fencer simultaneously prepared himself for attacking his opponent and readied himself for his opponent's attack on him (Castle 12). Various stances would in theory enable the fencer to parry any attack, although certainly some stances were better for parrying certain moves than others. Both Saviolo and di Grassi comment that while the use of the rapier may be combined with that of the dagger, the rapier is never used in conjunction with any defensive blocking instrument such as a target, buckler, or shield. The only blocking instrument regularly used with the rapier is the cloak, which engages a rapier, rendering one's opponent defenseless. Since, as di Grassi points out, not all blows may be warded with the cloak (H3r), he and his fellows repeatedly stress the use of the rapier and gloved hand, or the rapier and dagger, to project the defensive ward.

The defensive stance enables a fencer to ward off attacks to any part of his body merely by turning aside his opponent's weapon with a dagger, rapier, or gloved hand (hence, the term "ward").[10] Such a defense is effective because of the rapier's comparatively light weight and because its edges are not sharp enough to inflict a serious wound. Instead of relying on clumsy armor or a heavy and cumbersome shield, the fencer depends on his own agility and his superior strategy to protect him. Di Grassi describes an intimate connection between the protective ward and the body itself:

> Wards ... are as a shield or safegarde. ... For he who hath no skill to carrie his bodie and beare these weapons orderlie, which either cover, or easely maie cover the whole bodie, cannot be saide to stand in warde, insomuch that a man ought to use great diligence in the apt carriyng of his bodie and weapons. (C4r)

A ward is enacted by one's carriage: the defense is made *by* the body and *in relation* to it. In effect, the ward is the body's attitude of readiness: the weight and balance of the body, its position relative to the opponent's weapon.[11] Yet the ward obviously extends out beyond the torso itself, though not to the tip of the extended rapier. On the contrary, di Grassi says, the first two quarters of the sword closest to the hilt are "to be used to ward withall, because in striking they draw litle compas, and therefore carrie with them but smal force. And for that their place is neere the hande, they are for this cause strong to resist anie violence" (B1v). The ward, then, extends the fencer's sense of personal space as far as his outstretched hand or even to the point on the sword where it can parry most effectively. Like the shield, which di Grassi describes as "a wall before the bodie" (M1v), the ward defines one's personal space as the area within which any penetration is an aggressive intrusion.[12]

Saviolo implies that the ward extends the body beyond the physical frame: in explaining how to respond to an opponent's attack, he tells his pupil, "even at that instant that he moveth his foot in charging you, as you finde him open in any place, so seeke to offend him" (***3r). The suggestion to respond when "you finde *him* open" metonymically equates the opponent and his ward, as if the ward was perceived not only as a defensive blocking gesture but also as a parameter defining the physical limit of the combatant himself. While the ward functions as a physical marker demarcating inside and outside, it also protects the tender body within, ideally creating an impermeable barrier. The slight turn of the arm or the rapier creates a fence of crisscrossed gestures. Although they involve only one's physical extensions—one's arms or a steel blade—the wards function as a wall. To penetrate this wall is to penetrate an artificially constructed personal barrier; like breaching the wall of a dwelling-place, penetration intrudes on that which has been designated closed, personal, not to be entered.

Saviolo's terms characterize the ward as an extension of body space and the fencer's victory primarily as any intrusion into that space: "if [your opponent] bee skilfull in managing his weapon, take heede in anie case that you let him not get within you, or winne grounde of you" (I4r). To "get within you" is clearly not to wound you, but to thrust a sword within your ward (though that, of course, makes it more likely that he will also wound you). But the ward is like the outermost layer of epidermis: one is *already* penetrated when the ward has been penetrated.

The area within the ward functions as "critical distance"—the term Hall uses to characterize "the narrow zone separating flight distance from attack distance" among many animal species (11). Depending on the social structure of the animal species, a subordinate animal may yield room to a dominant of the same species, rather than intrude into this space (Hall 13). Many physical signs of discomfort at such penetration—even in quite neutral contexts—have been observed in both animals and human beings (Hall 11-37). The sense of this space is related to the sense of one's own body; intrusions into this space are indeed physical intrusions upon one's person. Saviolo repeatedly differentiates between breaking through the ward and wounding an opponent; the term for breaching the ward is almost always "to enter":

> [H]e may enter with his lefte foote and put you in great danger. (I3r)
>
> [I]f you bee not passing readie with your foot, and in turning your bodie wel and fitly on your right side, your enemie entering maye thrust you in the bellie with his Rapier. (I3v)

What the opponent *enters* is the ward. In technical terms, the extension of the ward is repeatedly characterized in terms of geometry (di Grassi A2v, A4r–B4r; Saviolo E4v–F1r). This extension, whose center may be the hip pivot, the shoulder pivot, or the wrist pivot, forms a curvilinear shape, a literal circle of power and a circle of protection. Once that circle has been breached, one's powers of defense are quite limited. One's ward, then, serves as a defense—a "fence"—in the sense that it is a protective barrier.

The use of other weapons may redefine the sense of space according to their length or the nature of their use. George Silver, the advocate of the short sword, views the ward in a different light. Like di Grassi, he endorses the use of physical barriers: the hilt, he says, "is a more sure and strong ward, then is the blade of the Rapier" (33, 52). For Silver, the rapier is *less* maneuverable than the short sword. Aside from its design, which he believes leaves the hand vulnerable to wounding, the rapier's length (four feet or more) makes the weapon difficult to manipulate.[13] Its limited use for attack (it cannot be used for edge-strokes, only for thrusts) is less worrisome in his view than its "inconvenient length, and unweildinesse" (9); fencers, he asserts, are "in danger of everie crosse, that shall happen to be made with their rapier blades, which being done...it is impossible to uncrosse, or get out, or to avoid the stabbes of the Daggers" (9). In his view, a physical barrier is stronger and more reliable than one depending, like the ward, on the uncertain skills of the fencer. But di Grassi warns that using the round target (a small shield) can hinder one's fighting ability because its weight can weary the muscles, and it can easily block sightlines, especially when raised to deflect a blow to the upper torso or head. Thus, a shield may not actually extend the physical sense of the body as well as the ward of the rapier fencer. Since sight is so necessary to effective combat, the shield might well feel to a combatant like a clumsy tool rather than an extension of the body.

In some perceptual sense, the extension of personal space may initially depend on actually extending the rapier, which is experienced as a part of the body. Nor is this sense unique to the sword; a twentieth-century hockey player, for example, may consider his stick a part of him.[14] This sense of the weapon has practical ramifications: a swordsman's assessment of distance and proportion depends upon the close relation of body and weapon. Di Grassi, who discusses both thrusts and edge-blows at length, points out that if one combatant attacks with a thrust and the other with an edge-cut, their relative distance is altered by their method of attack. If a combatant who plans to thrust

> perceive himselfe to be nerer by halfe an arme, he ought not to care to defend himselfe, but with all celeritie to strike. For as he hitteth home first, so he preventeth the fal of his enemies sword. (A4v)

Because he stands close to his opponent, his blow will land before that of the other. By contrast, if he stands at a greater distance, he will not be able to wound his opponent before the edge-blow makes contact, and so he should parry rather than attacking. In the actual thrust, the sword extends the reach of the arm, so the assessment of distance should involve not only the length of the arm but the added length of the sword as well (O4r); in the edge-blow, the sword describes part of a circle around the pivot-point, so the equation becomes more complicated.

But to Saviolo, the weapon is always the instrument of the man who wields it. He takes pains to emphasize that the rapier is a tool, not an extension of the body. Saviolo discourages any confusion for practical reasons, pointing out that the two elements can easily be separated: if you take hold of your opponent's sword arm, he may switch to a left-handed sword grip and confound you (F2r–F2v, H4v–*1r). Seizing the sword hilt, on the other hand, effectively ends the fencing match as such.

In his book *Paradoxes of Defence*, the reactionary George Silver goes even further by arguing that not all parts of the body can be used effectively to advance into the personal space of one's opponent. He views even certain extensions of the body as artificial—as elements that cannot indicate true possession of a physical space. Whatever is done with the foot, he says, is "false fight," because leading with the foot gives away your intentions to your opponent before the goal is achieved. For Silver, the hand is the swiftest and most trustworthy agent—it becomes less effective when its motions are combined with those of other bodily members.

Much of Silver's distrust of rapier-fight seems to derive from the strategies that, he insists, are entirely ineffective. But Vincentio Saviolo asserts that there are three wards that, properly learned, will defend the fencer from any and all attacks (D2r). Saviolo's insistence on the development of instinctive responses strongly suggests that the extended sense of physical space, once learned, may carry over into the fencer's general deportment. Saviolo stresses the importance of practice, disparaging those "which will thinke they knowe inough, but most commonly are deceived" (H1r). He places great emphasis on "readiness," a term that seems to describe for him an almost reflexive response to an attack. In explaining how to attack an opponent in a rapier and dagger combat, he comments that "you must bee verye well exercised in these passataes, for perfourming them with quicknes of the bodye, albeit you happen to faile of your purpose, yet your enemie shalbe able to take no advantage thereof" (***2r). The "exercise" or practice that he advocates produces a passata performed with "quickness of the bodye," an almost automatic action that enables the fencer to respond to the opportunity without needing to think. Although Saviolo advocates analyzing the combat as one fights, his recommendation suggests that certain maneuvers should be automatic. In the manual's dialogue, the scholar Luke asks the fencing-master why the student must practice stoccatas and imbrocatas so often. The fictional master Vincentio replies, "if you desire to bee made readye and perfect, practise these principles, learning well the time and measure, and therby you shall open your spirites in the knowledge of the secrets of armes" (*3v). "Proper time," according to the combat historian Egerton Castle, involves "reduc[ing] the motions of weapon and body to the strictly necessary ... so as to employ the least possible time in attack and parry" (12). "Measure" involves "keep[ing] out of easy reach when on the defensive, and, conversely, never to deliver an attack without being within striking distance" (Castle 11). But the term "spirits" derives not from fencing but from Galenic-Renaissance medicine, referring to what it is that amplifies stimuli to the body, thereby animating it (Roach 40, 41). Thomas Heywood, apologist for the theater, uses the term "active spirits" to refer to physical transformation, "an actual change in the actor's bodily shape between passions" (qtd. in Roach 42–3). Saviolo's phrase "open your spirites" obviously involves some similar notion of transformation. It suggests a number of possible meanings—first, to open oneself to fencing in order to gain a bodily knowledge of the defensive responses that should follow specific attacks. One's spirits also may refer to one's mood, one's buoyancy: the phrase suggests that exercise may improve one's spirits, perhaps through balancing the humors or "spirites." But in addition, the phrase suggests that through proficiency, fencers gain self-confidence that they express physically. These physical indications of skill would almost certainly be the body language expressing one's sense of extended personal space. Certainly, the fencer's development of expanded or extended personal space depends in part on his sense of ease in movement.

Yet that ease is not, of course, the final goal of training in fencing. Nor is the creation of an impenetrable ward, whose development, like its accompanying spatial assumptions, must be complicated by the need to defeat one's opponent. Because offense necessitates entering the personal space of one's opponent, one's own personal space also must be compromised when one attacks. What happens, then, to the sense of personal space when the fencer moves out of his ward?

Were the fencer's attack enacted at random without a sense of timing, the movement would indeed seem to burst the attacker's "bubble" of personal space. But the fencer is taught to attack only when he may seize the advantage. Fencers are engaged in a partner relation not unlike that of paired dancers: each responds to the other's movements. The manuals make frequent references to time and proportion, as if fencing was a sport set to music; in fact, Saviolo often describes the body's ward in action almost as one would dancing steps: "at that verie instant make three times with your feet at once, moving a little with your right foot, a little with your left; and againe a little with your right" (G4v). The similarity does not end with the set movements: when referring to the first ward he teaches his pupils, Saviolo describes a stance almost shockingly intimate. The instructor

Figure 2.2 Woodcut from *Vincentio Saviolo, his Practise* (London: 1595). This illustration demonstrates the reciprocal movements of teacher and pupil.

should "holde his Rapier against the middest of his schollers Rapier, so that the pointe be directlye against the face of his scholler, and likewise his schollers against his, and let their feete be right one against another" (D3v). This is what Hall calls "personal distance," about which he asserts, "This is the limit of physical domination in the very real sense" (113). At the near limit of this distance, according to Hall, "[t]he kinesthetic sense of closeness derives in part from the possibilities present in regard to what each participant can do to the other with his extremities" (112). The contest thus forces adversaries to be acutely conscious of their physical intimacy.[15] The intimacy and trust of the stance Saviolo describes between pupil and instructor resembles that of dance partners in the round dances enacted among both countryfolk and courtiers. But it is feasible only between teacher and pupil; in such a relationship, the pedagogical imperative has already established power relations that need not then be disputed.[16] The stance also indicates the degree of trust between teacher and pupil. Other relationships are more questionable.[17]

Significantly, the value of physical closeness to an opponent is disputed in the manuals. Simply put, any given distance offers equal advantages to both fencers, except perhaps in the moment of an initial attack and the defensive response. Timing, again, is all. Certainly it is agreed that a fencer who stands too close to his opponent loses the ability to thrust effectively. But what about the effective parrying of an attack? The obvious response to attack, retreat, was unpopular with many men who considered it cowardly to fall back (Saviolo *4v).[18]

The inherent psychological effects of physical intimacy may actually offer a shortcut to achieving the domination over another that is the fencer's ultimate goal. If an opponent closes in to press his attack, a fencer must choose either to back away or to stand his ground. If he stands his ground, that physical closeness prompts such responses as an increased heart rate and alteration in the size of the pupils.[19] Focusing the eye at such close range involves some muscle strain, resulting in physical discomfort. Pressing an opponent by closing in physically also makes it more difficult for either combatant to use his weapon effectively, because the rapier can be used only to thrust, not to cut. Combatants at this point may revert to a more primitive sense of aggression. At such a close distance, they can easily resort to their hands; indeed, there are several recorded instances of duels in which biting occurred toward the end of the fight.

Saviolo, discussing the use of the rapier, argues in favor of retreating: "If you be assaulted on the sodain, your enemy having gained time and measure, so that you are in evident danger to bee slaine, had you rather die than retire a foot?" (*4v). But describing a moment when neither side has the advantage, in recommending that the combatant "growe uppon" his adversary, Saviolo suggests a gradual incursion into his personal space. His words describe a strategic enlargement of one's own space, like an army attempting to gain ground. The idea is to force a slow retreat, perhaps one that the opponent is not even aware of, by stepping into his space: "seeke still to growe uppon him with your foote, that is, that your right foote bee without side of his right foote, and when hee gives the foresaide thrust…you shall onelye turne your Rapier hande inwarde, passing speedelie with your lefte foot to his right foote" (I4r). Eventually, the combatant moves onto the ground that the opponent occupied, taking the opportunity to force his adversary off balance. Gaining space seems less important than throwing one's opponent off balance by doing so. Maintaining a stable personal space seems to help the fencer keep a low center of gravity and remain well-balanced. Rather than be forced backward, to "give ground" himself, the combatant may use his opponent's momentum to enlarge himself—to exchange his personal space for that of his opponent and to avoid being boxed in or cornered. The intrusion Saviolo describes is a victory because the defendant maintains control of his body and its surrounding space at the very time when the attacker must work to recover that control.[20]

The intimacy of the combatants is heightened by strategies like these, which involve mirroring the movements of one's opponent. Di Grassi says in just so many words that imitating one's opponent may be the best way to gain an advantage; in discussing how to defend against the thrust of the high ward, di Grassi urges his reader "to endeavour to overcome the enimie, by the same skill by the which he himselfe would obtaine the victorie" (M2r). Saviolo says, "You must followe [your enemy] in moving his body: so shall you stil holde your advantage, and hit him where you will" (***2r). Perhaps the fencing-masters perceived imitation as a way of inadvertently gaining the skills of one's opponent; as a technique, it increases both one's own bodily awareness and one's powers of perceiving an opponent's movements. Perhaps one even learns what one's adversary is thinking when one imitates his body language.[21]

Such readings of these fencing manuals assume a certain freedom in the fencer's body movements; yet Georges Vigarello's detailed and provocative study of seventeenth-century French fencing manuals suggests just the opposite—that "[p]edagogical practice resorts to the formal precept of bodily uprightness and of a controlled deportment in spelling out various reasons for respecting them" (155). To make sense of the apparent differences between French and Anglo-Italian manuals, we must consider both cultural context and the actual directives of the manuals considered. Although Paris was one of the most popular centers for fencing schools at this time, the manuals I examine, which were published in London, characterize the body in substantially different ways than do the French fencing manuals of only a slightly later period. Those, as Vigarello asserts, emphasize elegance more than strength in teaching readers to maintain and to perfect their bearing (Vigarello 179). In fact, French training in a variety of physical exercises during that time was modeled on that of dancing.[22] Vigarello's study enables us to contrast English and French notions of style, thereby clarifying the assumptions inherent in the way these Anglo-Italian manuals construct personal space.

During the reign of the Tudors, demonstrated ability in skilled pastimes such as fencing, dancing, and poetic composition filled the gap left by martial prowess, which once had been the primary element structuring the social hierarchy among English noblemen. These new accomplishments not only distinguished courtiers from their country cousins and from wealthy merchants but also distinguished between aristocrats, offering a way to define and assess people's standing in this already-elite social scale.[23] To some, fencing, like writing poetry, might seem utterly useless; to others, it was a signally valuable social accomplishment. Some writers condemned it as a foreign custom, while others praised it as an aristocratic practice.[24]

In France, however, fencing was more established as an aspect of the male courtier's training, rivaling the training in the military academies founded by Richelieu and attended by a significant portion of the male aristocracy during the seventeenth century (when the warrior elite remained a proportionally significant element of the French nobility) (Vigarello 185). In England, where the role of the aristocracy was less clear and the need for a warrior elite diminished, fencing was not part of a military education—in England it was, in fact, unobtainable as such. Moreover, the cult of honor, alive and flourishing in seventeenth-century France, was regarded with disfavor in England by both monarchs and the merchant class, whose power was on the rise.[25] Together these two groups established stiff penalties for duelling, a practice that remained far more acceptable on the Continent. In contrast to the discipline of fencing in France, fencing in England was not imposed by reigning institutions and, in fact, it maintained a quasi-legal status that linked it with the disorder of a former elite.[26] Nor could the fencing in England be defined by reference to the modern military system, which, "as a technique of internal peace and order" in Foucault's view, "sought to implement the mechanism of... the disciplined mass, of the docile, useful troop, of the regiment" (168).

Anglo-Italian fencing manuals differ in many specific details from seventeenth-century French manuals: the Anglo-Italian manuals do not prescribe the containment of movement so much as they do the conscious use of movement.[27] While these manuals, like French ones, address the relation between art and nature, the results for the body seem very different. The Anglo-Italian manuals examined here bear more resemblance to *mid*-sixteenth-century French texts, of which Vigarello says that "their indirect influence on posture is more implicit than detailed" (156). Although the English texts, like the seventeenth-century French manuals, refer to the body of the addressee as one in need of discipline, they emphasize comfort and agility and the reliance on information from the senses. Specifically, they do *not* offer what Foucault, discussing French eighteenth-century infantry training, calls "a collective and obligatory rhythm, imposed from the outside... a 'programme.'... a web that constrains [gestures] or sustains them throughout their entire succession" (151–2). Although the discipline of this kind of combat emphasizes the skill and precision necessary for effective defense and offense, the acquisition of these skills, according to the Anglo-Italian manuals, is dependent on attention to the body's own messages. Control is not such an overwhelming concern as it is in Vigarello's French texts (176–80). On the contrary, in the Anglo-Italian tracts, "nimbleness" and "nature" replace "correctness" as catchwords. Although "order" is a concept of great importance, this term more often suggests a symbiosis of bodily awareness and mental attention than it does the artificial postures that Vigarello asserts were the norm in French circles.

These terms—and indeed the relation between French and English manuals—should be understood in the context of English attitudes toward foreign customs.[28] For the English, notions of rank were often inflected by positive notions of the English Saxon heritage (Jones, *Triumph* 214–71); thus, members of the gentry and even the aristocracy might choose to perceive themselves as representatives of an (idealized) English yeoman class, manifesting their ties to the land through such character traits as simplicity, straightforwardness, resistance to authority, or plainness.[29] Italian fencing techniques may actually have had a special appeal for English gentry because they oppose the rigidity of the French school of fencing. The body language of the skilled fencer indicated physical flexibility and confidence: it should not be associated with the uncivil behavior and lack of self-control that Anna Bryson analyzes.[30]

According to Saviolo and di Grassi, part of the success of the fencer depends on what his body language conveys—or keeps from conveying. Saviolo frequently characterizes the body in motion as a discursive field; much of his tutelage is based on the assumption that one's body, even in stillness, may betray one's intentions. Learning to assess the body language of one's opponent is a significant part of his treatise. Thus, when combatants imitate each other, they do so as a means of assessing or frustrating each other's intentions. Saviolo urges fencers to learn both to interpret the movements of their opponents and consciously to control their own movements so as to avoid involuntary communication. In addition, Saviolo teaches his pupils to deceive their opponents through body language: "one that would teach these principles and cannot plaie with his body, putteth himselfe in great danger to be hit on the face" (*3r). Saviolo seems to advocate almost a teasing display inviting a thrust that would give one the advantage. "To play" also means to perform, and the performance of the fencing-master might well involve an improvisational element. To "play" at that time also carried the negative meaning of "deceive" or "falsify";[31] yet, in a competitive context, the falsifying of movement was a legitimate strategic maneuver, an acceptable way to gain the advantage. The element of pranking and deceit (the xenophobic Silver's terms) is a strong suggestion in the word "play," fitting well with Saviolo's sportive context of a match envisioned between pupil and teacher.

Saviolo does urge straightforward communication through body language on occasion, especially when those motions can shape one's own sense of the combat: "Having taken weapons in hand, you must shewe boldnes and resolution against your enimy" (**3r). Resolution involves readiness, a physical attitude of preparedness that involves the body in the creation of the ward (I3v). A cool head and a constant awareness of the body are necessary to win the fight. Saviolo's injunction still directs attention to appearance. This directive assumes that the outward demeanor will match the inward state, although the emphasis is on manifesting that resolution. The directive opposes the stance taken in French fencing manuals that, according to Vigarello, warn their readers that strenuous movement "risks overstepping what is proper, since aristocracy had a duty to show complete and visible self-control" (180).

The necessity for keeping one's intentions hidden entails that the entirety of the performance is never revealed. Nonetheless, the playful element of fencing should be recognized as a courtly element.[32] The fencer's ability to feint sportively is an enactment of sprezzatura. Although the fencer must honestly acknowledge the body's signals, he may direct the body to offer inauthentic signals to others. In Castiglione's symposium, Count Ludovico da Canossa sparks a controversy by characterizing grace as the practice of sprezzatura, concealment of art (43). The fencer's playing with his body, in contrast, may be practiced, but appears to be achieved without planning, created on the spur of the moment. Such improvisation is the essence of nonchalance (sprezzatura)—the effect achieved without effort. Eduardo Saccone has pointed out the association of sprezzatura with Aristotle's *eironeia,* a form of pretense involving understatement and the intentional diminution of one's merits. Sprezzatura, Saccone argues, departs from the strict Aristotelian mean of *aletheia,* privileging instead a mode of understatement as a means of distinguishing between the general public and the initiated (56–9). The feint of the fencer is an ideal manifestation of that mode: it is a skill developed through training but must be enacted spontaneously as an improvisatory mode of confusing one's opponent. Castiglione's Count refers specifically to both the duellist's readiness and his daring, the two elements comprehending the training as well as the improvisatory element (37). The playful aspect transforms the art of fence into an opportunity to display one's personal style. Despite its ritualistic elements, the sport seems to offer a space for personal style rather than the conformity to an ideal dependent on bodily uprightness or conventional shape, as Vigarello sees in the later French manuals (155, 181).[33]

Yet the criticism of incontinent body language that Anna Bryson notes in English courtesy manuals is a notable aspect of the Anglo-Italian fencing manuals as well. Certainly, several courtesy manuals of the period indicate an assumption that swaggerers are indiscreet and quarrelsome men whose courage never comes up to their boasts. Obadiah Walker advises his readers that "Modesty is more gracefull then boldness, boldness then bashfulness, bashfulness then impudence" (225). Brathwait, in *The English Gentleman,* considers personal revenge proper, but describes in scathing terms the "raw and unseasoned Youth" who comes to London to learn the art of roaring:

> You may suppose him to have attained to some degree, so as he can looke bigge, erect his Mouchatoes, stampe and stare, and call the Drawer Rogue. ... But for all this, he hath not fully learned his postures: for upon discourse of valour, he hath discovered his Cowardize. (41–2)

Whether or not the fencer's expanded sense of personal space was conveyed by swaggering remains ambiguous. However, swaggering was depicted negatively because it conveyed a sense of self-importance contrary to the value of sprezzatura, and because it suggested the likelihood of a gap between appearance and performance.

Both di Grassi and Saviolo stress that a fencer's skill depends in large part on heeding the body's information about its natural capacity. These older teachers would probably agree with the value George Silver places upon the man who "standeth free in his valour with strength and agilitie of bodie, [who] freely taketh the benefit of nature" (71), although they would quarrel with the assumption that such a man must necessarily be untrained in fencing. Di Grassi warns against artificial prescriptions when he urges his reader not to use some arbitrary measure to indicate the distance of a pace. Because some men are tall and others short, he advises "everie man in al his wards to frame a reasonable pace, in such sort that if hee would step forward to strik [sic], he lengthen or increas one foot, and if he would defend himself, he withdraw as much, without peril of falling" (C1v). While di Grassi censures constant movement, he recommends that his readers step forward when they thrust, for "who so straineth himselfe to stand otherwise, as he offereth violence unto nature, so hee canne never indure it" (C3r). In discussing the low ward, he criticizes fencing masters who advocate stances that are only "for a small time to be endured"; he promises that, "casting all these aside, I will frame such a warde, as shalbe applyed, to time, to nature, and to safetie" (D1v).

Saviolo uses the words "nature" and "natural" more seldom than di Grassi; yet his recommendations also militate against constraint and stiffness. On the contrary, his constant catchword is "nimblenes," a term that stresses ease and quick movement. For Saviolo, a rapier fencer rather than a swordsman, the previously positive terms "stedfast" and "firm" describe "some...which seeme to be nayled to the place"; instead he endorses "readines and nimblenes," terms he applies to the fencer who stands "as though he were to performe some feate of activitie" (D3v). Vigor and lively movement are positive attributes in Saviolo's manual, and he also prescribes flexibility as one of the fencer's essential characteristics.[34]

Both di Grassi and Saviolo see the fencer as a three-dimensional body moving through space; their concern is both to make the fencer conscious of his movements and to ensure that he can direct his body in the most advantageous way. Both consider it important for fencers to understand the natural laws of physical objects and their relationships. Di Grassi explains the best strategy of attack by referring to the laws of geometry:

> First, that the right or streight Line is of all other the shortest: wherefore if a man would strike in the shortest lyne, it is requisite that he strike in the streight line.... That by these Rules a man may get judgment, it is most cleere, seing there is no other thinge required in this Art, then to strike with advantage, and defend with safetie. (A2v–A3r)

This image envisions the fencer himself as a center from which lines of attack radiate outward. Unlike the French fencer Thibault, whose use of geometry Vigarello criticizes, di Grassi does not create a "hierarchy of circular movements" that fails to take into account the joints of the limbs (Vigarello 158). On the contrary, di Grassi uses geometry here to avoid the arcs almost inevitably set in motion by the slashing gestures that broadsword fighters used in edge-blows.

Overall, these late-sixteenth-century manuals differ crucially from the French seventeenth-century manuals that Vigarello discusses: essentially, these three authors are more concerned with the fencer's own physical awareness than with a self-presentation directed at others. Despite certain elements shared with the later French texts (for example, the "code of compulsory bows" that Vigarello refers to [178]), these manuals emphasize the object of the sport and not the manner of its enactment. Saviolo and di Grassi repeatedly remind their readers of the goal: "[S]eeke all meanes to become victor, and so you shall maintaine your reputation" (Saviolo **2v). The object of the combat is to conquer one's opponent and to defend oneself successfully.

Many of the distinctions between Anglo-Italian and French manuals suggest strong parallels between the training of English fencers and the skills of English actors.[35] Much recent scholarship has dealt with the antitheatricalists' concern with actors' powers of improvisation and impersonation.[36] As we compare the French experience of fencing with that indicated in the manuals of di Grassi and Saviolo, we note the Italians' unique emphasis on the conscious use of movement, on understanding the significance of one's opponent's movements, and on being able to improvise, even to fake movements that confuse one's opponent or take him by surprise. The physical carriage of the fencer, with its indication of an extended proxemic area, would not necessarily be consciously noted by every passer-by, but it would have an effect. Few people would note the propriety of "active and sprightly" movements for young men or "slow and deliberate" ones for older figures as Obadiah Walker does (217); yet we respond almost instinctively to gesture, carriage, and mien. And just as the fencer was taught to become aware of what his body communicates, the Elizabethan actor would have been skilled at mimicry and at deciding what he wanted to communicate through his body. Thus, even though ordinary people might not have been aware of the fencer's extended proxemic limits, the experienced actor might easily be capable of recognizing and imitating them in his characterization of a role.

In *Elizabethan Stage Conventions and Modern Interpreters,* Alan C. Dessen reconsiders earlier stage historians' assumptions about attempts at verisimilitude in Elizabethan and Jacobean staging. With Huston Diehl and Catherine Belsey, Dessen suggests that many crucial scenes in early modern drama draw on the conventions of morality plays. Early modern players, he argues, would have been likely to present crucial gestures in a stylized, emblematic manner in order to create a "theatrical italics" indicative of a plot's symbolic or thematic logic (111).[37] My assumptions about early modern stagings of fencing and duelling derive from both Dessen's emphasis on allegorical effects and Joseph R. Roach's recent study of the early modern understanding of realism.[38] Given the trend toward more realistic drama in the early modern period, I posit that realistic stage effects at this time could be used specifically as commentary on dramatic modes—"modes" in Frye's sense: genres that function almost allegorically. In other words, I assume that combats and fencing expertise were staged realistically to delineate character in ways that structure the audience's sympathies and moral perceptions.

The very stance of the expert fencer, as I have already argued, could serve as the mark of a hero, thereby indicating assumptions about both morality and gender construction. Various aspects of proprioception specifically related to fencing skill also could be used to designate specific relationships among characters. This kind of subtlety might not be necessary to indicate obvious gender differences, but it could be instrumental in delineating subtle distinctions of social status. As Anna Bryson has commented, roaring boys acted incontinently, manifesting a body language more in keeping with a man of lower rank than with the gentlemen from whose ranks such figures generally arose. By indicating social rank, the character's carriage also could comment implicitly on ideals of masculinity, subverting or endorsing the assumptions of men in a given rank about appropriate behavior. The general idea is not new: any undergraduate familiar with Hotspur's scorn for the courtier who came to the battlefield carrying a pouncet-box "which ever and anon / He gave his nose and took … away again" recognizes that body language can indicate both distinctions in rank and distinctions in the understanding of masculinity (I.iii.38–9). In the drama, proxemic behaviors derived from fencing expertise or the lack of it could be manifested onstage to indicate rank and notions of manliness.

Ben Jonson's *The Alchemist* (1610), which deals largely with social distinctions and the possibility of their erasure, opens with a violent, yet comical confrontation that can be read either as a satire of the challenge to the duel or simply as a debased version of the duel itself:

> *Subtle*:   Ile gumme your silkes
>   With good strong water, an' you come.… I shall marre
>   All that the taylor has made, if you approch.
> *Face*: You most notorious whelpe, you insolent slave
>   Dare you doe this? (I.i.6–12)[39]

Physical combat is translated into invective, and combat itself reconceived as a physical expression of flyting, as corporealized rhetoric. Perhaps this scene could be interpreted as a brawl rather than a combat, but since Face later makes such a point of Subtle's knowledge of challenges and duels, performance values would demand for consistency's sake that the opening fight should have at least a thematic connection with the later pedagogical scenes.

The lesson that Subtle later gives the country boy Kastril in quarreling and duelling begins reasonably enough:

> *Subtle*: Charge me from thence, or thence, or in this line;
>   Here is my center: Ground thy quarrell.
> *Kastril*:   You lie.
> *Subtle*: How, child of wrath, and anger! the loud lie?
>   For what, my sodaine Boy?
> *Kastril*:   Nay, that looke you too,
> I am afore-hand.
> *Subtle*:   O, this's no true *Grammar*,
>   And as ill *Logick!* You must render causes, child,
>   Your first and second *Intentions;* know your *canons*,
>   And your *divisions, moodes, degrees,* and *differences.* (IV. ii.17–24)

But the lesson soon shifts from combat to rhetoric. Instead of teaching the physical combat as his initial directives seem to suggest he intended, Subtle redirects Kastril toward understanding the nature of linguistic mediation: look for causes, intentions, he urges. Through vocabularies of logic and rhetoric, Subtle emphasizes the importance of fine distinctions in choosing the correct signifier for signified. The discipline he urges on Kastril is the conscious understanding of the abstract nature of language.

From a mimetic viewpoint, however, Kastril's lesson represents the combat through verbal agility. When Subtle opens with the geometry of the fight—"Here is my center: Ground thy quarrell" (IV. ii.18)— we await an example of swordplay. But the combat fails to materialize: instead of watching a fencing exhibition enacted by Subtle, played by an actor who might have been skilled at swordplay, the audience sees the rogue retreat to lessons in verbal preliminaries and then turn almost immediately to seducing the Widow Pliant. Subtle's fencing skills are never revealed; instead, Face describes them, and the audience must deduce what it can from his discussion of the subject. Verbal agility substitutes for physical skill.

This scene is by no means an anomaly in the play. In *The Alchemist*, Jonson represents the duel as a way of making one's word good; it is related to plain or honest speaking and opposed to both bombastic and poorly conceived speech. This play offers an extended fantasy in which speech does not need to be tied to actions. Only in the final scene is the gap between word and deed closed. Throughout most of the play, duelling appears to be merely one form of transformation offered by the would-be alchemists Subtle and Face—transformations that include gambling, fortune-telling, and alchemy itself. But at the conclusion, these elements melt away, while the actual swordfight produces material gain. At the play's denouement, the bipartite structure of the duel is acknowledged. The duel's conventions, its preliminary insults and challenges can be used as rhetoric to manipulate those unskilled in language, but its mystique rests on the skillful use of the sword, executed by the representatives of legitimate institutions. Although the cozeners dangle the performance of the duel before us throughout the play, it is Lovewit who finally enacts it in defense of property interests. In the denouement, when swordplay actually occurs, the duel becomes realigned with law, property, and legitimate institutions generally. Throughout the play, the duel is represented as the conquest of aggression through the command of language, but the violence of the duel is aligned at the conclusion with both language *and* law, as if Jonson, finally perceiving himself as a figure of some stature, chose to give his best strategies to the figure who represented property interests.

Recognizing the play's thematic complexity, we must consider how staging of the opening scene might help set up these ideas. Do both con men possess equal knowledge of the art of fence, or do their levels of expertise differ? When the play opens, dialogue indicates that Face is threatening Subtle with a sword while the alchemist brandishes a vial of acid. Subtle's later scenes indicate that he, not Face, is presumed to possess knowledge of the art of fence; yet his bait-and-switch tactic, which shifts from the teaching of fencing to the teaching of the challenge, raises the possibility that his expertise is faked. On the other hand, Face's honorific of "Captain" suggests that he ought to have knowledge of military weaponry at least. Both characters, as residents of London, would have seen exhibitions of the Masters of Defence, but the actors themselves would have had to decide whether a servant or a sharp-eyed vagabond could gain more skill at a gentleman's art like fencing.

Mimicry of the master is a staple of plays with clever servants, whether in comedies like Plautus's or in modern dramas like Strindberg's *Miss Julie*. Jean, the valet in that play, learns to imitate the gentry from going to the theater; he pleases his young mistress, Miss Julie, by playing the role of a gentleman but finds himself incapable of action when confronted by riding boots, a potent and symbolic metonymy for their owner, Julie's noble father. Jonson's Face might be capable of approximating some fencing moves learned from watching his master; yet one would assume that years of service would make it difficult for him to perform the physical part of a man of authority. Given the details that Subtle provides about Face's life as caretaker of the house, it is clear that Face himself was Subtle's first object of transformation. Face could only profit in petty ways from the opportunity offered by his master's absence until Subtle "*Sublim'd* [him], and *exalted* [him].... Put [him] in words, and fashion.... made [him] fit / For more then ordinarie fellowships.... Giv'n [him his] othes, [his] quarrelling dimensions" (I.i.68–74). In the opening fight, Face would almost certainly be trying to project a householder's status by overcompensating for his servants' training. The actor playing Face might swagger and gesture broadly; his previous life as a butler would be evident in his excessive cowering and his quick retreat at Subtle's every gesture with the vial of acid.

Guessing at the body language of the actor who first played Subtle is more difficult. The character is probably not meant to know anything of the art of fence; yet he has made a career of improvisation based on close observation and, living in London, would have had many opportunities to note the carriage of gentlemen and aristocrats.

Doll's successful masquerade in front of a knight as a great lord's sister suggests that Subtle would have been capable of some similar feat. More than Face, then, Subtle could probably imitate a fencer's extended sense of personal space fairly plausibly. His vulgar gestures (indicated by dialogue such as "I fart at thee" and "lick figs / Out at my—" [I.i.1, 3–4]) might contrast markedly with his behavior when facing front, intentionally creating a comic effect. The possibility of his extended space is supported by his verbal aggression: though Face is the first speaker, Subtle is the first of the two to speak at length, aggressively taking the floor to describe his colleague's pitiful state prior to their collaboration. Given the inequality of their weapons (which recalls Jonson's story of his duel with the actor Gabriel Spencer, in which the playwright triumphed although his opponent's sword was ten inches longer than Jonson's), we have to assume that Subtle had some physical or psychological advantage that prevented Face from winning their combat by use of his sword. That advantage could be depicted as Subtle's superior imitation of a fencer's stance or by his more subtle manifestation of the trained swordsman's proxemic assumptions. Subtle could respond with reciprocal gestures to Face's stichomythic insults and interruptions and then move forward decisively at the point when he found the opportunity to silence Face with his own words. He might advance initially with a gesture of the vial, following up with acidic invective rather than actual acid. This advance might be enacted *as if* following up actual rapier-thrusts with shifts in weight from one foot to the next, but emphases in speech might be substituted for the appropriate arm gestures. Face, in response, might cower and then resort to derisive gestures, abandoning his dignity as Subtle draws his own together with such rejoinders as "I doe not heare well" and "I wish, you could advance your voice, a little" (I.i.24, 32).

Subtle's imitation of the fencer's spatial assumptions, however, could not be allowed to outdo Lovewit's real confidence at the play's conclusion. All in all, there are there are five characters whose body language or fencing expertise comes into play as an indicator of status, propriety, or morality: Subtle, Face, Doll, Kastril, and Lovewit. I include Doll because she eventually stops the fight: the Folio offers the stage direction "She catcheth out Face his sword: and breakes Subtles glasse." Although, as I shall explain in the next chapter, women learned proxemic assumptions directly opposed to those learned by fencers, the training detailed in conduct-books for women seems to have been directed primarily toward gentle and aristocratic women. Doll's ability to seize the men's weapons indicates less about her status than it does about that of the men. When a woman's actions put an end to the argument, they either derogate fencing as a manly endeavor or reveal both men's skill as bogus. Either way, Doll's actions reveal a truth about Subtle and Face, though that truth could refer either to the validity of the masculine ideal to which they aspire or to their ostensible achievement of higher social status. In other words, her way of wading into the quarrel and seizing the weapons diminishes the stature of the two opponents and reduces them to childish brawlers or to self-deceiving pretenders. Her words suggest the latter: she mocks Subtle with her sarcastic comment, "And you, too, / Will give the cause, forsooth?" (I.i.129–30). Calling the two men stinkards, perpetual curs, murmuring mastiffs, and good baboons, she reminds them of what they have come from, concluding by pointing out that only *if* they agree and work together, then they may merit the honorifics they have bestowed on themselves. Her words back her actions: despite her excellent acting ability, Doll's faith in their schemes rests primarily on the superior power of words, which seems to transform all of them despite the lack of corresponding substance in the physical world. This faith, however, will prove to be misplaced when property interests return home in the person of Lovewit.

Kastril's proxemic assumptions must indicate his status as a yokel and an oaf. He has no knowledge of fencing, and his equal admiration for those who quarrel and those who take tobacco suggests that he admires roaring boys for their finesse and sophistication—that is, for what their behavior represents and not for the level of skill manifested in the actions themselves. As a member of the country gentry, Kastril would have been trained to use older weapons, most likely the broadsword and, perhaps, the battle-ax, the pike, or the bow. Thus, his body language might indicate this expertise. As a man accustomed to wielding heavy weapons, he would take care to plant himself with a secure center of gravity, stomping around like a Brothers Grimm dwarf. As a bumpkin, Kastril might be portrayed as entirely unaware of personal space, intruding into other characters' space at certain times and attempting to make contact from too great a distance at others. Heavy and ponderous movements might easily yield comic effects if, for example, he overbalanced as he brandished a light but overly long rapier at his fencing lesson with Subtle.

The amusement of the audience at Kastril's antics would be shared by Surly in Act IV, scene vii, when Kastril disports himself with both words and weapons in an effort to prove himself to Subtle and Face. Surly's attempt to reveal their shifts to Kastril and the Widow Pliant is the first serious threat to the cozeners' control of the dramatic community. When Surly unmasks himself, Face and Subtle manipulate Kastril into acting on their behalf to throw him out. As Face urges, "[Y]ou must quarrell him out o' the house" (IV.vii.35). This penultimate staging of the duel mocks the practice on several levels. It mocks Kastril's verbal and physical clumsiness; it mocks the formulae that he ought to have mastered; and it mocks the trivial causes for which gallants often shed blood. Kastril's words and his corresponding body language would work together at this point to derogate the ritual of the duel:

> *Kastril*: Where is he? which is he? he is a slave
> What ere he is, and the sonne of a whore. Are you
> The man, sir, I would know?
> *Surly*: I should be loth, sir,
> To confesse so much.
> *Kastril*: Then you lie, i'your throate.
> (IV.vii.4–7)

The comedy of this exchange derives from mutual misunderstandings: while Surly is not the man Kastril describes, he is the man Kastril wishes to address. As Surly continues his attempt to set Kastril straight, the game they are playing begins to comment on its own assumptions:

> *Kastril*: Sir, if you get not out o'dores, you lie:
> And you are a pimpe.
> *Surly*: Why, this is madnesse, sir,
> Not valure in you: I must laugh at this.
> *Kastril*: It is my humour: you are a Pimpe, and a Trig,
> And an AMADIS *de Gaule,* or a *Don* QUIXOTE.
> (IV.vii.36–40)

Kastril's comparison of Surly to heroic literary figures should more properly apply to himself. His comment subverts the assumptions of the chivalric epic by suggesting that the mad heroes of the romances, supposedly motivated by high aspirations, may have resembled this egotistical rustic in more than their outward behavior.

Kastril uses the lie with no sense that he is creating a disjunction between word and world. The proposition "If you do not leave, you lie" makes no logical sense. His ignorance of fitness in language makes him into a slapstick object of humor, like Bergson's jack-in-the-box, "something mechanical encrusted on the living" (84). His attempt to "carry" a duel demonstrates the precariousness on which the cozeners' verbal empire is based.

The alienation from the physical world so evident in Kastril's wild words is a function of the con that Subtle and Face perpetrate. Their deceptions depend on the victims' increasing reliance on verbal mediation that replaces their own experience of the physical universe. Kastril's fantasy that he acts as a sophisticated city-gallant becomes increasingly ridiculous as he is matched against Surly. Of course, in contrast to Kastril, Face and Subtle demonstrate a considerable command of language. But duelling and quarreling alike demand the actor's awareness of their mediation of the physical universe in order for that mediation to be successful. It becomes clear that the cozeners' empire is falling apart when they call on Kastril as a defender.

The person who truly masters the quarrel is the one who does not appear until the end of Act IV—Lovewit, whose return reunites might with right and aggression with defense of property. As possessor of real estate, Lovewit is both master of the law and controller of the stage. His house, from which he can exclude interlopers, is the set of the play: thus, he can control the invasion of inside by outside at will.

Upon Lovewit's return, word is finally matched with deed. Language in the play has increasingly come to represent abstraction and fantasy; now it returns to simple representation of the signified. Lovewit closes the disjunction between word and deed most firmly when he defends his property with the sword. One of his first acts as Face's new associate has been to marry the Widow Pliant, whom he finds waiting in his house for the husband the con men have promised her. When Kastril appears, ready to beat his sister for her gullibility, Lovewit intervenes on his bride's behalf:

> *Kastril*: 'Slight, you are a mammet! O, I could touse you, now.
>   Death, mun' you marry with a poxe?
> *Lovewit*:   You lie, Boy;
>   As sound as you: and I am afore-hand with you. ...
>   Come, will you quarrell? I will feize you, sirrah.
>   Why doe you not buckle to your tooles? ...
>   Here stands my dove: stoupe at her, if you dare. (V.v.128–35)

Lovewit's combination of threats and insults, entirely appropriate in this context, impresses Kastril, but what bowls over the rustic is his new brother-in-law's evident ability to make good his threats. Lovewit's challenge to Kastril suggests a protective pose: one arm around the widow, the other holding a sword in a position of readiness. This promise of imminent violence offers much more concrete results than did the words of Subtle and Face. Lovewit's naked rapier, his confident stance, and what would almost certainly be his taking of central stage all show his readiness to act on his words. Subtle and Face, for obvious reasons, never indicate any such immediate result. The master's willingness to use his sword merges popular notions of masculinity with the more sophisticated notion of authority produced by various forms of power. In this case, the enactment of the contemporary male gender role is not equated with authority—instead, the performance of the manly role becomes a strategy for manifesting the authority he already has. The symbolic suggestions of his action are underlined by his words to Surly:

> Good faith, now, shee do's blame yo'extremely, and sayes
> You swore, and told her, you had tane the paines…all for her love;
> And then did nothing. What an over-sight,
> And want of putting forward, sir, was this!
> Well fare an old Hargubuzier, yet,
> Could prime his poulder, and give fire, and hit,
> All in a twinckling. (V.v.50–8)

Sex and violence are part of his display of traditional masculinity; this performance may be even more definitive than his repossession of the house.

At the play's denouement, combat moves from the verbal to the physical plane; simultaneously, its associations shift from illicit activity to lawful and authoritative behavior. Despite the attractions of the cozeners' linguistic agility, Jonson uses duels and the staging of them to endorse property interests rather than verbal skill, straightforward and honest characters rather than manipulative ones, the moral rather than the amoral stance. Conquest, and thereby masculinity, is aligned with the values of small gentry—but to achieve this aim, Jonson needs such subliminal devices as proxemic markers to make his audience accept the sudden turn away from carnivalesque values.

It seems fairly clear that training in the art of fence marks the trainee through his physical carriage and increased bodily awareness. But the explosion of popularity for both fencing and duelling in early modern England made these marks of the fencer much more significant. They help to designate certain behaviors often described in historical documents and to distinguish these movements from others that were censured or mocked. If we accept the idea that the fencer's sense of his body eventually became a class marker beyond the population of actual fencing students, we gain an understanding of how men of a certain rank wished to present themselves. These ideas are linked (but not dictated) by the *doxa* of such Italian conduct manuals as *The Courtier* and, to a lesser extent, by those of other countries' manuals, particularly older ones such as Erasmus's *De Civilitate Morum Puerilium*. Preferring certain manners over others and attempting to emulate certain physical styles, the gentry and aristocracy were responding in complex ways to institutional imperatives that were often obscure or contradictory. Though their behavior as a group seems to have been consistent (given the statistics), their shift in behavior was one that valorized self-shaping. The limitations of such shaping, however, are clearly dramatized in Jonson's play. The characters' actions and options are determined by their status, and theatrical presentation of these characters can even use the carriage of the fencer to direct audience sympathy toward legitimate interests. The body language of the fencer does not indicate that lines of status may be easily breached; instead, it helps us to understand the link between status and masculinity and the way that both were recognized and represented in the realm of the non-verbal.

CHAPTER 3

SEXUAL STATUS AND THE COMBAT

The previous chapter examined training in the art of fence primarily to understand class distinctions as they might be manifested by the proxemic assumptions resulting from such training. This chapter shifts the focus to two other ways of conceiving manhood: manliness in opposition to womanliness and manliness in opposition to boyishness. Neither axis should be perceived as a simple adequate / inadequate dichotomy. The contrast between the dicta of women's conduct books and those of the fencing manuals reveals an implicit analogy between the feminine body and the conquered body. The language of combat in fencing manuals furthers implications about the gendering of leakiness and permeability that recent scholars have noted in medical texts. The resulting association between conquest and effeminization suggests that masculinity may be understood as a sign not only of sexual difference but of sexual maturity—that the conquered body is most literally affiliated not only with the passive, permeable woman but also with her alternative, the immature male. This suggestion is borne out in the anonymous *Swetnam, the Woman-Hater,* in Massinger's *The Unnatural Combat,* and in Shakespeare's *1 Henry IV*—plays that depict fighting between neophytes and more experienced men, or between youths who perceive combat as a rite of passage in which a victory designates them adult males. Proxemic assumptions not only differentiated upper-class men and women; they created expectations about personal space that strengthened the sense of competitive masculinity, the sense that one's manhood was linked to the derogation of another man's. Although duelling was more widely practiced by young men than by men of mature years, a duellist's victory construed the winner as a man, the loser as a boy. Such constructions were not entirely universal, but they were common, and demonstrate the counterintuitive nature of many common assumptions about gender at this time.

As we have seen, physical competition, particularly fencing, brought a sense of power to aristocratic Englishmen of the early modern period through the assumptions that they learned in fencing about the relationship between their own personal space and that of others.[1] Comparison to the training of female bodies further clarifies the distinct ways that gentlemen understood the relationship of body to surroundings. During the period under examination, while men of wealth and status learned to manifest assertiveness through their bodies, women at the same social level were taught to efface themselves physically.[2] The male experience of inhabiting the body encouraged expansiveness and aggression; women's discipline encouraged stillness and receptivity. Many different aspects of female training taught proxemic assumptions directly opposed to those that men learned from fencing.

The emphasis in courtesy books for women on *containment* and *restraint* supports Gail Kern Paster's argument that the many disparate texts characterizing women as leaky vessels do so with reference to women's perceived lack of self-control (25). Based on her own examination of these texts, Ruth Kelso has asserted that a woman's modesty was indicated in her "behavior, carriage of the body, use of the eyes, gestures, and the choice and wearing of clothes" (*Lady* 25). Much of the training of the gentlewoman involved the skills of housewifery; yet certain dicta regarding body language and personal space (referring, essentially, to proxemic assumptions) were imposed upon women in order to ensure that they assumed the proper demeanor. Important traits that women were urged to develop included humility, constancy, temperance, and the fear of shame, tellingly known as "shamefacedness." Kelso quotes Barnaby Rich, who characterizes shamefacedness as

> a restraint to withhold [good and virtuous women] from those artificiall abillimentes that do either smell of vanitie or breed suspect of honesty: for Bashfulnes is it that moderates their thoughts, makes them modest in their speeches, [and] temperate in their actions.... (Rich 22; qtd. in Kelso, *Lady* 43)

The French text "Le Doctrinal des Princesses" urges that "if shame does not preside, / Shame has a place and honor is assaulted / Without good deportment" (94). Such directives indicate what proxemic assumptions women learned during an upper-class education.

Women were taught to keep their eyes downcast; timidity was encouraged and the blush considered a sign of reverence and maidenly virtue (Bruto f.44a; qtd. in Kelso, *Lady* 43–4).[3] Brathwait's *The English Gentlewoman* (1631) urges women to "[be] *still* from the clamours and turbulent insults of the *World; still* from the mutinous motions and innovations of the *flesh*" (49, qtd. in Ziegler 86). The body language of the young girl was firmly governed by those in charge of her; conduct books urged that she be trained to stand composedly with her feet together, avoiding unnecessary body movement (Kelso, *Lady* 50). Her gait should be a medium stride performed "slowly, but not too slowly lest she be taken to be loitering for a purpose" (Kelso, *Lady* 50). When she dines, "she should sit erect with feet and knees together, to be known as a virgin and not a prostitute" (Kelso, *Lady* 50). Significantly, these strictures greatly resemble those directed toward young boys, who were similarly taught to efface themselves in order physically to convey their subordination to adult males (cf. Correll 58–76). F. Seager's pamphlet "The Schoole of Vertue, and booke of good Nourture for chyldren" tells its audience in Chapter Seven ("How to behave thy selfe in taulkinge with any man"),

> Low obeisaunce makyng,   lokinge him in the face,
> Tretably speaking,   thy wordes see thou place.
> with countinaunce sober   thy bodie uprighte
> Thy fete juste to-gether,   thy handes in lyke plight.
> (235)[4]

Postures such as these eliminate any self-assertiveness expressed through gesture, making the person who enacts them a still figure, an icon rather than a living human being.[5]

Women were also taught not to perceive the physical proximity of others as an intrusion. Adult women, even those of high status, were expected to endure the approach of others, and even to endure attacks on their bodies. As Kelso writes,

> Woman's whole life was a lesson in submission to the will of another. Obedience...included the acceptance of correction, even blows, in all humility, subjection, fear, sweetness, and patience without provoking either parents or, later, husband by talking back, babbling, or running away. (*Lady* 44)[6]

Women were discouraged from physical resistance to aggressive seduction or even sexual coercion; these, in their potential to damage one's reputation, might be more detrimental to one's life than spousal abuse. Kelso alludes to Bouchet's advice about importunate lovers: refuse to hear them speak but avoid any show of violent anger that might provoke them to revenge (Bouchet Epist.10, f28a; qtd. in Kelso, *Lady* 51).[7]

Because of the concern with limiting female body language, even some early modern writers who endorsed the education of women argued that women should not develop any skills that could encourage a flamboyant demeanor.[8] Music was often criticized as an opportunity for women's unseemly public displays.[9] And, while Vives would permit women to study rhetoric, Leonardo Bruni would not.[10] Regarding women's physical activity, Vives recommends only that girls should play ball together in a secluded garden or orchard (qtd. in Kelso, *Lady* 52).[11]

Women were also associated with sexual receptivity (Trexler 32), a posture that might, of course, also be ascribed to specific men. Soft voices, gesturing with hands and wrists, and the practice of singing were considered womanish, perhaps because they were perceived as signs of receptivity.[12] Such constructions of the female may be seen in Shakespeare's "The Rape of Lucrece," as when Lucrece's rapist describes his experience of her affection for her husband: "'And how her hand, in my hand being lock'd, / Forc'd it to tremble with her loyal fear!'" (ll. 260–1). Later, as Georgiana Ziegler comments of lines 302–59, "the house prosopopoeically takes Lucrece's part, and even more intimately, the chamber metaphorically represents her 'self,' her body with its threatened chastity" (80):

> The locks between her chamber and his will,
> Each one by him enforc'd retires his ward....
> As each unwilling portal yields him way,
> Through little vents and crannies of the place
> The wind wars with his torch to make him stay. (ll. 302–3, 309–11)

These images of female receptivity, female permeability suggest certain assumptions about the nature of femininity, characterizing "a particular kind of uncontrol as a function of gender" (Paster 25). Paster has analyzed such images as they appear in medical texts, iconography, and proverbs, positing that iconic depictions of "the female body as a leaking vessel display that body as beyond the control of the female subject, and thus as threatening the acquisitive goals of the family and its maintenance of status and power" (25). What, then, should we make of the imagery in the fencing manuals that figures men as permeable because of their vulnerability to attack?

Fencing, like several other aggressive sports, endorses the aggressive penetration of the space of others. Images of penetration and permeability resurface in the language of fencing manuals, but with a difference: the fencing manuals figure *men* as permeable in the context of their physical vulnerability. For a man to be permeable is to be shamed; to attack and to penetrate, on the other hand, is to dominate other men physically. Inherent in the duel is the negotiation of status between combatants: the victor's status increases, while the loser is shamed by defeat. The proxemic assumptions learned in fencing practice are severely compromised by loss: the duellist's personal space has been violated, and even if he is not killed, his bloody wound weakens him both literally and symbolically. Whereas the victor may experience an expansion of his personal space as a result of the duel, the loser (if he lives) is likely to perceive his personal space as smaller, and as violated.

As I said in the previous chapter, the fencer's extended sense of personal space must be altered by both the need to attack and the possibility of being penetrated. Penetration was further complicated by Galenic beliefs about bodily fluids. Blood, semen, and breast milk were all understood as various transformations of bodily fluids (Laqueur 35–62; Paster 64–84). Involuntary bleeding, as with a wound, was associated with feminine processes such as menstruation and with failings such as excessive desire, which could weaken men if desire resulted in frequent orgasms that dried men out too much (Laqueur 40–52).[13] In Paster's terms,

> Man is naturally whole, closed, opaque, self-contained. To be otherwise is both shameful and feminizing.... The male body, opened and bleeding, can assume the shameful attributes of the incontinent female body as both cause of and justification for its evident vulnerability and defeat. (92)

In this way, the extended personal space of the gentleman could be reduced by the shame of a wound that possessed both social and physical implications. Unlike wounds proudly gained in war, wounds gained in defense of personal honor could signal shame and loss. Saviolo dictates that the man who has lost a duel should not be permitted to enter into another: "The dutie of gentlemen is to preferre their honor before their life, and he whosoever goeth the looser out of the listes, sheweth that hee accounted more of his life than honor.... if afterward he would challenge any man, he ought to be refused" (Ee3v–Ee4r). Losing the duel thus comprised both loss of honor and loss of manhood (although, as I have said before, such abstract injunctions were more severe than the practice that actually resulted).

That bleeding wounds could be perceived as effeminization should not surprise us. Though bloodletting as such could be "construed as an issue of bodily voluntarity and self-control" as Paster suggests, involuntary bleeding places the subject who bleeds in the camp of the weaker, uncontrolled sex (78). By association with sexual congress, penetrating and being penetrated were perceived in the early modern period as gendered behaviors: to be conquered was to be emasculated.[14] Combats among men have always provoked bawdy language that acknowledges the phallic significance of the sword; Saviolo's manual is replete with references to entering and thrusting (for example, I3r, I3v, and K1r). At one point, Saviolo urges the pupil to observe his opponent carefully, commenting, "[B]y howe much the more strongly hee thrusteth, and the more furiouslie hee entereth with the passata, by so much the more easilie may you hurt him.... Furthermore, if you finde his Rapier long..." (K1v). Such unintentionally suggestive language makes it impossible to avoid perceiving the duellist as penetrable, permeable, and open to assault of a sexually ambiguous nature.

The question soon becomes *not* "Do the wounds gained from losing a personal quarrel diminish a fighter's masculinity in the eyes of others?" but, "How are the wounds and the defeat of a fighter understood by those who see them as signs of his loss of masculinity?" Though Paster perceives men's bleeding as a sign of effeminization, I suggest that the combatant's penetration can redirect our thinking from the axis of gender to that of maturity—to perceiving permeability not as necessarily feminine but as opposed to mature masculinity. Because of his open wounds and because he eventually yielded to the victor, the defeated duellist was perceived as unmanly. This category of "unmanliness," however, was as likely to be construed as the realm of preadolescent boyhood as it was to signify feminization. In other words, the duellist's loss could suggest his physical immaturity instead of or in addition to effeminacy.

Immaturity and the passive role in homosexual intercourse had been linked in the minds of early modern gentlemen since the resurgence of interest in Greek texts. In classical Athens, the passive partner in male/male intercourse was generally either a slave, or an adolescent boy who permitted the practice as a favor to an older man, as he expected it would be permitted to him once he attained full maturity (Dover 73–109). Penetrating a slave simply supported the foundations of the Greek patriarchal master/slave system; penetrating a boy of good family reinforced the rigid social hierarchy that designated physical immaturity in males as a specific social category distinct from that of other kinds of males. In classical Athens, however, as in the early modern period, social distinctions were perceived as destabilized by practices that reversed standard hierarchies of power and prestige. Man/boy practices were accepted in Greece (they tended to be overlooked in early modern England); consensual man/man sex in either culture was generally censured.[15] In such situations,

> the issue is not the identity of sex but the difference in status between partners [or lack of it] and precisely what was done to whom.... It was the weak, womanly male partner who was deeply flawed, medically and morally. His very countenance proclaimed his nature: *pathicus*, the one being penetrated; *cinaedus*, the one who engages in unnatural lust; *mollis*, the passive, effeminate one. (Laqueur 53)[16]

The axes of gender and physical maturity are equally likely to be used as explanations for the hierarchy of dominance established by the outcome of the duel: the figure who is conquered is subordinated to his conqueror; moreover, his humiliation diminishes his manhood at the same time as his loss is likely to diminish the spread of his personal space. In his provocative discussion of ancient Greek practices and their relevance to the early Iberian contacts with the many peoples living in the area now called Latin America, Richard Trexler describes

> a universe of penetrative penality: a context in which the male threat to penetrate other males was as much a part of the cultural superstructure as was heterosexual rape.... power among males was conceptualized in part as the rule of active adult men over passive adolescents or "boys." (37)

By the phrase "a universe of penetrative penality," Trexler means a society in which private acts of chastisement often took the form of sexual humiliation. Society, in fact, may be structured by a hierarchy in which this mode of domination is a testing ground for a male's place in his community. Although Trexler characterizes ancient Greece by this term, he points out that such traditions are not unknown in late medieval or early modern Europe, citing as a case in point the thirteenth-century English law that allowed a cuckolded husband to castrate his wife's lover if he caught them in the act of adultery. Trexler also cites a story in Boccaccio (day 5, tale 10) that seems derived from an anecdote in *The Golden Ass* about a husband who rapes a youth who has cuckolded him (22, 190).

Gary Spear supports Paster in his interpretation of what he calls "the penetrated male body" and its symbolic representation of "the essential vulnerability of manliness":

> To represent the male body as open to sexual or homoerotic penetration is to contest the cultural presumption of its inherently closed nature and to pluralize the avenues of sexual contact.... To be effeminated is thus to become sexually passive, to be symbolically feminized. (418)

We may also see the axis of sexual maturity used in a non-gendered context to define growth from youth to adulthood in Shakespeare's Caius Martius Coriolanus. As Janet Adelman has shown, Coriolanus's speech links bleeding wounds with the dependent infant's open mouth. To avoid such weakness, Coriolanus hardly acknowledges the need for food as natural or human ("Anger's my Meat" 131). Adelman argues that this Roman hero's masculine identity "depends on his transformation of his vulnerability into an instrument of attack.... Cominius reports that Coriolanus entered his first battle a sexually indefinite thing, a boy or Amazon (II.ii.91), and found his manhood there" ("Anger's my Meat" 132). In Adelman's view, Coriolanus is so anxious to prevent any appearance of an open orifice (which Adelman reads as a sign of regression to infancy) that he refuses to acknowledge ordinary human needs. In turn, Paster observes that, during battles, Caius Martius insists that the blood loss resulting from his wounds should be regarded as "both voluntary and therapeutic":

> Martius effaces the evident fact of his permeability through the hyperbolic assertion of personal control in a therapeutic idiom. He has allowed to flow, he has *dropped* only excess blood. The protestation that his body is not yet "warm'd" implies that he could stand to release even more blood as a matter of promoting greater "solubility." (96)

Adelman uses a classic Freudian framework to explain the effect of Aufidius's final insult as an infantilization of Coriolanus: "Since [Coriolanus's] manhood depends exactly on this phallic standing alone, he is particularly susceptible to Aufidius's taunt of 'boy'" (*Suffocating Mothers* 151). One can easily historicize Adelman's interpretation, reasoning that the warrior's anger at the term derives less from the implied infantilization than from the implication that his manhood has been compromised by his affections (whether for his mother or for his alter ego, Aufidius himself).

The connection between wounds, penetration, sexual humiliation, and physical immaturity recurs in contexts far beyond duelling, and in places far removed from early modern England. Trexler discusses at length the construction of the coward in Mediterranean antiquity as an effeminate—that is, as one who manifests traits generally ascribed to women, such as weakness, gentleness, softness, and delicacy (32). Such constructions seem to depend less on a masculine/feminine dichotomy than on the "one-sex model" described by Laqueur as a system in which "the boundaries between male and female are of degree and not of kind" (25). We can read such constructions as applying not merely to degrees of maleness but also to social relations, to concerns with dominance and subordination that are as appropriate to defining man/boy relations as male/female relations. In depictions of the permeability of the defeated male body, these two dichotomous categories—sex and maturity—were portrayed as parallel, if not actually interchangeable. Stephen Orgel draws attention to "the importance of the analogy between boys and women in the culture" (51).[17] Emily Vermeule, discussing *The Iliad*, asserts that

> A duel at close quarters may be treated formally as a love-struggle.... In a duel, an isolated world inside the main battle, one soldier must be the female partner and go down, or be the animal knocked down. It is a role naturally marked by unwillingness to cooperate. (101)[18]

We have already seen the importance to early modern duellists of models of classical heroism such as those presented by Homer.

Although the duel as it occurred in the early modern period is not the only context in which penetration could carry suggestions of sexual humiliation or of physical immaturity, it is one whose surrounding practices make these connections more likely. While duelling is not a sexual contest, it is one replete with sexual metaphors: phallic weapons, penetration, yielding, and conquest. Billacois points out that French duellists often inspired a sense of fraternity in one another: although duels resulted from insults, the combat "permitted the realisation of... the theme of the 'brother enemies' or 'antagonistic complementarity'" (214). But, as Vermeule says of combats in battle, the sense of fraternity that brought respect for one's opponent in a duel could also become a hierarchical relation redefining gender roles in the instant of victory. Even during the early modern period, this hierarchical relation developed in many structured kinds of combat beyond that of the duel. After battles, conquering warriors frequently mutilated enemy corpses, often in ways intended to debase the virility of the former opponents: genitalia were amputated and orifices frequently enlarged—"violated"—by the insertion of foreign objects. The symbolism of such gestures seems particularly germane in case of the duel, because the rapier was designed to pierce and to penetrate; the wounds it made were punctures that often caused internal injuries rather than the slashing cuts that resulted from using broadswords.

Such associations may be noted in many disparate dramatic contexts. The duel's covert homoeroticism and the sexual element in the shame of loss are hinted at when Scanfardo enrolls in fencing school in the anonymous play *Swetnam the Woman-hater*. Scanfardo, a naive servant, comes to Joseph Swetnam's recently created fencing school in Sicily. He wants to learn fencing because he plans to marry soon and "they say, / Then or never, is the time for a man to get the mastery" (I.ii.106–7).[19] The fencing match becomes a trope representing the same mastery in marriage: the active subordination of a wife to her husband's will. Scanfardo's interest in fencing expertise, however, actually opens up the possibility of doing without women when a bit of byplay suggestively shifts the focus to male-male relations:

> *Scanfardo*: I was now comming to be entred, Sir.
> *Misogynos* [Swetnam]: That you shall presently. My Rapier, Swash.
>   Come, Sir, I'll enter you.
> *Scanfardo*:   What meane you, Sir?
> *Misogynos*: You say you would be entred; if you will,
>   Ile put you to the *Puncto* presently.
> *Scanfardo*: Your Scholler, Sir, I meane. (I.ii.70–5)

The joke plays upon the word "enter," meaning both "to enter within one's ward" and "to enter as a pupil in a roll-book." But a bawdy joke is evident as well: to enter, as in "to penetrate sexually."[20] Scanfardo's stated desire to "be entred" can be perceived as a teasing suggestion on the author's part that Scanfardo may shortly enact the passive role in anal sex with Misogynos. As the butt of this joke, Scanfardo runs the risk not of effeminization but of humiliation—being reduced by defeat to the level of a boy who must submit to a mastery both violent and sexual. His droll correction of "Misogynos" suggests that duelling and woman-hating (Swetnam's chief attributes in the play) both result from a social dynamic of dominance and subordination in which one must conquer or be conquered.

Staging this dynamic would have been easy; in discussing effeminacy and "uncleanenesse," Bishop Lancelot Andrewes refers to Sirach (*Ecclesiasticus*) 9:27: "When a man seeth a man, he may know him;

the apparell, laughter gesture, and gate, will declare what is in him (773). Andrewes actually offers a list of signs by which practitioners of unclean acts may be recognized: "1. they goe on tiptoe: 2. they have...stretched forth necks: 3. *nutantes oculos,* the rolling of the eyes: casting them scornfully on the one side first, and then on the other: and 4. they have *minutos passus,* a mincing gate: they goe as if they were...shackled" (771). On the other hand, as Gary Spear points out, exaggerated masculine behaviors also were perceived as possible signs of the effeminate; a blatantly overacted performance of manliness could create "a series of emasculating reversals—from man to woman to animal" (414)—and, as I argue, from man to woman *or* from man to youth. Actors enacting signs such as those provided by Andrewes could easily indicate how the audience should perceive certain characters in ambiguous situations, such as Scanfardo, the son in Massinger's *The Unnatural Combat,* even Shakespeare's Coriolanus or Harry Hotspur.

Wounds, sexual humiliation, and physical immaturity come to the fore in Massinger's *The Unnatural Combat* when the villain uses the male/female axis of difference to characterize his duel with his son. Throughout the play, the term "unnatural" recurs several times, always with reference to Malefort Senior. The unnatural combat of the title refers to both the duel between this character and his son and the combat within Malefort Senior between his lust for his daughter, Theocrine, and his knowledge that such feelings are wrong. More broadly, the theme of perversity derives from the overturning of social hierarchies as characters of lower social status attempt to stop Malefort Senior from raping his daughter. (Malefort Senior triumphs over all of them, and only after Malefort Junior and Theocrine die do the heavens intervene with a bolt from the blue, killing Malefort Senior during a storm with a flash of lightning.)

The confluence of weakness, womanliness, blood, and wounding is evident early on in the play, supporting Paster's assertion that bodily fluids were perceived as both interchangeable and representative of effeminate weakness. In Act II, Scene i, an acquaintance of Malefort Junior recalls the young man's frequent oaths: "We shall meete cruell father, yes we shall, / When i'll exact for every womanish drop / Of sorrow from these eies, a strict accompt / Of much more from thy heart" (26–9).[21] Malefort Junior hopes to redeem his own womanliness, manifested by his tears, by augmenting his manhood when he makes his father drip with blood from a mortal wound. As we shall see in *1 Henry IV,* blood is perceived as a measurable substance that helps keep a bookkeeper's account of manliness. Malefort Junior expects to reduce the stature of his father, a respected soldier and Admiral of Marseilles, by symbolically feminizing him, penetrating him with his own sharp weapon. (Perhaps Malefort Junior also imagines the image as a symbolic revelation of his father's unnaturalness, the wound as a means of rendering visible what is within.) The son's success seems likely, and he regrets his own appearance of unnaturalness in his desire to duel with his father. Malefort Senior, by contrast, is pleased at the challenge, although he refuses to permit anyone to serve as his second: "For me to borrow / (That am suppos'd the weaker) any aid / From the assistance of my Seconds sword, / Might write me downe in the blacke list of those, / That have nor fire, nor spirit of their owne" (II.i. 89–93).

At this point in the play, Malefort Junior still comes off as the villain since, to protect Theocrine's reputation, he refuses to state his father's crime overtly (and the plot has not yet revealed it). When father and son meet and the scion characterizes his father's depravity only "in a perplext forme and method," Malefort Senior selfrighteously exclaims against any need to justify his conduct to his child:

> must I plead
> As a fearefull prisoner at the bar, while he
> That owes his being to me sits a Judge
> To censure that, which onely by my selfe
> Ought to be question'd? mountaines sooner fall
> Beneath their vallies, and the loftie Pine
> Pay homage to the Bramble. (II.i.149–55)

The father strategically casts the charge of unnatural behavior back onto his son. In doing so, he reinforces standard early modern assumptions about the child's relation to his father, in which no amount of aging can alter the father's superior status. Any chance of a more balanced, perhaps more cyclical representation of the generations is eliminated when, against all likelihood, Malefort Senior triumphs in the duel. Immediately before the combat, the father has asserted the impossibility of any other outcome by arguing that his son's strength and skill with the rapier flow directly from the father:

> *Malefort Junior:* This sword divides that slavish knot.
> *Malefort Senior:* It cannot,
>   It cannot wretch, and if thou but remember
>   From whom thou hadst this spirit, thou dar'st not hope it.
>   Who train'd thee up in armes but I? (II.i.165–68)

The father perceives the father/son relation almost as an invisible umbilical cord through which manhood flows from father to son. Cutting the knot that ties them together would be like severing a cord—it would disrupt the flow that energizes the son's desire to fight.

Conquering his son is a way for Malefort Senior to prevent the youth from attaining full manhood; in taunting him before the duel, he reiterates that the boy has no masculinity of his own:

> All that is manly in thee, I call mine;
> But what is weake and womanish, thine owne.
> And what I gave, since thou art proud, ungratefull,
> Presuming to contend with him, to whom
> Submission is due, I will take from thee. (II.i.176–80)

Though his terms depend explicitly on the axis of masculinity versus femininity, the implication seems clearly to revert to that of manhood versus boyhood, maturity versus immaturity. Malefort Junior expects to achieve manhood by righteously killing the father; the father is determined to permit no such thing. Malefort Senior tropes his own perversity by twice characterizing the fluid that he shares with his son as poisonous venom rather than blood, semen, or some metaphysical fluid. Directly before the contest, he pledges, "Expect not / I will correct thee as a sonne, but kill thee / As a Serpent swolne with poyson, who surviving / A little longer, with infectious breath, / Would render all things neere him, like it selfe / Contagious" (II.i.181–6). After killing his son, he addresses himself, saying, "Were a new life hid in each mangled limbe, / I would search, and finde it. And howere to some / I may seeme cruell, thus to tyrannize / Upon this senslesse flesh, I glorie in it. / That I have power to be unnaturall, / Is my securitie" (II.i.204–9). He reduces his son to the level of a serpent, satanic in its power to corrupt. Yet he himself is, of course, the agent of corruption; he himself is the limb that must be dismembered. His unnatural character is clarified as soon as Malefort Junior has fallen, and the rest of the play serves to reveal it and to bring about dramatic retribution.

There is some hint from the duel's very outcome that a universal law has been overturned for a time. The father's admission of some perversity within him is in some sense unnecessary; his degeneracy is evident from his lack of compunction at killing his son—a reversal of the process of generation. Massinger strategically reverses the common expectation for such duels-as-trials-by-combat in order to darken the atmosphere of his drama. The duel is still conceived so basically as an initiation of youth into manhood that we cannot fully recognize our expectations until they are frustrated, as in this play. On an archetypal level (for the early modern mind, on the level of the prose romance) the duel is an opportunity for a hero not to prove himself as he is already but to gain a new place within the community of adult males. This use of the duel is most obvious in a play such as *1 Henry IV*, in which the passage from boyhood to manhood is a repeated theme. In that play, Shakespeare restructures history to stage a combat that, although it occurs within the context of a battle, manifests numerous traits of the duel.

The mechanics of dominance are evident in *1 Henry IV*'s varied representations of violence. Presenting the deterioration of a chivalric system in which honor and respect were generally assumed between opponents, this second play in Shakespeare's tetralogy exposes the ease with which these assumptions could be manipulated by machiavels. Throughout the play, we see the theme of erotic aggression played out in the Hal/Hotspur rivalry, which culminates in Hal's physical domination over Hotspur's corpse. Manhood is repeatedly defined over and against boyhood, as immaturity and femininity function yet again as alternative Others that define masculinity. When Shakespeare revises history to make Hal and Hotspur both youths just entering adulthood (historically, Hotspur was Henry IV's contemporary), not only does his choice create notable thematic complexities, it renders resonant the gendered epithets for these youths that reappear throughout the play.[22] In *1 Henry IV*, conquest is represented verbally by terms that construct the losers as women or as boys. The two youths each intend to prove their own manhood on the body of the other, as Hal eventually succeeds in doing.[23] Both anticipate their encounter in terms of embraces and sexual consummation, not only with reference to good-fellowship but also with overtones of sexual dominance. Framed by the narration of the Welshwomen's affront to English corpses after battle and the elision of the warrior Douglas's groin injury (which forces him to surrender), the contest between Hal and Hotspur plays out the violent power dynamic in both gendered and developmental terms.[24] The contest is capped by the (fictionalized) single combat that represents within the play the prince's accession to manhood after an arguably effete boyhood. Although the battle of Shrewsbury was fought with broadswords, pikes, and more primitive weapons (and although the play's original staging probably mustered up similar implements), the language of sexual conquest that recurs throughout seems to allude to the emasculation effected by early modern duelling. The broader framing of war and its humiliation of the conquered body contextualize the combat and highlight the power of victory to construct winners as princes of assured power.

The play begins with the king's description of political and natural disorder. Nature and society seem to make war on each other: men bruise the earth's "flow'rets with the armed hoofs / Of hostile paces" (I.i.8–9); the earth, in turn, "daub[s] her lips with her own children's blood" (6). These metaphors are paralleled by the unnatural sexual reversals enacted on the English dead, as Westmerland brings news that Mortimer has yielded to Glendower and

> A thousand of his people butchered,
> Upon whose dead corpse' there was such misuse,
> Such beastly shameless transformation,
> By those Welshwomen done as may not be
> Without much shame retold or spoken of. (I.i.42–6)

By castrating the corpses and placing their genitalia in their mouths (Abraham Fleming's account of the atrocity), the Welshwomen have enacted a not unheard-of gesture of dominance over and contempt for their enemies.[25] Trexler cites similar actions among ancient Aztecs and Incas in the sixteenth century, explaining the significance of such actions in this way: "[W]e see women and other dependents... effectively effeminizing the enemy. The very dependents of the winners were seen to be more masculine than the humiliated enemy males" (72–3).[26] Such behavior grossly violated English feudal customs, which generally permitted losers of a battle to collect their dead in order to give them Christian burial.

Shakespeare's elaborate elision of this "barbaric" expression of dominance (which would have been known to many of the educated audience members) is balanced at the end of the play by the playwright's equally notable displacement of a castration, one seemingly symbolic of the unmanning powers of defeat. Douglas, Hal recounts, had fled the field when he saw the battle lost. The man whom Falstaff had described as he "that runs a' horseback up a hill perpendicular.... but afoot he will not budge a foot" (II.iv.343–54) is reported as having "Upon the foot of fear, fled with the rest, / And falling from a hill...was so bruis'd / That the pursuers took him" (V.v.20–2). Douglas's reputation as a man who stands and fights against all odds is belied. Unable in this case to control nature (or gravity), he is defeated by the natural phenomenon he had conquered in the past. Holinshed tells us that the steeply rising hill almost literally mastered him: "the earl of Dowglas, for hast, falling from the crag of an hie mounteine, brake one of his cullions, and was taken" (Bullough IV:191, qtd. in Evans 881, n. 21–22). Shakespeare alludes to, yet conceals Douglas's damaged testicle, avoiding any outright reference to the humiliation of the loser.

Such references to the conquered body effeminized by conquerors offer a new view of the fraternity expressed by several pairs of worthy opponents in the play. François Billacois comments that early modern French duellists "owed it to themselves to honour their opponent in order to honour themselves" (213), but these half-concealed elements of England's history in this play indicate the pleasure that common people took in the sexual humiliation of their fallen adversaries. Although both Shakespeare's Hal and his Hotspur seem to adhere to the chivalric code upon which Billacois expatiates, the affection is, to some extent at least, an anticipatory love of conquest. The affection that each expresses for his opponent is ultimately the expectation of conquering his manhood.[27]

Hotspur is characterized early on in the play as the epitome of masculinity. He is described as a phallic sapling—"Amongst a grove the very straightest plant" (I.i.82). But immediately undermining that image is the expression "sweet Fortune's minion," the darling of fortune (83). The term "minion" derives either from the Old High German word for love or from the Celtic word for small. This word expresses the king's mingled admiration for and frustration at Hotspur; according to the OED, it was mainly used in a contemptuous sense to refer to one's mistress. The secondary meaning is "a favorite of a sovereign, prince, or other great person," but also "especially opprobriously, one who owes everything to his patron's favour, and is ready to purchase its continuance by base compliance, a 'creature.'" Hotspur, "sweet Fortune's minion," is, then, doubly subservient: more fortunate than worthy, he is the paramour of fickle fortune, with all the suggestions of lightness and insubstantiality that detractors ascribed to such Elizabethan favorites as Essex; and he is a minion because, in Shakespeare's play, he is a youth. Before the first act has concluded, Northumberland will link that youth with effeminacy, chiding his son as a "wasp-stung and impatient fool…[who] break[s] into this woman's mood" (I.iii.236–7).

Hotspur's masculinity is continually threatened by womanish traits that bubble up within him. Like Geoffrey Whitney's emblematic leaky barrel, he blabs his intentions; Lady Percy inquires into his affairs on the strength of the information she gained from hearing him talk in his sleep (II.iii.47–55). Like the starling he plans to train to irk the king, Hotspur obsessively utters his cousin Mortimer's name throughout Act I, scene iii; later his wife refers to him as a "paraquito" (II.iii.85). Concerned for him, she compares his sweaty face to a lately disturbed stream whose bubbles indicate hidden disturbances (II.iii.57–62).

Hotspur disdains the debilitating powers of love; he channels his sexuality into war, not eros. Not only does he disdain his cousin Mortimer's uxoriousness, he banishes his wife from the marriage bed. During the early modern period, it was believed that because sex involved the expenditure of seminal fluid, masculine vitality could be lowered by frequent sexual intercourse (Paster 171). Humoral theory asserted that the body circulated the blood in progressive refining processes. Laudable blood, "a subtle and thinne body always mooveable, engendred of blood and vapour, and the vehicle or carriage of the Faculties of the soule" was supposed to flow to the heart (Crooke, *Microcosmographia* 174; qtd. in Paster 72). The final refining process took place in the spermatical vessels, where blood was refined into semen (Paster 71–2). Hotspur involuntarily gives information to his wife while he sleeps, but where he can control his outflow, as in sexual intercourse, he is vigilant. Lady Percy perceives his earnest attempts to contain himself as unnatural; she expresses her concern that his behavior may manifest a humoral imbalance:

> Tell me, sweet lord, what is't that takes from thee
> Thy stomach, pleasure, and thy golden sleep? ...
> Why hast thou lost the fresh blood in thy cheeks,
> And given my treasures and my rights of thee
> To thick-ey'd musing and curst melancholy? (II.iii.40–6)

Hotspur is preserving not only her safety by his silence but also his bodily fluids for the taxing efforts of the rebellion. Only when he is horsed and ready to go will he willingly say, "I love thee infinitely" (II.iii.102).

However, as Phyllis Rackin asserts, "Desire for another man ... fails to compromise [a character's] masculinity; instead, it reaffirms it" ("Foreign Country" 70). While Hotspur's passion for battle cannot be shared with Kate, he sounds like one of Billacois' duellists when he speaks of Hal:

> [B]e he as he will, yet once ere night
> I will embrace him with a soldier's arm
> That he shall shrink under my courtesy. (V.ii.72–4)

Hotspur's passion for fighting is here displaced onto his opponent. Whereas the sword keeps an opponent at more than arm's length, Hotspur envisions drawing Hal into his personal space, there to engage in a wrestler's embrace. The embrace that will end in death is far more important to Hotspur than the embrace that brings the "little death." Hotspur's erotic energy is directed toward the worthy opponent that Hal, surprisingly, turns out to be.

While Hotspur disdains flesh-and-blood women, he describes powerful forces in clearly feminine terms. Late in the play, he refers to his initial attack on the king's forces as a defloration, with results that will take the form of a pregnant Fortune. Knowing that Northumberland cannot lead his troops to join them, Hotspur sees his father as a weapon held in reserve: Northumberland can either press their advantage or prove a refuge "[i]f that the devil and mischance look big / Upon the maidenhead of our affairs" (IV.i.58–9). If the outcome is swelling trouble, then Northumberland may be able to contain or even abort the king's efforts at retaliation; if all goes well, Fortune's pregnancy should be brought to term with a new monarch delivered from the disorder. Hotspur and his cohorts are the ones whose actions may prove a potent seed to Fortune; they hope that she will conceive a happy outcome.

Many of Hotspur's images present all-powerful women who seem to grow from eating rather than from impregnation: he vows that he will kill the king's troops, sacrificing them to Bellona "all hot and bleeding" as if they were roasted oxen. He plans to offer Mars a tribute that will overwhelm him, drown him "[u]p to the ears in blood" (IV.i. 117). Hotspur conflates sex, violence, and the act of eating in a synaesthesic cluster of images:

> I am on fire
> To hear this rich reprisal is so nigh,
> And yet not ours. Come, let me taste my horse,
> Who is to bear me like a thunderbolt
> Against the bosom of the Prince of Wales.
> Harry to Harry shall, hot horse to horse,
> Meet and ne'er part till one drop down a corse. (IV.i.117–23)

The violence is characterized as a passionate embrace (bosom to bosom) that concludes in death. This vision of the combat, involving meeting "hot horse to horse," suggests a sexual contest, a union in sexual riding in which death and orgasm are indistinguishable. Hotspur desires a "taste" (test) of his horse, as if the practice of the action will bring him the satisfaction of its successful enactment—the full meal of wholesale slaughter. Despite Hotspur's asexual nature, his vision of himself-and-horse plunging like a thunderbolt into the prince's chest sounds like sexual penetration—or like the Tumucuan and Incan practice of sodomizing their prisoners with weapons before killing them (Trexler 68). This plunging into "Harry's" bosom suggests an entrance not only into his space but into his very body, a symbiotic union between the two Harrys.

Hotspur seems to take sexual pleasure in satisfying hungry Bellona; yet the sacrifice that will light up her eyes will float the god of war away. The flowing liquid that excites Hotspur is meant to satisfy another vampiric creature than the mother earth that King Henry initially envisioned tasting her children's blood. Bellona, unlike Mars, can take it all in. In this play, the female characters are few in number and only Glendower's daughter seems to have a satisfactory sexual relationship with her husband. Most of the female characters might, like Mistress Quickly, refuse the names by which women are defined because they resonate as "whore." The allegorical women, the ones more frequently invoked in this play than the wives, are indeed whores: Fortune is fickle, and Bellona is a frighteningly insatiable devourer.

Hal, in contrast to Hotspur, is described in terms that both parody and valorize phallic and martial power.[28] Falstaff contrasts his friend's slim frame with his own obesity, calling Hal "you dried neat's tongue, you bull's pizzle, you stock-fish! ... you tailor's yard, you sheath, you bowcase, you vile standing tuck!" (II.iv.244–8). The imagery develops from piscatory terms often used to refer to the woman's vulva, to slang for phalluses ("pizzle" and "yard"), containers for weaponry, and finally to a weapon itself.[29] The tuck, or rapier, is an anachronism in this context, when sword and buckler was indeed the standard equipment for the swordfight. For the most part, however, Hal's masculinity is figured on another level. His linguistic ability renders him akin to the rapier in its demand for agility and the ability to improvise; moreover, he is also "sharp" like a tuck. Not only is he clever and witty, but he has from his first scene indicated the sharp practice by which he hopes to win the people's hearts.

Hal compares linguistic flexibility to skill at swordfighting when he responds to Falstaff, "Well, breathe a while and then to it again" (II.iv.249). The comparison is an old one, but one can amplify it by arguing that Hal's eventual victory over Hotspur is figured in rhetorical displays of sprezzatura. Hal's flexibility and ability to improvise become increasingly evident as the Percy rebellion moves toward confrontation. He plays hide-and-seek with his own nobility, increasing its potency by refusing either to own or to disown it.[30] Lacking Hotspur's years of education on the battlefield, Hal nevertheless enacts the role of the *chevalier* seemingly without effort. The implicit contrast is underlined by Hal's early mockery of Hotspur as the tongue-tied warrior who "kills me some six or seven dozen of Scots at a breakfast" and then says, "'Fie upon this quiet life! I want work!'" (II.iv.102–5). Hotspur—in fact the truer warrior—resembles the warrior Castiglione describes "who not only declined [to dance] but would not listen to music or take any part in the other entertainments offered him, but kept saying that such trifles were not his business" (33). Hotspur disdains courtly accomplishments and, like Castiglione's messer Roberto, "we clearly see him making every effort to show that he takes no thought of what he is about, which means taking too much thought" (Castiglione 44). In contrast, Hal's effort at self-presentation is so well concealed that neither his biological nor his spiritual father is aware of it. His effort at sprezzatura is only revealed in his pride that he is "so good a proficient...that [he] can drink with any tinker in his own language during [his] life" (II.iv.17–20). In Hal, Shakespeare gives us the courtier, the man of natural grace, who conquers the career soldier because he *can* perform and *can* prove that he is "essentially made."

Because Hal cannot point to past achievements, he defines himself in relation to more stable, clearly established referents such as his father and Hotspur. This choice necessitates placing himself in a subordinate position relative to these well-tried figures. Speaking to Henry IV, Hal stresses, "I will ... / Be bold to tell you that I am your son" (III.ii.132–4). Much of the strength of this communication comes from his wish to indicate both a similitude to his father and a regard for him. Like his father, he will prove his strength in arms, and his prowess will indicate his desire to redeem his father's good opinion of him. Decked in the blood of his enemies, Hal will prove that his own blood is noble—and in that revelation, the implied stain on his father's honor will be wiped away.[31] Hal hopes to achieve this proof by meeting Hotspur on the field:

> And that shall be the day, whene'er it lights,
> That this same child of honor and renown,
> This gallant Hotspur, this all-praised knight,
> And your unthought-of Harry chance to meet. (III.ii.138–41)

Hal implicitly contrasts himself with the all-praised knight but also links the two as fellow youths—son and child.

When Hal and Hotspur finally meet, Hotspur says, "[W]ould to God / Thy name in arms were now as great as mine!" (V.iv.69–70).

The comment reinforces the mirroring that Shakespeare wants us to see: Henry Percy first contrasted to, then mirrored by "that same sword-and-buckler Prince of Wales" (I.iii.230). The king's wish that Hal could be proved a changeling and Hotspur his true son is never gratified, but the two are depicted throughout the play as brothers, paired emblems of political ambition.

When Hal conquers Hotspur, he becomes for the first time an unironic man-on-top, with Hotspur the shrunken, humiliated Other.[32] The visual scene at the conclusion of the combat clarifies Hal's role as heir and his place in the physical world relative to Hotspur. Hal is now the dominant figure of the two; visually, the corpse that was Hotspur is a peripheral element.[33] As Hal himself says, referring to Hotspur's body,

> When that this body did contain a spirit,
> A kingdom for it was too small a bound,
> But now two paces of the vilest earth
> Is room enough. (V.iv.89–92)

At Hotspur's death, as Hal stands like a Colossus over his prone body, the reference to Hotspur's need for space during his life strikingly delineates his body as conquered space—not merely threatened but destroyed as an autonomous individual. With Hotspur's death, Hal assumes not only Hotspur's honors but even his voice: "[L]et my favors hide thy mangled face, / And even in thy behalf I'll thank myself" (96–7). As others have pointed out, Hal assumes the role of both elegiser and elegised; with Percy gone, he himself can perform the roles they formerly shared. For Hal, "to be a person is to be his father's son, which is to be his father's heir, which is to be a soldier" (Traub 472). To be a soldier is to engage in a hierarchal dualism in which one is perpetually below or above the other. Hal's victory establishes both his conquest of Hotspur and his similitude to the more firmly ensconced monarch, his father, from whom he will inherit the throne.

I have used the instruction given to fencers (primarily aristocrats or wealthy men) to show how the masculine sense of bodily knowledge is formed. Fencers placed a high regard on nimbleness, dexterity, judgment, and an awareness of one's center of gravity—knowledge derived from attentiveness to one's own body and observation of the movements of others. Insofar as fencing involved interaction with another individual, it heightened a sense of intimacy that may have made men increasingly uncomfortable, possibly prompting behavior that resulted in status-raising violent encounters. Overall, training in fencing taught men comportment that was likely to lead to physical confrontation, whereas women were taught to comport themselves in such a way as to avoid drawing any attention to themselves. These lessons in physical deportment created a different experience of inhabiting the body for men than for women. The spatial assumptions that resulted served to distinguish between the sexes and helped to structure the early modern sense of gender difference.

The fencer's proxemic assumptions help us to understand the enormous significance of failure in the duel, of being wounded by a rapier. Having one's skin pierced, bleeding from a wound created a sense of unmanning reinforced by the fencer's assumptions about the impermeability of his physical space, although the belief in the impermeability of the male body (according to Paster and Laqueur) was probably shared by the general population. Yet, for a fencer, having one's space invaded was not only to be threatened but to be lessened as an autonomous individual. The physical carriage of the fencer literally embodied his assumptions about his place in the physical world. Because of the link between wounding and loss of a duel, the resulting loss of face was also linked to humiliation that might possess a sexual valence. Such evidence of his own permeability lessened the loser's sense of his own manliness and made him feel effeminate or infantilized. These concepts, though related, were not synonymous; the fear of being reduced to the level of a boy through the humiliation of loss was particularly strong for those who perceived victory in combat as a rite of passage to manhood. The terms of the duel in *The Unnatural Combat*, both in vocabulary and dramatic structure, indicate the power of this dynamic in the fight between the Malefort father and his son. The manhood/boyhood dynamic is yet more pronounced in *1 Henry IV*. Although Hal and Hotspur engage in a single combat that differs greatly from the early modern duels of honor, their references to one another manifest the same sense about proxemic penetration. Their language sexualizes conquest and recasts it in terms of domination of an immature male by a mature male, suggesting that masculinity was understood not only as the antithesis of femininity but also as physical maturity opposing effete immaturity. This dynamic is one that tempered the understanding of the words "masculinity" and "femininity"; it should be acknowledged as a significant component in the early modern understanding of gender.

Chapter 4

Misperceiving Masculinity, Misreading the Duel

This chapter examines how status-based notions of honor modified the idea of manliness when the phenomenon of duelling became popular in early modern English society and on the dramatic stage. The texts I examine are in some sense working through the contradictions in humanist thought about the relation of essence to being; as social documents they work out the answer relationally, by offering different answers to men of different ranks. Status alters both one's definition of honor and one's valuation of it. Because the authors of anti-duelling tracts failed to comprehend the significance of honor for the gentry and aristocracy, their publications failed in large part to mitigate the popularity of the duel. Only James I acknowledged the importance of honor in his edict against duelling, but by assuming that royal recognition was the fount of all honor, he, too, failed to perceive the instability of the concept.

The social understanding of masculinity is further altered when the duel is mimetic, staged as part of a drama. Because playwrights wrote commercial dramas rather than social criticism, their portrayals of the duel were based on dramatic imperatives. Yet in many ways the dramatists' understanding of the duel resembles that of the authors of the anti-duelling tracts. The common thread between duellists and their dramatic counterparts is their concern with social status. But playwrights tended not to use quarrels over precedence as the motivation for duels that capped the climax of serious plays; instead, the quarrels that instigated staged duels usually sprang from serious family wrongs. The causes leading to the duel were reinterpreted in this way so that the audience might more easily empathize with the story; more trivial provocations were generally presented only in satiric contexts. Yet the skepticism of the middling sort appears in the staging of the duel, which seldom figured prominently without comedic or skewed elements in the surrounding context. Even in tragedies, the playwrights had difficulty maintaining the high seriousness of the duel as a cultural rite. In *A Fair Quarrel, Hamlet,* and *The Revenge of Bussy D'Ambois,* the characters' motivations and situations are treated quite seriously. Yet the staging of the duel and the surrounding elements undermines the earnestness of the first play and the high tragedy of the latter two. The duels fail to bring the satisfying closure offered by revenge tragedies; on the contrary, they seem to undermine the possibility either of closure or of tragedy itself. The rite of the duel seems to "get out of hand"; like the poisoned foil that slips out of Laertes' grasp during the fencing exhibition in *Hamlet,* the performance of the duel seems to develop its own trajectory despite the playwrights' best intentions. Although these writers structure their plots to give the situation the gravity it deserves, their unease with and alienation from the code of honor results in some deflation of aristocratic pretensions.

However, though the representation of the duel is problematic both in terms of verisimilitude and dramatic effectiveness, the larger social context of the duel is preserved. Its derivation from a masculinist ethos is presented in the theater as a recreation of masculine community. In plays in which combat is a central element, we see repeatedly that the rite serves to consolidate homosocial bonds and to render women peripheral. Whether the bonds are formed with the duellist's opponent or with the observers, the result is a valorization of a military elite in which women have only a secondary role. Perhaps these bonds are strengthened because the duellists of the plays are depicted principally as family representatives—not as individuals jockeying for private fame, as they more often were in Jacobean England. But at the broadest level, despite these differences, both staged and real duels endorsed the patriarchal structure that nurtured the dynastic system.

Anti-duelling tracts crystallize the conflict that the courtier had to negotiate between individualism and law. Was familial honor more truly augmented by individual effort or by royal favor? Bacon says in his 1614 tract against private combats that duels are inspired by a false concept of honor, since "[t]he fountaine of honour is the King, and his aspect, and the accesse to his person continueth honour in life" (17). The metaphor of the king as a source of honor expresses a common notion of honor as it developed under the Tudors. According to Mervyn James, the concept of honor shifted in the sixteenth century as the state asserted its "monopoly both of honour and violence" (309). For several previous centuries, the most basic element of honor had been one's obligation to the family and "kinship group":

> a man's very being as honourable had been transmitted to him with the blood of his ancestors, themselves honourable men. Honour therefore was not merely an individual possession, but that of the collectivity, the lineage. Faithfulness to the kinship group arose out of this intimate involvement of personal and collective honour, which meant that both increased or diminished together. Consequently, in critical honour situations where an extremity of conflict arose ... the ties of blood were liable to assert themselves with a particular power. (M. James 325)

These ties created a complex network of relationships, each involving a clearly demarcated superior and inferior established by "lordship, kinship, friendship, and the code implicit in honour itself" (M. James 313).

Although the importance of the extended family diminished in the sixteenth century, childrearing practices continued to reinforce the patriarchal family structure. In reading the common analogy between king and subjects, fathers and dependents, critics have focused on its indication of how the king *wished* to be perceived, but the analogy depends for its effectiveness on how the father *was* perceived.[1] The head of the household commanded absolute obedience at all times (Stone *FSM* 171–2, 195). According to Stone, the child's subordination, evident in an extraordinarily deferent code of conduct, lasted as long as the parents remained alive (*FSM* 172–3).[2] Stone's evidence suggests that strong feelings of regard and admiration, or the family loyalty that Mervyn James describes, might easily be derived from the excessive show of respect that was expected. Moreover, the English reformation reinforced the important role of the head of household, thereby strengthening the regard other family members had for the patriarch.[3]

When family ties were paramount, the honor of an aristocrat consisted of two elements: loyalty to the family whose pedigree had brought him honor, and steadfastness to any pledge in which he gave his word. In fact, this code of honor created a secondary code of private morality in which men could lie and cheat without losing their honor so long as they took no oaths in the course of their deceptions. A promise "gave the essence of honour, will and intention, the public status which enabled both to be brought into question" (M. James 340). But during the reigns of Elizabeth I and James I, the code of honor altered as the monarchs consciously sought to break up the influence of the great dynasties. While blood and lineage were not discounted as elements of honor, "uncertainty about the status of heredity in relation to other aspects of honour increased, with a proneness to present honour, virtue and nobility as detachable from their anchorage in pedigree and descent" (M. James 375). The potential for conflict increased because it was not always clear who was "entitled to deference and [who was] required to accord it" (M. James 314).

More conflicts resulted not only because status was less clearly defined but also because the Crown was attempting to manipulate the idea of honor for its own ends. Mervyn James draws a connection between "the visitations, and the state-centred honour system" and an attempt to direct community loyalties "solely to a single centre, the crown" (338). Humanists like Sir Thomas Elyot encouraged the perception that honor was created by the king's recognition of virtue or valor in his subjects (M. James 338–9). Mervyn James also recounts stories of local resistance to such changes.[4]

During this period, the ideas of the Italian humanists also affected the English court's perceptions of honor. Haniball Romei, author of *The Courtiers Academie,* draws a distinction between *honor natural,* "a common opinion, that he honored, hath never failed in justice, nor valor," and *honor acquired,* "a reward, manifesting an action of beneficence" (80, 82). These terms derive from Aristotle's; as Romei says, "[I]t is by the Philosopher, two manner of wayes defined, in the first booke of his Rhetorike, saying: Honor is a signe of beneficent opinion: and in the fourth of the Ethikes, Honour is the reward of vertue" (82). Thus, "beneficent opinion" is the generally good opinion of others, or honor natural, whereas honor acquired refers specifically to recognition by a sovereign power of an individual's qualities or actions.[5] The humanists were not naive about the relation between honor natural and honor acquired. Although Count Gherardo Bevelacqui, a character in Romei, compares the honor of the honored person to the whiteness of milk as an inherent attribute, Romei's character Gualenguo alludes to a line from Cicero: "Vertue for guide, but Fortune for companion, I would have" (Romei 109, 114), implying that a man must be both virtuous and lucky to be honored. Romei also discusses whether it is honorable to strive to gain recognition for one's acts. As Mervyn James suggests, the honors from one's sovereign seem less important in themselves or in their source than in the fame they bring, "the immortality which honorable deeds conferred, their memory being preserved and celebrated in the community to which [the man of honor] belonged" (324).[6]

As I have implied, the aristocrat's notion of honor was shaped by his understanding of the family structure, by royal policies instituted during the Tudor regime, and by Italian humanist notions of courtesy. But the idea of honor among the middling sort, while heavily influenced by Italian humanism, was also affected by English civil law and by the advent of capitalism. For this group, a good name developed in a different way and was formed along different lines; its destruction had different consequences than for an aristocrat. Those who wrote against the custom of duelling derived almost entirely from the middle ranks. Because they failed to see that the defense of his honor was part of the role of the aristocratic man, their arguments could not dissuade young men of higher social status from the custom. Nor, for the most part, did these writers recognize the desire for social status that motivated the untitled to ape the nobility. The arguments of the antiduelling tracts depended on warrants that their audience did not share.

Even among the aristocracy, there were many different conceptions of honor. Examining the sixteenth-century duelling code in 1710, Scipione Maffei found that authorities on honor had given nearly twenty different definitions of the term; based on his findings, the modern historian Frederick Bryson suggests that "variations in time and place cause honor to depend upon features which contradict one another" (Maffei 186; qtd. in Bryson 10–11). Yet one constant remains among this plethora of meanings: the equivalence of honor and manhood, and, up to a certain time in the English Renaissance, an almost universal understanding of honor as the spiritual quality that enables a man to gain glory in feats of war. Discussing two works about honor that circulated in England during the fifteenth and sixteenth centuries, the *Boke of Saint Albans* and Llull's *The Book of the Ordre of Chyvalry*, Mervyn James points out that "[i]t was virtue which made the potential honourable quality of a man actual" (310). "Virtue" here is a composite of enumerated virtues, all "related to conduct in war and battle" (310–11). This martial emphasis recurs in early Elizabethan tracts on honor (M. James 312). But in the Renaissance, "virtue" could be reconfigured as a synonym for honor itself. The Latin term *virtus* is, after all, closely related to the word *vir*, man. Though the commonest meaning of *virtus* was manliness, the word could, like the late medieval "virtue," refer to the primary traits of warriors: bravery and courage.

*Virtus/vertu/*virtue, however, may be distinguished from honor by its emphasis on spiritual qualities. Phyllis Rackin distinguishes Renaissance notions of gender from our own by characterizing our modern gender ideology as constructed "on the basis of physical difference" whereas during the Renaissance, "masculine superiority tended to be mystified in the spirit, feminine oppression justified by the subordinate status of the body" ("Foreign Country" 76). In other words, men in the Renaissance did not consider themselves superior because of their physical strength but because they believed that strength was governed by their spirituality—their virtue. Honor, then, can be understood as the spiritual component of physical strength. We, too, have this notion, invariably described in slang terms: "the right stuff," *cojones*. But—and this is another significant difference between the early modern English and the contemporary American mind—we tend to locate this quality in groups of lower social status, whereas in the Renaissance it was a mark of nobility. For us, there is some effeminacy implied in being a "suit," but in Shakespeare's time the possessor of virtue is always the superior element of a dichotomy: aristocrat/plebeian, man/woman, spirit/body, as Rackin says (75–6), and, as I would add, Englishman/foreigner as well—the only dichotomy of this culture valorizing those of low social status.

The English monarchy's continued efforts throughout the sixteenth century to establish honor as the gift of the king were, of course, resisted by the hereditary nobility (M. James 336–9). The new notion of honor was more widely accepted among the middling sort, whose commercial interests were in any case opposed to the violence of an honor-oriented society. Much of the material in the antiduelling pamphlets attacks the aristocratic privileging of reputation. Two different anti-duelling tracts, "Duell-Ease" and "The Christian Knight," both refer to the story of Constantine's picture:

> Constantine the Emperour, his picture was drawne with a singular representation of great Majestie. ... A most idle fellow, found an opportunitie to cast filth on it. ... Well friends (saith Constantine) you tell mee of a fellow that hath disgraced mee, and contemptuously cast dirt on mee ... but nothing doe I feele upon Constantine: I see Constantine cleane, the glasse sheweth no ordure in my face: your conceit may

terme my face fowle and filthily abused; but my conceit telleth mee nothing of it, how then can I be angrie? ("Duell-Ease" 57–8)

The author goes on to compare Constantine's picture to the reader's name and credit, calling them "vocal images" and "a picture in the air." The analogy functions effectively on the literal level: a name is a verbal representation, just as a portrait is a visual one. Reputation, however, a "good name," is an abstraction, distinct from the person it characterizes. To injure a reputation is not to harm its owner physically but to harm a person's standing within the community. If that person values social standing, such an injury is grievous, though it has no effect on his or her physical well-being. The analogy fails because, as the author of "Duell-Ease" points out, Constantine was the "Emperour of the rising and setting Sunne" (58); his standing was not affected by the defacement of his portrait, and his decision not to punish its defacer increased rather than decreased the regard that others had for him. Were Jacobean courtiers as secure in their standing as Constantine, they would have had no reason to challenge those who diminished them. But in the court's shifting hierarchy, among his equals "the man of honour was expected to assert his 'preeminence,' a requirement which imparted a note of tension even to ordinary social intercourse and daily conversation" (M. James 313). In other words, an early modern nobleman's position in court society cannot be compared to an emperor's undisputed preeminence precisely because a nobleman can rarely bring himself to act with such imperial nonchalance. Lacking the emperor's greatness, he responds to slights with an anxiety that confirms his unstable status. Though the story was intended to show that the truly great can disregard such signs of impudence, most noblemen could not rise above the insecurity of their positions.

At times, even the authors of the anti-duelling tracts recognize that the notion of honor is a variable cultural construct. William Wiseman, author of "The Christian Knight," dismisses those who consider their reputations injured if they fail to respond to injuries: "I little weigh what they say, that are carried away with a vice *regnant*. ... For this present I say no more but this. He that hath revenge in his power, hath also judgement of honour" (P4v). Any individual who is wronged may define for himself whether honor consists of responding to or ignoring the injury. G. F., the author of "Duell-Ease," attempts to shift the paradigm by characterizing injury as "a distemper meerely in fancy" whose cure is a draft of "bloud...of men... yea the stoutest" (Epistle Dedicatory). Repeatedly the intention of fighting is described as a disease, with references to humoral theories about excessive choler. Yet G. F. makes his argument two ways: while invoking the trope of pugnacity as a disease, he discounts the notion, implying that only willful obstinacy induces men to fight. Bacon's rhetorical strategy constructs honor as a trick: in his "Charge ... touching Duels," he asks the nobility "for true honors sake, honor of Religion, Law, and the King our Maister" to support his prosecution of "this fond and false disguise or puppetrey of honor" (34). Bacon links duels to the exhibitions that drew members of the underclass; he compares honor to a puppet show—a performance manipulated by a showman, a mountebank's trick. Throughout the "Charge," Bacon attempts to construct the combat as both low and foreign. This image of honor as a trick indicates his unwillingness to recognize the notion of natural honor; in fact, as a self-made man, Bacon would have had some stake in debunking the association between lineage and honor.

In arguing against the practice of duelling, Wiseman suggests that honor was once a stable entity now adulterated by foreign and effeminate fashions: "How farre is this from the ancient doctrine of manners, or manhood, now corrupted wholly, by the upstart humours of a number of desperates; who if it were a fashion to ride out in the raine, and leave their cloakes behind them, no doubt they would follow it" (S1v). He seems aware that abstract notions of manhood have changed over time, and he offers several interesting dichotomies: he distinguishes between the manhood of common sense and the manhood of fashion, using this duality to explain the "corruption" that, in his view, has altered an essential concept. He also acknowledges the insecurity of court life in his differentiation between ancient doctrines and "upstart humours," disdaining the more recently made knights of James's reign. Thus, he shows less concern with ancient families than with the gentry and those of merchant status who follow the fashion, disregarding their own well-being for the sake of public approbation.

Although Wiseman's assessment of the duellist's motives is accurate, he couches his analysis in terms that deride the custom. Failing to acknowledge the validity of the aristocrat's definition of honor, he can hold the duellist up to ridicule without reaching the essential issue. At one point, he alludes to Cicero's saying, "*Quam quisque novit artem, in hac se exerceat,*" "Let no man goe out of his element, or skill" (R1v). In Wiseman's view, if a man does not possess honor through his lineage, he should not attempt to gain it through the notoriety of the duel:

> Let merchants deale with merchandize, and schollers with bookes: every man meddle with his owne profession. It sufficeth a man to bee

honest, though not honourable. What should a shoomaker goe try his honesty in the field with a hatter, that challengeth him; but rather challenge him againe (as one did) to shewe him as good a Hatte, as hee can shewe a shooe. (R1v–R2r)

Wiseman uses the shoemaker/hatter combat partly to chide parvenus for trying to rise out of their rank. His point is that although duelling is a defining act, it cannot redefine those below a certain rank. Some should be content with honesty rather than aspiring to gain honor. This application of the more basic saying, "Shoemaker, stick to your last," invokes traditional pride of place to warn potential roaring boys that they may become ridiculous rather than illustrious if they attempt to master a craft not their own. G. F. similarly criticizes those who aspire to gain honor through duelling: "by the baser creature, a Challenge is thrust on, as not being able to creepe into Honour, but by the casualty of a combat" (Epistle Dedicatory). These writers perceive the duel not as a result of hotheadedness but as an attempt at social climbing.

Recognizing the writer's power to alter the cultural meaning of certain significant abstractions, Wiseman and Bacon both do their best to demonize the practice of the duel by aligning it with clearly negative practices. Wiseman urges his reader not to "forget" themselves, a useful term because it can refer either to degrading oneself or to attempting to rise above one's station. Wiseman perceives two kinds of "memory lapses": the forgetfulness of hot blood, responsible for brawls, and that of cold blood, which results in hubristic acts of revenge (N2v). He goes on to the provocation to the duel—the quarrel. This act, he says, belongs only to the hasty or choleric man; "an other man as good as hee, will never doe it, but leave it to scouldes in allies, and alehouses" (N3r). He invokes the old argument that angry words are the province of powerless, perhaps even low-ranked, women.[7] Bacon sarcastically suggests that "the year books and statute books must give place to some French and Italian pamphlets, which handle the doctrine of Duells" (10), attempting to rouse his readers' xenophobia.

These criticisms of the duel express a fear of uncontrol that seems to have been a major source of anxiety at this time. Just as antitheatricalists feared that watching plays could somehow hypnotize audiences into performing morally repugnant acts, Wiseman and Bacon express a fear of some sort of unholy possession.[8] Wiseman fears that the reading of chivalric romances has resulted in a sort of mass Quixotism. Bacon is even more specific; he alludes to "bewitching

Duells": "[f]or, if one judge of it truely, it is noe better then a sorcery that enchanteth the spirits of young men, that beare great myndes, with a false shew, *species falsa;* and a kind of satanicall illusion and apparition of honour" (12). In both cases, the writers suggest that the glamor of the duel compels young men to act against their wills—their understanding is confused and their moral sense perverted. The obvious wrong of killing is distorted in the duel to appear honorable.

Wiseman is particularly concerned with false analogies; he quotes Galen's Latin tag *Similitudo mater erroris* to argue that men need to be capable of making fine distinctions to avoid the wrong conduct. "Pride is like magnanimity... envy like justice... gluttony like naturall appetite, and therefore men bee ravenous," he says, arguing that the excessive practice of any virtue becomes a vice (V1r). In the opening of his charge against duelling, he complains of those who "were never officers in the field, and yet if they have beene at the University a while, and have read a little of Livie, or Plutarks lives; and then come new to court, or Innes of court: they thinke themselves straight to bee Scipioes, or Hannibals, and fall to practising" (N2r). University men, he suggests, learn pugnacity and vainglory by literary example. Reading about dictators creates dictators. But while these men act like roaring boys, they conceive themselves as following in the footsteps of military leaders. If his assertion is true, then these literary models confuse young men as to the proper course of action: the military model is proffered at the expense of the civic model of citizenship. Were these young men taught Cincinnatus instead of Scipio, they would be able to distinguish between the behavior proper for war and that proper for peace.

Certain misapprehensions, however, derive not from the culture of the university but from the court. Bacon says of court culture that

> it is so punctuall, and hath such reference and respect unto the receyved conceipts, whats before hand, and whats behinde hand, and I cannot tel what, as without all question it doth, in a fashion, countenance and authorise this practise of Duells. (16)

In other words, the emphasis on etiquette makes people overly attentive to triviality; the valorization of the small detail justifies quarreling over an imagined insult or a casual slight. G. F. lists some of the pretexts for the duel: "a false smile of a beauty; a simple conceit, of some hollow friend: a light mistake of a foe, things all of no value, a challenge must passe, must have its answer: else honour goe exiled for ever" (5). The combat, as James I said, violates the grounds "aswell of Naturall, as of Legall Justice," because the satisfaction of the duel greatly overbalances the "weight and measure to the wrong" (60). Bacon acknowledges that in this culture the duel seems "as if it had in it some-what of right," but he does so while decrying the culture as a whole (16). His is the outsider's view that defines but does not justify a culture's values. Bacon praises the Roman republic, where insults were recognized as a theatrical game. In the course of statesmen's orations, "exquisite reproaches were tossed up and downe in the Senate of Rome"; yet words were not understood as a diminution of honor but as "mere breath" and an opportunity for sport (27). Bacon sees the Roman practice as a sovereign example, for the citizens "eyther despised [insults] or returned them, but no blood split about them" (28). The anti-court bias is evident here, as in Wiseman's scathing comment, "Men be never souldiers untill they fall out: and then every country man is a cavaleer" (R1r). The term "cavaleer" combines the worst elements of Hotspur's courtier and Hotspur himself: a "cavaleer" is both overly precise and overly eager to perform any deed that will bring him honor.

Most of Wiseman's arguments seem to be directed toward convincing the middling sort not to ape their superiors, as Bacon's are aimed at preventing the aristocracy from acting like their inferiors. Wiseman grapples with the old argument that the extra-legal duel, like the trial by combat, permits the hand of God to indicate the more righteous combatant. Wiseman tropes this argument as a violation of the boundaries of social rank: "Wee must not looke to heare God speake, but by deputies and magistrates; we ought not expect miracles, nor bee our owne Judge" (R2v). The expectation of a direct message from God is a direct transgression of the religious hierarchy. Wiseman manifests a firmly Anglican notion of divine communication; his view goes against the more radically Protestant emphasis on a personal relationship with God.

Bacon is less consistent than Wiseman: he sees aristocratic duelling as both an appropriation of common law and as a degradation of a good name. He astutely observes that the practice of duelling implies "two lawes, one a kind of Gowne-law, and the other a law of reputation" and sarcastically urges, "if they be in the right, *transeamus ad illa,* lets receive them, and not keepe the people in conflict and distraction betweene two lawes" (10). Bacon's quip is intended to point out the impossibility of reconciling two opposing codes of conduct and the preposterousness of according the duelling code the respect that is granted to civil law. The duelling code was not congruous with common law as the trial by combat had been, nor could it serve

Figure 4.1 Frontispiece of *Duell-Ease* [detail] (London: 1633). This illustration indicates God's displeasure with the duellist who has initiated the combat with a challenge: God as superior duellist.

adequately as a substitute for the monarch's central authority. The duelling code depended on the existence of common law to define it as a sort of shadow, an adjunct that governed a narrow elite; as such, it might have been tolerated if it had not grown so widespread and so public that its practice looked like a flouting of the king's law.

Bacon therefore attempted to discourage the practice among the aristocracy, specifically by asking them to note how public the practice had become. He begins his tract by noting his surprise that aristocrats should continue in a practice grown so common: "I should thinke (my Lords) that men of birth and quality will leave the practise, when it begins to bee vilified and come so lowe as to Barberssurgeons and Butchers, and such base mechanicall persons" (6).[9] The consciousness of rank was indeed a strong force for shaping behavior; as Elias has shown, the nobility often rebuked their children for sloppy behavior by characterizing it as churlish.[10] Yet Bacon seems more disingenuous here: implying that base persons have embraced duelling in imitation of their social superiors, he attempts to make this imitation sound unique. Referring to butchers and barbers duelling, Bacon offers a distinction without difference, since the lower orders habitually aped many noble practices. Bacon, moreover, fails to distinguish between the motivation of the aristocrat and that of the roaring boy. While Wiseman criticizes the general attempt to do as aristocrats do, Bacon never considers why aristocrats are willing to risk their lives over trifles.

In contrast to his Attorney General, James I granted the validity of the aristocrat's concern with reputation: in his edict against duelling, he deplored "verball wrongs" "[f]or by this meane all men may bee robbed of that reputation, which as a Birth right they brought with them into the world, and cannot forfait nor forgoe, without some acte done by themselves unworthily" (43–4). He describes a good reputation as a birthright (the *honor natural* of Romei) that can only be lost by one's own failure. It is that failure that James seeks to redefine throughout a large part of his edict. While Bacon endorsed the response of Charles IX of France, who proclaimed "That the King him-selfe tooke upon him the honor of all that tooke them selves grieved or interessed for not having performed the Combat" (Bacon 15), James takes a different approach. One strategy he uses is to point out the instability of the concept of reputation. Giving the lie, he points out, has only been framed as an insult during this age. Like Bacon, he refers to the Romans "that are worthily reputed the purest and best Interpreters of all words that originally are drawne from themselves, [among them] the Lye was thought to be no other, then an earnest negation of a bold affirmation" (48). Not only does James emphasize the denotative rather than the connotative meaning of the word "lie," he also refers his audience to a period in which the word bore no particular connotations at all.

James recognizes, however, that the code of honor had the force of religious belief for his courtiers. He refers to the common perception that "many had wonne Honor by the losse of their lives, upon this worthy ground, and those should bee the Saints, whose names they would insert, by limning them in red letters, into Honors Calender" (27). Surprisingly, James takes pains to outline this point of view, validating it rather than condemning it. He even suggests that the gentlemen "not so sensitive of smart, as fearful of dishonor" fight from understandable motives (14). This sympathetic approach is reinforced by his account of his reluctance to prohibit duelling (15). He grants that abolishing duels and keeping potential duellists content will be difficult because it involves mediating continually between pairs of proud men (19–20).

The edict offers several different approaches to resolving the problem of duelling: it pledges to make legal satisfaction easier to obtain; to punish duellists more severely if they agree to fight; and to redefine duelling in a way that will make it easier for men to refuse the duel while maintaining their honor. First, James suggests that judges will soon raise the amount of damages granted by common law when they realize the value that aristocrats place upon their honor (34). But the monarch also realizes that "how grievous soever Penalties may seeme, that are layed either upon the Persons, or the Purses of Our Subjects... yet they neither worke Repentance or remorse in themselves" (91). To achieve that end, James states his intention to detain those who have planned to fight a duel until "they have confessed under their owne hands, a grosse errour in the judgement of all sorts of men, wronging Honour asmuch as Duetie" (91). James is, of course, constructing the intention to fight as a sort of thought-crime.[11] In doing so, he dangerously blurs the distinction between intention and action. Not only does he recognize a link between word and deed, acknowledging that one may instigate the other, he implies that even thoughts may be punishable because they are the origin of premeditated crime.

What James objects to as much as to actual bloodshed, of course, is the challenge to his own authority. Whether the duellist sees himself as able to augment his own honor (110–11) or "seekes his reputation from the maniest voyces among the people" (113), he indicates that the king's favor is secondary to other elements in his concept of the formation of honor. James hopes that the threat of punishment will intimidate those who remain unaffected by the fear of losing his favor. The edict's combination of threats and cajoling seems intended to convince the nobility that "it had beene better for them to have borne the rashe imputations of greene wits, that will bee satisfied by nothing but the sword, then the grave Judgements of Superiours" (38). With this passage, James reverts to his usual autocratic method, with a hint of the patriarchal role that he believed the king played in relation to his subjects.

But James does not depend solely on threats to procure his subjects' obedience; he also attempts to redefine honor once again. At the close of the edict, James spends ten pages explaining the relation between courage and the law. If no quarrel other than the king's can serve as grounds for combat, then no law-abiding subject will fight in a duel. To challenge another under these circumstances is "rather a demonstration of pusillanimitie and cowardise, then an acte of resolution and fortitude" (114). According to James, those who abide by the law are as incapable of fighting as those who are lame, in prison, or in orders, "For, who can deny that man to live in the state of a prisoner, whom so many bands of duety and obedience deteines from answering a person that is past himselfe?" (116). An attempt to provoke such men should be considered base, even cowardly, because these men simply don't hold the same freedoms as the one who cares nothing for the king's statutes. Thus, James attempts to define volition ("would not") as inability ("cannot") and lay the onus on the man who sends a challenge with the knowledge that it will not be accepted. By throwing the charge of cowardice onto the figure who offers the accusation, he attempts to remove the nobleman's sense that his honor depends on accepting the challenge. The strategy probably would have been effective if most aristocrats were, as he assumed, less "sensitive of smart … [than] fearful of dishonor" (14). The actions of James's subjects suggests that many still resisted the notion that honors were conferred by the king; indeed, their behavior shows that they believed that they could augment their honor through deeds that would win the admiration and wonder of the people.

Like the authors of "The Christian Knight" and "Duell-Ease," most playmakers derived from the middling ranks. But whereas the duel was the *raison d'etre* of the anti-duelling tract, in the drama it was simply a plot device to build an effective play. Actual staged duels occurred seldom; more often the combat was anticipated but avoided, or recounted as an offstage occurrence. Combats form natural climaxes, and skillful playwrights used them to structure dramatic action. (A notable exception, Massinger's *The Unnatural Combat,* which presents a duel in Act II, remains lopsided despite the playwright's attempt to build on the duel as a trope for the rest of the dramatic action.) Though the duel could be (and often was) satirized onstage, it could also serve to cap a tragedy.

Where the staged duel functions as a significant plot element, its presentation suggests that the dramatist's goal was good playwriting rather than verisimilitude or social criticism. As we have seen, many duels in this period were motivated by a desire for fame. Individualism not only destabilized the social hierarchy but also valorized popular honors on the basis of even temporary fame. Young men sought for a name among their peers as a measure of social success; relatively arbitrary aspects of court life were the measure of a man's status. In the drama, however, those characters who subscribed to this viewpoint were satirized.[12] Playmakers chose not to portray quarrels over individual honor positively; indeed, such subjects are rare. Instead, the theater linked honor once again to family concerns. The phenomenon of duelling was given dramatic weight, particularly in tragedies, by association with serious family matters. In plays in which the duel figures largely, the playwrights usually chose to deviate from reality. Rather than attempting to imbue relatively trivial causes with gravity, they used the duel to resolve matters such as the murder of a character's family member or a deliberate attempt to destroy a character's status. Plot elements create the grounds for tragedy and lead steadily toward the play's final confrontation. Yet when the duel is staged, more often than not something in its presentation threatens to undermine the magnitude of the event. The playwrights' skepticism about the resolution promised by the combat becomes evident in what results from the attempt to take the rituals of honor seriously. In this respect, we see the playwrights unable to control their own perceptions of aristocratic mores.

Although the rituals of the combat may produce a grotesquely tragicomic effect, the psychological results for the characters are oddly consistent and oddly realistic. These stage-duels create an economy of exchange that excludes women while strengthening the bonds between men. Whether the affinity develops between two combatants or between duellist and supporter, the result is a tie that precludes heterosexual bonds. In some cases, women are pushed to the periphery of the drama; in others, they form subordinate same-sex communities of their own; in yet others, they merely serve as a means of exchange that brings men closer. In all the plays, however, manhood is structured as the willingness to take on the role of the family representative, acting as the man whose behavior stands for the integrity of the family he represents.

In Middleton and Rowley's *A Fair Quarrel*, reputation is initially interpreted as a Cratylan label that expresses "the essence of each thing in letters and syllables" (Plato, *Cratylus* 369). The insult that leads to the challenge to the duel is treated as if reputation could define one's essence:

> *Captain Ager*: You left a *coward* here?
> *Colonel*: Yes, sir, with you.
> *Ager*: 'Tis such base metal, sir, 'twill not be taken;
> It must home again with you. (III.i.115–17)[13]

Ager's pronoun referent (" 'Tis") alludes not to "coward" but to "insult"; his statement is an informal challenge to the Colonel to fight, "an indirect method of giving the lie," as Bowers puts it ("Duelling Code" 62). In saying, " 'Twill not be *taken*," does Ager mean that the insult cannot be swallowed, as in a metaphor of digestion? That it will not stick to him, as in a reference to his exterior composition? That he refuses to accept it, as if it were bad coin? The currency metaphor seems likely; it reinforces the distinction between counterfeit and true valor. Moreover, this metaphor is later used repeatedly in the play with reference to another character.[14] Or could "taken" mean that the insult will not blend in with his essence, as in a metaphor of essential elements? The pun in "such base metal" supports this interpretation, meaning that the fine quality of Ager's own mettle (or metal) cannot assimilate the lowness of the insult. Repeated imagery shows that for Ager, reputation and honor inhere within his own body. The elements of his composition must reject anything base as foreign. Ager's expression suggests that the imputation of cowardice is concretized in the word coward itself, as if the word were a physical entity that must find a home with either the Colonel or himself. If words are swords, as one character asserts earlier in the play, this is an ugly and ill-made sword whose point Ager intends to turn back on its owner. He will not accept it as his own, as a sign that expresses a truth about him.

A Fair Quarrel examines shifting ideas about reputation in the context of the challenge to the duel. While some writers have read the play as an endorsement of duelling and others as a condemnation of it, we can see in this play a satire that interrogates the received ideas on the subject (with the exception of the final scene, which offers an idealized and artificial conclusion that begs the questions the play has raised).[15] The play's protagonist, an idealistic and scrupulous young soldier who must decide what a "fair quarrel" is in order to fight one, offers the most clearly articulated idea of honor. But despite the widespread critical assumption that his perspective is the one the play endorses, the play as a whole offers a much wider view of the issue.[16] Overall, the dramatists' ideas of honor are structured by the concept of action as a continuum ranging from entirely verbal, rhetorical gestures to physical, non-verbal acts. Much of the play involves comic business based on different characters' ideas of where to locate the challenge and the duel on this continuum.

A Fair Quarrel portrays both honor and reputation as dangerously unstable. Although Ager is depicted quite seriously, his scrupulousness may seem laughable. To clinch the matter, the scenes about the roaring school in the secondary plot satirize Ager's deep concern for exact truth by using nonsense words to emphasize the arbitrary nature of language. Like *Hamlet* and *The Revenge of Bussy d'Ambois*, this play portrays the duel as a ritual that strengthens fraternal bonds, specifically between the combatants. Its authors show the English regard for reputation as shortsighted, comical in the context of this romantic comedy but potentially tragic outside it.

The main plot of *A Fair Quarrel* concerns the punctilious concern for reputation shown by both Captain Ager and the Colonel, his superior officer. Hearing a soldier equate the two men's valor, the Colonel is incensed—and appalled when Ager does not immediately concede his superior's greater worth. As an indirect result, the Colonel calls Ager a "son of a whore." Ager, incensed in turn, challenges his commander to a duel. Comic complications ensue as Ager, ostensibly manifesting his scrupulousness, decides to check the truth of the charge with his mother before he goes to the combat. His mother, though virtuous, decides not to deny the insult in order to prevent her son from endangering his life in her defense. Ager responds to his mother's magnanimity with contempt. He condemns her supposed inchastity and goes to cry off the combat. But when the Colonel calls him a coward, he rejoices at receiving an insult over which he can in conscience fight. He fights and critically wounds his commander. At death's door, the Colonel repents of his insult and revises his will to make Ager his heir and his sister's bridegroom. The Colonel miraculously recovers in time to preside over his sister's wedding.

The play's plot may seem silly, almost Pythonesque, when briefly summarized, but the quarrel about reputation between Ager and the Colonel embodies a significant conflict of the early modern period. The sense of self cultivated by an aristocratic military elite came under attack when elements as diverse as economic shifts and the new science further destabilized the changing feudal order. The Colonel, who had perceived his position as a stable one in a clearly defined hierarchy, learns that the beliefs and behavior of a subordinate can call his position into question. The quarrel does not derive from a disagreement about precedence but from one about dismantling an old hierarchy and replacing it with another that appears dangerously mutable. Although the Colonel is not an aristocrat (he seems to be a gentleman, nothing more), his sense of self derives from a military hierarchy like the one eroding in *Othello*. Like Iago, he is worried that showmanship and personal graces may replace years of meritorious behavior as the measure of a man's worth. He has devoted his life to a career that appeared to guarantee him a well-defined place; in a chance conversation, he finds that the requirements for that place have changed.

Ager's understanding of reputation seems to his superior officer dangerously chaotic, lacking a sense of order; Ager's view threatens the Colonel's sense of reputation as a creation built over time. The Colonel's reputation is, as he says, life of his life, the thing most highly valued in the military. When his status is challenged by the overheard conversation in which one man considers Ager the Colonel's equal, the higher-ranked officer feels that he must engage in combat. Ager does not see why his valor should not be compared with the older man's; he says to the Colonel's friend, "What should ail you, sir? There was little wrong done to your friend i' that" (I.i.66 7). Ager's sense of honor derives from the self-consciously chivalric military ideal that prompted Castiglione to urge that

> whenever the Courtier chances to be engaged in a skirmish or an action or a battle in the field, or the like, he should ... do the outstanding and daring things that he has to do in as small a company as possible and in the sight of all the noblest and most respected men in the army ... for it is well indeed to make all one can of things well done. (99)

For Castiglione, selectively conspicuous bravery is part of the ethos of sprezzatura, the performance of all deeds in such a way "as to conceal all art and make whatever is done or said appear to be without effort" (43). The aristocratic figure that is Castiglione's subject is, despite his military prowess, named the Courtier, not the Soldier; he performs actions not primarily to achieve concrete goals but to impress others in the court—most specifically, the prince. Ager's perception of military valor is based on this reinterpretation of it; he presumes that by performing notable acts of valor, he will receive official recognition fairly quickly. In contrast, the Colonel perceives high military rank as the signifier of a long and successful career; as in Bacon's edict, honor consists for him in a monarch's public recognition of years of meritorious service.

Given the veneration of order and degree in the early modern period despite various shifts in the social order (Stone, *CA* 29–49), Ager's insensitivity to the Colonel's claims severely lessens his credibility as the moral arbiter of the play. In this opening scene, Rowley pointedly exhibits Ager's insensitivity to the precedents of rank:

> *Colonel*: What can you dispute more questionable?
>   You are a captain, sir; I give you all your due.
> *Captain Ager*: And you are a colonel, a title
>   Which may include within it many captains;
>   Yet, sir, but throwing by those titular shadows,
>   Which add no substance to the men themselves,
>   And take them uncompounded, man and man,
>   They may be so with fair equality. (I.i.75–82)

Ager here dismisses the naming power of words to which he will later show himself exaggeratedly attached. Simultaneously, he writes off the degrees in military rank, a significant and respected form of order. The Colonel's rank is, presumably, the kind of reward that Romei intended when he spoke of acquired honor. When Ager assumes that the name of Colonel is merely a titular shadow (significantly, "Colonel" is the only name this character is given), he fails to recognize how actions generate names. The Colonel's rank *is* his identity, which he has attained through the medium of a long career in military service. It is far from a "titular shadow" for him, but a measure of his manhood.

Ager's failure to acknowledge the Colonel's rank as deserving of esteem is followed by a disregard for his friend's superiority in years. To the Colonel's outraged comment on his impudence—"Y' are a boy, sir!" (I.i.83)—Ager replies insouciantly that manhood and youth each possess their own virtues. His refusal to respect degrees of order contrasts strongly with the Colonel's willingness to restrain his temper for the sake of his impecunious kinsman Fitzallen. Ager, comparatively insensitive to the labels of social hierarchy, soon loses his temper over another sort of label. In this scene, he is curiously blind to the ways that reputation's labels might alter his own behavior.

When Ager begins to quarrel seriously with the Colonel, he responds to a challenge to his honor natural and not to one of honor acquired. The Colonel's insult, "son of a whore," casts aspersions on Ager's mother and names him a bastard. This condition renders one's honor and status questionable; Romei asserts that the loss of natural honor entails the loss of any acquired honor (83–4).[17] George R. Price rightly observes that a great deal is at stake for Ager:

> If he does not immediately refute the charge with his sword, his father's, his mother's, and his own honor are all lost, including the glory he has recently won by remarkable feats of valor in battle. Henceforth no gentleman need respect him, his career as an officer will be blighted, and no advantageous marriage will be possible. (xxi–xxii)

Ager does not recognize that his own notion of honor is part of a new and destabilizing social system, but he is fully awake to the Colonel's threat to his status in the old one. Therefore, he steps up to the challenge to defend not only his recently won personal glory but his position as the representative of a good family.

Ager's perception of the duel as a means of disproving insults conflates the extra-judicial duel and the trial by combat. When Ager overcomes the Colonel, he self-righteously exults, "Truth never fails her servant, sir, nor leaves him / With the day's shame upon him" (III.i.165–6). He sees the duel as a way of clearing his name from his opponent's imputation. Yet he also sees the combat as a way of gaining glory, *increasing* the reputation he has gained through his military prowess: "Then shines valor, / And admiration from her fix'd sphere draws, / When it comes burnish'd with a righteous cause" (II.i.129–31). The defense of the family's reputation functions separately (and differently) for him from the actual combat. By acting as the defender of his family's honor, he enhances the status he has already gained for himself as a soldier. Although he is concerned with upholding his family's reputation, he also sees the episode as an opportunity to gain admiration from others for his behavior; he conceives of war as a sun that draws admiration from others. This view is reinforced by the comments of Ager's seconds, one of whom urges him to the duel by professing the beauty of the Colonel's insult, its perfection as an excuse for combat:

> Why would you cozen yourself so and beguile
> So brave a cause, manhood's best masterpiece?
> Do you ever hope for one so brave again? (II.i.228–30)

The perception that the duel offered a valuable opportunity for self-aggrandizement was common in Jacobean England. In addition to the antiduelling tracts, accounts of private quarrels derived from such sources as private letters or memoirs like Naunton's *Fragmenta*

Regalia indicate that this motivation often played a part in quarrels.[18] Ager's beliefs do represent those of the small gentry and court aristocracy of the time, many of whom were military officers as well. In Ager's mind, insults, like weapons, mark the victim, indicating his physical or moral weakness. Because insult possesses the power to alter the recipient's identity, it must be requited at any cost. But the fight will also increase his standing by bringing him general recognition.

The most basic challenge to Ager's view that words label and define people in an essential way comes from the minor character Chough. Chough's interest in the duel focuses entirely on the preliminary insults, which he mangles in a comedic demonstration of language's arbitrary nature. In the later additions to the play (known as Issue 2, Quarto 1), Chough and his man Trimtram encounter two whores and a pimp and accost them using the language they have learned in roaring school:

> *Chough*: Deliver up thy panagron to me.
> *Trimtram*: And give me thy sindicus.
> *Captain Albo*: Deliver?
> *Bawd*: I pray you, Captain, be contented; the gentlemen seem to give us very good words.
> *Chough*: Good words? Aye, if you could understand 'em; the words cost twenty pound. (116, ll.74–80)

The would-be roarers demonstrate the elaborate terms they have learned, which, while meaningless in themselves, gain a functional significance from the value placed upon them. Chough views his new words primarily in economic terms. They are valuable because he has paid a large sum for them. Despite their cost, however, their value is lessened by his inability to use them properly.[19]

Eventually Chough and Trimtram engage in an aggressive bout of roaring against the whores and their protector. This verbal attack parodies the degrees of rhetoric that lead to the duel and highlights the meaninglessness of the actual words, somewhat as Touchstone's famous parody of duelling rhetoric does in *As You Like It*. But while Touchstone's story involves courtiers practiced in linguistic flights, the comedy in *A Fair Quarrel* derives from the participants' ignorance of the conventions. Albo and his whores are nonplussed at the series of insults because Chough's terms do not build to a climax as Touchstone's do. Failing to make themselves understood, Chough and his manservant proceed to offering direct threats, quite contrary to the law of arms. The conclusion is reached when Trimtram promises not only to charge a captain (Albo), but to "discharge upon him, too."

Turning his back, he wins the field by farting (as Richard Levin wittily observes, "an early anticipation of modern gas warfare" [227]), parodying both the duel and the military sally, and reducing the ideals of military honor to a set of animal behaviors.

Victory or loss aside, the arbitrary meanings assigned to Chough and Trimtram's nonsense words call into question the power of words to define essential nature. Chough's curse on a tobacco seller is empty rhetoric unless he can demonstrate some result from it; the Colonel cannot prove Ager the son of a whore simply through the use of the term.[20] Although Ager hopes to *dis*prove the insult through combat, in fact the charge must remain unanswered, for in the play's period, few actually expected to learn truth from the combat's outcome. Criminal trials had come into use for serious cases of defamation (Baker 506–8), but instances of gratuitous insult like the Colonel's remained unresolvable charges best treated as words emptied of constructive meaning.

Other characters, more aware of the powers of rhetoric, show a sophisticated understanding of the relation between word and world. Russell, Lady Ager's brother, sees words pragmatically, as the airy nothings that the author of "Duell-Ease" would have his audience understand them. Hence, he is quite unconcerned with such issues as reputation. As Levin points out, Russell inhabits a different society from Captain Ager—"the bourgeois society of the city—with entirely different attitudes toward the questions of honor that dominate the lives of his sister and nephew" (224).[21] Yet Russell also acknowledges the emotional force of words, holding that words themselves can function as weapons and that they should, for that reason, be hedged round with the same restrictions that combats are.

Russell indicates his sense of words as weightless, fleeting, but dangerous and able to wreak harm as he acknowledges the injury committed by the Colonel's insult to his sister:

> And I must tell you, sir, you have spoke swords,
> And 'gainst the law of arms poison'd the blades,
> And with them wounded the reputation
> Of an unblemish'd woman. (I.i.353–6)

The Colonel's insult has not *engendered* swords, but itself functions *like* a sword—that is, it wounds. Russell responds in kind, not with a threat of violence, but with a reply that parries the accusation: a verbal defense of his sister. He seems most angry, not at the verbal attack itself, but at the treacherous poison in the insult, the potential for great loss of reputation for an innocent woman. But Russell can counter the Colonel's speech-act with another. Once having contradicted the insult, Russell feels no need to threaten physical force in order to make the other man retract his words. He finds combat unappealing not because he lacks belief in deeds but because words cannot provoke him to violence. A rationalist convinced that words can only offer emotional arguments, he treats them essentially as weightless.[22]

The merchant Russell demonstrates a pragmatic view of linguistic power not shared by all of the middling sort. The lawyer was commonly considered to exalt the powers of language through the practice of his trade and, in fact, the lawyer's profession was perceived as related, if not akin, to duelling. During the early modern period, the duellist was popularly linked with rhetoricians and lawyers as much as with soldiers: Ager's concern with exact truth and an entirely justified cause derives from the Renaissance lawyer's emphasis on the subtleties of civil law. Sometimes the connection was inverted, as with the lawyer's common reputation as a quarreler. Ager's delicacy itself parodies the wordy scruples of a group perceived as overly concerned with details of rhetoric. Saviolo argues in *Vincent Saviolo His Practise* that the phrase "Thou sayest not true" is grounds for a challenge, while "That which thou sayest is not so" is not (S2r). The power of fine distinctions to get a person into or out of trouble must have seemed quite punctilious to those untrained in the precise nature of language and law. With these precedents in mind, Romei actually argues that the combat derives from the precedents of civil law more than from those of the military.[23]

By the time Ager and the Colonel actually fight, Ager's notion of honor has been severely compromised. Although Ager is taking the man's part by taking on the quarrel, the play enlarges upon the Falstaffian concept of honor as a word, implicitly challenging the notion that manhood can be constructed by a regard for words. True, the fight breaks down the continuum of words and actions, unequivocally demonstrating the essential difference between words and deeds. But simultaneously the combatants' seconds try to label the combatants' movements with fencing terms, suggesting the debasement of the once-unitary meanings of these formerly valued abstractions:

> 1 *Ager's Friend*: An absolute punto, hey?
> 2 *Ager's Friend*:   'Twas a passado, sir.
> 1 *Ager's Friend*: Why, let it pass, and 'twas; I'm sure 'twas somewhat.
>   What's that now?
> 2 *Ager's Friend*:   That's a punto.
> 1 *Ager's Friend*: Oh, go to, then,
>   I knew 'twas not far off. (III.i.154–7)

The watchers struggle to legitimize the duel by defining its parts, but their words divorce the violence from its context, making this technical language seem as meaningless as Chough's acquired gibberish. Their inability to articulate the action as it occurs maintains it as something entirely different from speech. The violent action of the physical sphere proves unassimilable to the continuum of language—some things cannot be adequately represented in words.[24] Chough's sense of the difference between the language and the action of the duel thus proves more than valid. He refuses to permit words to lead to actions, perceiving roaring as a discipline in itself rather than as a prelude to duelling. For Chough, the show of rhetoric gives more opportunity for pure performance than does the actual combat. Ager and the Colonel, in contrast, put aside verbal competition and seek proof in action.

Despite their quarrel, Ager and the Colonel eventually end up better friends than they were before. The bonds between them are particularly evident when Ager attempts to soothe the Colonel's feelings: "I never thought on victory, our mistress, / With greater reverence than I have your worth, / Nor ever lov'd her better" (III.i.55–7). Their pursuit of a common mistress in their pursuit of victory brings the two men closer, while it elides actual women. Note that victory, traditionally conceived as a cruel, unreliable, and fickle mistress, is yet more desirable than a flesh-and-blood woman. Pursuit of such a mistress creates strong homosocial bonds at the expense of heterosexual ones; these men undergo essentially the same dilemma as Benedick and Claudio in *Much Ado about Nothing*. Victory becomes not the ultimate goal but the means to draw men closer, as we see in the Colonel's subsequent behavior. Believing himself mortally wounded, the Colonel tells his sister that he wishes her to inherit his wealth on condition that she marry Ager. To her aghast response, he explains that, having robbed Ager of "fair fame," he wishes to make some sort of expiatory payment and that she is "the fairest restitution" he can think of. (He forgets that Ager's victory will have regained for the captain the reputation he might otherwise have lost and that he, the Colonel, now owes nothing.) In a grotesque reversal of the *wer-geld* custom, the Colonel sends a flesh-and-blood woman as payment for his attempted theft of Ager's "honor."[25] By leaving his property to his sister as a dower that he intends Ager to control, the Colonel makes an arrangement in which the woman functions primarily as a gift-exchange and as a means of putting her brother's property into Ager's hands. His sister's marriage to Ager ends by bringing the two men together, just as their pursuit of honor did.[26] While the bride is entirely silent in the final scene, like the cipher she is, the two men praise each other volubly and conclude by clasping one another in their arms. The feminine is elided: while a woman is useful for channeling masculine aggression, she is unnecessary when men are in harmony with one another.

As the playwrights attempt to convince us, if one gives of one's substance (as the patriarchs of the play have until the conclusion been unwilling to do), then honor will take care of itself. Freehandedness will result in closer links among all friends, and women will be the glue that brings intergenerational males together. With this conclusion, the play seems to endorse the French view of duelling described by Billacois: that duelling creates masculine intimacy (198). The bond cemented by marriage in this play is begun in blood lust, which is often described as akin to blood-brotherhood. Ager marries into the Colonel's house by duelling with him. Their combat further eliminates questions of reputation by providing a proof of their essential natures: only courageous men can acquit themselves well in combat. Thus, the slippery and unreliable medium of language can be bypassed and trustworthy, "true" men admitted to the exclusive brotherhood of honor. While duelling is by no means a method of discovering truth, much less a revelation of God's judgment, its excuse seems to be its ability to create fraternal bonds between its participants.

Despite the play's happy conclusion, it remains far from an endorsement of single combat. The outcome of the duel actually undermines more than one traditional rationale for the ritual. Several elements of the play destabilize the concept of honor, which is presented as a slippery and manipulable abstraction. The concept of reputation functions as a paper tiger, easily erected at need but more easily destroyed by even the clumsiest rhetorician. Other words are similarly problematized: the terms "cause" and "insult" are reduced merely to anger and aggression, elements that dissolve the bonds of fellowship characterized as most essential.

When we turn to tragedy, we find the dramatic intensity of the duel similarly undermined. In *Hamlet*, Shakespeare eventually presents the duel as a figure for a certain ethos of manliness. But the character Hamlet regards this ethos with almost as much ambivalence, it seems, as Shakespeare does. Although the duel is represented as Hamlet's best opportunity for emulation of his father, the occasion—when it comes—proves to be the wrong time after all. The oddly botched fencing match comes to suggest the impossibility of Hamlet's following his father; as numerous critics have remarked, each belongs to his own age.

When the play opens, Hamlet seems aggressively to be pursuing a mode of humanist individualism. His mourning clothes, "the trappings and the suits of woe" (I.ii.86), publicly bespeak his determination not to play a public role—to stay out of the sun. His black attire urges the community not to attempt to include him. Hamlet wishes to grieve privately, believing the private sphere appropriate to a good son. When Horatio offers his condolences, saying, "I saw him once, 'a was a goodly king," Hamlet responds by praising his father specifically in gendered but otherwise essentialist terms: "'A was a man, take him for all in all, / I shall not look upon his like again" (I.ii.186–8). Unlike Fortinbras, whose eulogy upon Hamlet's corpse is, "he was likely, had he been put on, / To have prov'd most royal" (V.ii.397–8), Hamlet does not see his subject's primary virtue in his royalty but in his masculinity. Although Hamlet's comment seems on the surface almost tautological, insofar as his father was a man like all men, it actually indicates the belief that nobility is inherent in manliness rather than an adjunct to royalty or rank.

Hamlet's father has been primarily a warrior, of which type the most conspicuous living representative in the play is Fortinbras.[27] Before we see Prince Hamlet, we hear how the father looked when he "the ambitious Norway combated" in single combat, how he "frown'd... when in an angry parle / He smote the sledded Polacks on the ice" (I.i.61–3). In the second scene, Claudius offers an alternative model of kingship, presenting the ruler as politician and negotiator.[28] Yet his jovial urging to Hamlet, "Be as ourself in Denmark" (I.ii.122) seems disjunctive. The comment, intended to urge Hamlet to feel comfortable, offers a Machiavellian pattern for the prince. To be "as Claudius" is to condition, to manipulate: these patterns of behavior are evident long before the question of Claudius's treachery or treason arises. "Be like me" eventually comes to mean, "Be like a traitor and an assassin; come to resemble a regicide."

Hamlet does. He comes to resemble Claudius not only in that he plots to kill a king but that he plots to kill him in circumstances similar to those of Hamlet Senior's death—"Cut off even in the blossoms of [his] sin" (I.v.76). As long as Hamlet considers how he will kill Claudius, he acts as the revenger who inevitably becomes corrupted by his crime.[29] In contrast to Laertes, who shouts and roars, Hamlet works by stealth. His plan must be executed without the king's knowledge.

The model of manhood that Hamlet admires, however, is his more noble father.[30] In the closet scene he offers Gertrude a blazon in praise of her husband:

> See what a grace was seated on this brow:
> Hyperion's curls, the front of Jove himself,
> An eye like Mars, to threaten and command,
> A station like the herald Mercury
> New lighted on a [heaven-] kissing hill,
> A combination and a form indeed,
> Where every god did seem to set his seal
> To give the world assurance of a man. (III.iv.55–62)

The speech emphasizes man's godlike stature; it further describes King Hamlet's physical presence as manhood embodied. These words create the notion of masculinity through specific signs which, taken together, offer a pictorial, almost emblematic representation of virility. Significantly, in this blazon the eye is not primarily an organ of apprehension; instead, it enacts unspoken imperatives, shaping the responses of those on whom the king glances. Hamlet Senior uses his eyes in a gesture of command. His mien compels not by demonstrating force but by implying his capacity to shift to action.

Hamlet the son soon finds that his reflective mode of mourning is not enough: he must also take revenge. Such an act must necessarily have a public component, as he is a prince and the son of a king. To kill Claudius is to become involved in the political arena. Action, then, is equivalent to taking a part, both in the sense of being partisan and in the sense of acting publicly, under the eyes of others. The notion of taking a part makes Hamlet uneasy, however, particularly because such a part would involve behavior that could be divorced from true feeling. He disdains the public grief of his mother and uncle: since it so quickly yielded to rejoicing, it must have been mere hypocrisy. "I have that within which passes show," he says, "These but the trappings and the suits of woe" (I.ii.85–6).[31] The theatricality of the players both attracts and repels him: "What would [the actor] do / Had he the motive and the cue for passion / That I have?" he asks (II.ii.560–2). Yet after ranting in theatrical fashion, he chides himself for substituting words for action. In this courtly context, Middleton and Rowley's continuum of action is reconceived as a dichotomy once again. Only women resort to language, Hamlet implies; it offers relief for the frustration of powerlessness (II.ii.582–7).[32]

Hamlet's decision to act, however, is slowed by the need to understand all the roles that have been assigned to him. Chief among these are man and son.[33] Hamlet learns from the ghost that his role as avenger *depends* on his identity as son:

> *Hamlet*: Speak, I am bound to hear.
> *Ghost*: So art thou to revenge, when thou shalt hear.
> *Hamlet*: What?
> *Ghost*: I am thy father's spirit. (I.v.6–9)

The ghost's assertion of their relationship assumes that the moral imperative of revenge is concomitant on their blood connection. To combine private and public is, for Hamlet, both to unite "that within" with forms and shapes, as he says (I.ii.82), and to join the role of son with that of prince. While the role of prince by itself could be that of the classic protagonist of revenge tragedy, Hamlet's desire to follow his father's model of masculinity makes him perceive such an enactment as shrill and theatrical. When Hamlet blazons his father, the reference to his stance "like the herald Mercury / New lighted on a [heaven-] kissing hill" (III.iv.58–9) recalls Quintilian's assertion that action in oratory is "a discourse, and sometimes ... a certain eloquence of the body" (II: 340). When speech and action are in harmony, their combination creates a sense of authenticity, of truth in argument. A public role for Hamlet must both derive from inward feeling and offer an acceptable presentation of himself as his father's heir.

Hamlet begins to work toward a solution in the course of his manic behavior. During this interlude, he reflects on the legitimacy of kingship in the case of monarchic incapacity or incongruity: "The body is with the King, but the King is not with the body. The King is a thing.... of nothing" (IV.ii.27–30). As G. Blakemore Evans points out, Hamlet refers to the legal concept of the king's two bodies—the separation of monarchic dignity from the monarch's mortal body (p. 1170, n. 27–8). Just as the royal aspect of the monarch can be distinguished from his corporeal aspect (an idea related to the one expressed in the anecdote of Constantine's portrait), manhood need not be inherent within the body but may be conferred or removed by rites of one sort or another.

When Hamlet realizes that he is in the midst of a duel, he recognizes that this is the rite that will enable him both to act publicly and to express his interiority without misgivings. The final scene departs from the original version of the story, in which, significantly, Hamlet is resolute and unhesitating.[34] Creating the false fencing exhibition enables Shakespeare to present the scene as the moment when everything falls into place for the prince. Yet even calling Hamlet a duellist somewhat distorts his situation; in this instance, I read *Hamlet* somewhat differently from other critics who have addressed this issue. S. P. Zitner argues that Hamlet seeks to attain "a state of mind that proceeds from ethical contemplation, social awareness, a quenching of passion, and. ... the disinterestedness that abandons private will to the will of God," assuming that Hamlet follows the precepts of Vincentio Saviolo, whose writings proscribed vengeful duels (Zitner 8; Saviolo Y4r). Along similar lines, Joan Ozark Holmer comments, "in light of Saviolo's ethic for honorable combat, Hamlet's words and deeds, within the context of Shakespeare's innovative fencing match, merit him the praise he earlier bestowed on his father" ("Shakespeare's Duello Rhetoric" 18). But Hamlet is not a duellist in Zitner's sense. Far from attempting to kill in a moral frame of mind, he does not even definitively plan to kill his stepfather by means of the sword. He does not reject the treacherous stab in the back because it is an ignoble act but because it punishes Claudio ineffectively, permitting him (Hamlet assumes) to rise to Heaven purged of his sins. What Hamlet seeks throughout the play is a way to perform the part of a man according to his father's model.

Such a mode is that of the duellist. It corresponds to Hamlet's needs in several ways. First, the verbal challenge that precedes the duel establishes a connection between word and meaning that destroys the seeming/being dichotomy. Second, the duel harks back to medieval trial ordeals, not least by its use of the challenge.[35] In the judicial duel, the challenge functions as a speech-act: a pledge to back one's word with one's body. The combat that results guarantees the good faith of the statement that precedes the combat. Moreover, the duel's antecedents invoke both historical tradition and the attempt by civil law to involve a heavenly tribunal. In addition, the custom of the duel bears strong overtones of courtliness and chivalry that enable young Hamlet to act publicly in a princely manner. Finally, within that courtly context, the duel embodies the notion of manhood, both through the correspondence of word and deed and through the implicit legitimation of vigilantism (and, by extension, individualism) as a means of achieving justice.

Hamlet's full understanding of his own role is not entirely apparent to him until he is in the midst of the fencing exhibition, yet we can see the notion of the swordfight working upon his mind somewhat earlier. He envisions the conflict between himself and Claudius as a combat, explaining that Rosencrantz and Guildenstern were foolish to come "[b]etween the pass and fell incensed points / Of mighty opposites" (V.ii.61–2).[36] The image recurs when Laertes describes his distracted sister's charms as so outstanding that "if praises may go back again, / Stood challenger on mount of all the age"

(IV.vii.27–8). These images are, of course, embodied in the false fencing match between Hamlet and Laertes, Claudius's tool. The frequency of this metaphor may be explained by a circumstance recounted to Laertes by Claudius: that the report from Paris of Laertes' skill with the rapier "[d]id Hamlet so envenom with his envy / That he could nothing do but wish and beg / Your sudden coming o'er to play with you" (IV.vii.103–5). Later, when the challenge to the exhibition has been issued, Hamlet tells Horatio he has hopes of winning because "since [Laertes] went into France I have been in continual practice. I shall win at the odds" (V.ii.210–12). Fencing (although a transparent anachronism) functions thematically as a link to Old Hamlet's single combat with Old Fortinbras.[37] In Renaissance England, it served as the courtier's modernization of the old aristocrat's ethos of the military elite. Hamlet's evident ambition to shine as a courtier, as well as his wish to model himself on his father, explains his rapier skill.[38]

When Hamlet wakes to the knowledge that he is in the midst of a duel rather than a fencing match, his desires fall into place. Laertes' final words—"the King, the King's to blame" (V.ii.320)—offer a new accusation that may be proven in blood. Hamlet is suddenly offered the opportunity to avenge his father's murder openly—both to enact the role of avenger publicly and to differentiate himself from the stealthy Claudius. The charge offers him an appropriate public face for his grief, one that also enables him to imitate the figure who epitomizes manliness for him. This open killing suits Hamlet: it is a task fitting for a prince, especially one who perceives himself as the rightful heir to the monarch's seat of judgment. Thus, this violence is the embodiment of his feelings, a public display, a chance to write his story, and an assumption of his royal prerogative as claimant to the throne.

It would seem as if Shakespeare is making a bold bid for the ritualistic powers of the duel—as if the final scene were indeed, as Ralph Berry puts it, "Hamlet's coming of age. ... his rite of manhood. ... the triumph of a public figure" (28). But the potential resolution of the combat is marred almost simultaneously with its introduction. The first challenge to the combat's transformative power occurs when the fencing match is proposed to Hamlet. Osric's account of the proposed fencing match stresses the formal nature of the exhibition. He emphasizes the courtliness of Laertes, hinting that the nature of any entertainment in which he takes part will be equally elegant:

> Sir, here is newly come to court Laertes, believe me, an absolute [gentleman], full of most excellent differences, of very soft society,

and great showing. ... you shall find in him the continent of what part a gentleman would see. (V.ii.106–11)

Osric's euphonious description of the proposed combat and his account of Claudius's and Laertes' wager both call attention to the courtly character of this ludic competition. Osric puts forth the combat as a sport of gentility, a combat in spirit and in class closer to the tilt than to the swordplay exhibitions of early modern England. Yet even before Osric speaks, Hamlet undermines the credibility of his perceptions, describing Osric to Horatio as "a chough ... spacious in the possession of dirt" (V.ii.87–8). The coded terms should immediately recall for us Hotspur's court popinjay and such Jonsonian creations as Sir Amorous La Foole and Sir Politic Would-be. Throughout the scene, Hamlet mocks Osric's linguistic formality, suggesting that Osric's taste is for the overelaborate, the foppish, and the effeminate. In this context, we may perceive the fencing exhibition as both a ludic test of manhood and a foppish competition.

When the match begins, it is neither a game nor a duel per se, but a rite that functions differently for each person there. As James V. Holleran points out, "the duelling scene consists of three different rites: a funeral banquet for Ophelia, a court entertainment for Gertrude and Hamlet, and a murder plot for Claudius and Laertes. And each rite is maimed" (88). The courteous and formal speech of the two participants suggests the fencing will be well governed, controlled, regulated by the ceremonies of courtesy. But the ceremony has been designed by Claudius, the devious, false monarch. Although the challenge to this combat characterizes it as an entertainment, not a duel, one participant (Laertes) and one watcher (Claudius) are aware that the combat will be lethal. This knowledge restructures the nature of the match; along with Claudius and Laertes, we know that this will be a fight to the death. Yet the rapier fight appears sportive and friendly at first. Hamlet actually asks Laertes to judge one of his hits. In the crucial bout, in which each wounds the other with the envenomed rapier, they appear at first to be in earnest; Claudius calls out, "Part them, they are incens'd" (V.ii.302). But when Hamlet refutes this, he and Laertes face one another again. It is only when Gertrude cries out at the poison and Laertes admits his treachery that disorder breaks out. The match, which had seemed a lawful entertainment, reveals itself as a ploy of the monarch, created by the king's design and yet unlawful.

The first overt violence has occurred earlier—in the almost comical struggle between Hamlet and Laertes in Ophelia's grave. That brawl occurs in a grotesque, disjunctive setting; its location shows how unpromising combat is as a means of resolving disputes when it takes place without ceremony or due process. That combat is replayed in the public entertainment, when the display of competition again carries its participants beyond the bounds set by the social circumstances.[39] Throughout the final scene, Shakespeare exploits the dynamics of violence as he had in *As You Like It*. As Cynthia Marshall says of the ludic match in that play, one character (here, Laertes) sees violence as the sign of sincerity, authentic feeling, while another character (Claudius) sees "the formal violence of [a contest] as open to manipulation" (268–9). For the court onlookers, a performance that began as a game has exploded its boundaries, breaking out of ceremony and playfulness to become brutal, sly, and real.[40] The fencing match has become several fragmented rituals at once, not one of them whole, entire, or enacted with sincerity.

At the play's conclusion, we also find that one of the duel's intended objects has failed: it has not necessarily brought closure to the events that led up to it. Horatio urges the necessity of recounting the events leading up to this bloodbath "[e]ven while men's minds are wild, lest more mischance / On plots and errors happen" (V.ii.394–5). The courtiers in the Danish court may not have recognized Hamlet's intentions as the justified slaying of a regicide; on the contrary, they may be unclear as to the motives, let alone the justice, of Hamlet's actions.

Whereas most revenge tragedy concludes with a bloodbath that effectively purges society of its corruption, *Hamlet* concludes with another delation.[41] As the Ghost bids his son "Remember me," Hamlet, too, uses almost his last opportunity for speech to ensure that his story will be told. Dying, Prince Hamlet prevents Horatio from committing suicide and implores him to remain alive to "tell my story"—essentially, to justify his actions. Upon Fortinbras's horror at the pile of corpses, Horatio begins his role as Hamlet's chronicler, promising Fortinbras

> So shall you hear
> Of carnal, bloody, and unnatural acts...
> Of deaths put on by cunning and forc'd cause,
> And in this upshot, purposes mistook
> Fall'n on th'inventors' heads: all this can I
> Truly deliver. (V.ii.380–6)

Horatio promises a re-living of the events, a loop back to the opening as a response to the need for an explanation. As Patricia Parker has argued, such delations or amplifications delay the closure of a story ("'Dilation' and 'delation'" 54–74). This one in particular seems to offer an infinitely receding series of frame narratives, as each retelling concludes with another promise to retell, to loop back to the beginning. While such delations may be the stuff of Othello's drama, they would seem to short-circuit the closure appropriate to tragedy, closure more clearly indicated in Shakespearean works such as *Macbeth* or *King Lear*. The need to clear Hamlet's name results in this perpetual repetition, accomplishing Hamlet's directive by avoiding the expected closure, refusing to let go of the past. Horatio's promise of explanation and justification expands the play beyond the "diminished society" that Frye says results at the end of a dramatic tragedy (5–6). Instead of a new society, Horatio promises to keep the dead in constant remembrance, preventing the community from ever moving decisively on to a new generation.

This ending also foregrounds the exclusion of the feminine. Horatio's desire to die with Hamlet is not unique, but it expresses a specific hierarchic relation between two men. In a way, Hamlet asks his friend to play midwife to his story, to bring him the immortality that he, Hamlet, would otherwise lack. Horatio fulfills the role of confidant so that he can later become the chronicler. And having this friend, Hamlet needs neither mother nor lover.[42] Both Gertrude and Ophelia die, both arguably out of love for Hamlet.[43] The person whose survival is necessary to Hamlet is the one to whom he is closest, the man whose intimacy enables him to bear Hamlet's story to the next generation. If we accept Adelman's hypothesis that Hamlet is disgusted at human sexuality, we can easily see how the Hamlet/Horatio relationship promises another kind of immortality for the prince.

Chapman treats similar themes in his two plays *Bussy d'Ambois* and *The Revenge of Bussy d'Ambois:* the philosopher-malcontent's place in society, the corrosive poison of ambition, male competition and love, the nature of one's obligation to one's kin.[44] However, Bussy and his brother Clermont (the protagonist of the second play) stand in relation to members of France's royal family as Horatio stands in relation to Hamlet. The editor Robert J. Lordi sees Clermont as "an enlarged portrait of Horatio" (16); in contrast, Robert Ornstein obtusely comments that the suicide of Clermont is "ludicrous": "Can we imagine a victorious Hamlet stabbing himself because Horatio has been slain?" (75). No, of course not; but we do see Horatio remaining alive only at the dying Hamlet's behest. Both of Chapman's Bussy plays focus on the power relations among those courtiers close to the royal family, in contrast to *Hamlet*, a play whose bare bones approximate a family romance in a royal bed. Chapman's plays present the court from the perspective of Horatio or Laertes, and they thus dramatize the difficulty of being the "creature" of men with more status. These plays offer the opportunity to see how playwrights perceived the aristocracy's enactment of masculinity in a court context.

These plays present the corrupt court typical of many revenge tragedies; neither Bussy nor Clermont, however, succeeds in changing that society.[45] Whereas Bussy represents what Eugene Waith has called the Herculean hero, Clermont, according to numerous critics, exemplifies the Stoic type.[46] While each protagonist manifests the magnitude that Aristotle demands of the tragic hero, that magnitude is qualified by Chapman's use of the duel.[47] The combat that successfully glorifies its instigator is the three-on-three combat between Bussy, his friends, and his enemies; the fight is recounted by the Nuncius, whose vivid description alludes to Greek heroes, mythical animals, and natural phenomena, conjuring up a more magnificent scene than any dramatic production at that time could have offered. Yet the great Bussy never duels onstage; that action is left to Clermont. Clermont's challenge to the Count of Montsurry results in a farcical scene that degrades the very ritual of the epistolary challenge. Although the combat itself redeems Montsurry somewhat, his arrant cowardice eliminates the suspense of the combat and changes the staged duel from a moment of judgment to an episode with an assured outcome quite incidental to the broader question of how the world will accommodate Clermont. As Chapman's original play glorified the Herculean hero, so *The Revenge* offers a type and a philosophy that improves upon the earlier hero.[48] Chapman's more modest Clermont seems preferable to Bussy because of his lack of interest in renown; as the drama unfolds, Clermont becomes an alternative model, less worldly and more concerned with duty.[49] In this context, honor is redefined as independence from worldly concerns, and the virtues that earned Bussy renown are reexamined with more skepticism.

In the first play, the combat is glorified by the Nuncius in terms of its promotion of fraternity and the valorization of honor over life. He begins in epic fashion by calling on the height of Mount Atlas and Mount Olympus to animate his words so that he can describe the event in an appropriate style. The predominant image in his account is of fire—the fire of choler and the flame of honor.[50] Each combatant's desire to acquit himself well is fed by that of the others; all burn with the desire for glory. Repeatedly Bussy is described as "fiery" or "free as fire," emphasizing the sense of something bright and uncontrolled.

Chapman skillfully draws us away from imagining the fight from moment to moment. As the audience hears of Bussy's sword "like a pointed comet," the fall of Bussy's opponent likened to an uprooted oak tree, and the attack of Bussy likened to a unicorn's charge, our imaginations elide potentially disturbing elements of the fight: Barrisor's facial wound or the possible comedy in L'Anou's fall onto his dead opponent's sword.[51] Only when the account has been brought to a decorous close do Bussy and Monsieur reenter the stage, and Bussy prepares to plead for pardon as humbly as he fought proudly for honor in the recounted fight.

The sheer scale of Bussy's achievement—killing two enemies and surviving both his friends—and the immediate squabble between Monsieur and the King draw our thoughts again toward the code of honor that Bussy has upheld. Only the caviller is likely to recall the petty insults that instigated the quarrel. Because these insults were transparently designed to provoke a duel, the fight that rests on such a basis would similarly appear petty and degrading if our attention were not distracted.[52] Instead, Chapman leads us quickly from the cause to the performance, enhancing Bussy's status with the audience not by the contest itself but by the rhetoric that characterizes it.[53]

Clermont, the hero of *The Revenge of Bussy D'Ambois*, is at once more mild and more revolutionary than his brother; he declines to tell Monsieur what he thinks of him when asked (I.i.212–20) but casually derogates the criteria that structure court society. His comments on the arbitrary nature of birth amount to a backhanded denunciation of his questioner:

> You are a king's son born...
>   And a king's brother...
> And might not any fool have been so too,
> As well as you?... You did no princely deeds
> Ere you're born, I take it, to deserve it;
> Nor did you any since that I have heard;
> Nor will do ever any, as all think. (I.i.280–90)[54]

Yet this dismissal of birth cannot be taken at face value, for Clermont's character is defined by the accident of birth: the fact that he is Bussy's brother gives him his identity and structures his behavior. Clermont, however, demonstrates a self-conscious knowledge of what his birth has made of him, while others "take their births and birth-rights left to them / (Acquir'd by others) for their own worth's purchase" (I.i.299–300). Clermont aspires to become

"The splenative philosopher that ever / Laugh'd at them all" (I.i.354–5) but deviates from his notion of virtue after the spirit of Bussy implores him to avenge his death (III.ii.109–12). At this point, he determines to act openly: as Baligny explains, "in the noblest and most manly course, / ...he resolves to send / A challenge to [Montsurry], and myself must bear it" (I.i.90–2). This openness is at variance with court culture, of which the two-faced Baligny is the best example. But for Clermont, the noble course is to "wreak our wrongs / So as we take not more" (III.ii.103–4). In a way, Clermont's virtue becomes its own reward; when seized by the King's hirelings, his well-known virtue enables the Guise to persuade the King to release him.

In contrast, Montsurry, Bussy's killer, lives by the mores of the court. His character is consistent from one play to the next: after he tortures his wife to learn her lover's name, he lures Bussy to the lovers' meeting-place and attacks him with a band of hired bravos.[55] In *The Revenge*, Montsurry barricades himself within his house for fear that he will be challenged to a duel for his honor. Baligny, Clermont's brother-in-law, must gain entry to the house through a ruse in order to deliver the challenge. When he states his intention, Montsurry refuses to accept the letter:

> *Montsurry*: Challenge! I'll touch none.
> *Baligny*: I'll leave it here then.
> *Renel*: Thou shalt leave thy life first.
> *Montsurry*: Murther, murther!
> *Renel*: Retire, my lord; get off. (I.ii.134–6)

When Renel and Baligny face off, Montsurry is frightened for his own life and not for Renel, who is ostensibly defending the premises.

This pusillanimous noble presents an extreme example of the French court's corruption. With the honor drawn from lineage so obviously absent, the concept of the challenge becomes ridiculous. A society in which requests for plain speaking are manipulative acts cannot offer a meaningful memorial to Bussy, a blunt but honorable soldier. With the nobility incapable of acting as their birth demands, Clermont's adherence to this idealistic and outmoded system becomes ludicrous. His decision to avenge his brother gains a larger significance as a failed attempt to recuperate aristocratic society, a repetition of his brother's attempt to reform society through plain speaking. While Clermont's Stoicism would lead him out of court society altogether, he follows his brother's mores in avenging him. But Chapman makes Clermont's own ethos increasingly attractive as society further alienates us from the dead Bussy's engagement. When Baligny promises to follow Henry to

> betray for you
> Brother and father: for, I know, my lord,
> Treachery for kings is truest loyalty;
> Nor is to bear the name of treachery,
> But grave, deep policy. (II.i.30-4)

he exaggerates to farce the attitude that James was attempting to inculcate in his people.[56] Bussy's code of honor, which Clermont tries to emulate, seems equally out of place, as much so as a Wall Street trader in King Arthur's court. This society has no room for honor so long as everyone below Henry, Monsieur, and the Guise are striving for advancement—and so long as this trio is struggling for domination. There is no reason to strive for a good reputation among such people; social rank is hopelessly confused, as when the nobly born Clermont complains to the French captain of being seized by lackeys, only to learn with disgust that his captors are soldiers in lackeys' garb. The deception indicates not only the soldiers' lack of integrity but their lack of personal pride in their status as military men. No one is interested in reputation; profit motivates almost everyone, and the code of honor is bankrupt, appearing comically picturesque.

When Clermont duels with Montsurry, he tries to infuse the ritual with the gravity of the trial by combat. Yet Montsurry's cowardice forces his challenger to use tactics that push the scene toward tragicomedy.[57] Clermont appears before Montsurry by rising out of the secret vault that had been Bussy's secret passageway to Tamyra's bedroom. Montsurry repeatedly lies prone on the floor and refuses to fight—not, he says, out of fear, "But to prevent and shame [Clermont's] victory / Which of one base is base" (V.v.27-8). As he says, there will be no glory for Clermont in killing a coward. His argument inverts James's assertion that it is unmanly to challenge anyone whose allegiance to his king forces him to refuse the challenge.

Clermont tries to invigorate Montsurry by stressing the equal nature of the combat (one on one) in contrast to the way Montsurry killed Bussy; he points out that their solitude prevents anyone from helping or hindering them:

> Put it to fortune now, and use no odds....
> All doors are sure made, and you cannot scape
> But by your valour. (V.v.18-22)

The deciding factor is courage or resolution, the elements that have already made Clermont an object of admiration in French society.

Yet Montsurry refuses to fight, cavilling about his weapon, his probity, and the conditions of the combat. His abjection continues until Clermont offers the prone man to Tamyra for her to torture as Montsurry had tortured her. Then Montsurry rises, saying, "I did but thus far dally"; they fight until he pauses to say, "Now give me breath a while" (V.v.61, 68). The fight continues until Clermont's sister, disguised as a man, enters and begs to be allowed to finish the combat. Although Montsurry asks Clermont to consent, Clermont insists on finishing off his opponent.

The interruptions and comic refusals lower the level of dramatic discourse yet again. Not only does the character of Montsurry debase Bussy's code of honor, he also prevents the fight from functioning as an effective suspense technique. By the time he dies, they have fought three times, pausing for dialogue between. The fight, an event that commonly draws in the audience, becomes tiresome. The audience cannot empathize with Clermont because of the alienating pace of the duel. A potentially useful plot twist becomes formal if not tedious, awkward if not droll.

Although the play's title suggests that its focus is Clermont's revenge upon Montsurry, the political aspect of the drama shifts the focus to the relation between Clermont and the Guise.[58] The curve of the career of the Guise becomes the arc of the play; with Clermont's discovery of the Guise's death, the play draws to a close. Each has a public role to play; as the Guise says,

> Come, away!
> Perform thy brother's thus importun'd wreak;
> And I will see what great affairs the King
> Hath to employ my counsel, which he seems
> Much to desire, and more and more esteems. (V.i.194–8)

Thus twinning their tasks, he draws a parallel between Clermont's revenge and his own service to the State. This, too, emphasizes similarities between him and Clermont.

For Clermont, Bussy is a sort of absent twin whose death leaves a void that Clermont is compelled to fill. But the Guise is another kind of twin—a fellow-follower of Stoicism and another noble nature. When Clermont fells Montsurry, he is almost immediately visited by the ghost of Bussy. It leads "the Ghosts of the Guise, Monsieur, Cardinal Guise, and Chatillon; they dance about the dead body and exeunt," amazing Clermont because he has not yet heard that two of these players have died (V.v. s.d.). When Clermont and the Guise discuss the Countess, Clermont dismisses men's love for women as mere appetite, adding that

> when love kindles any knowing spirit,
> It ends in virtue and effects divine,
> And is in friendship chaste and masculine. (V.i.186–8)

This love between men follows the Roman model, strengthening masculine ties and attenuating heterosexual ones. Although Clermont's actions throughout are structured by his role as the brother of Bussy d'Ambois, his closeness to the Guise eventually becomes equally significant. While Charlotte, Clermont's sister, attempts to incite Clermont to avenge Bussy's death, it is Bussy's spirit that succeeds in doing so. When the Guise dies, Clermont sees no reason for living. This mode of being derives from Clermont's Stoicism but is fostered by the masculine code of honor that compels Clermont to undertake the challenge of Montsurry. The void created by Bussy's absence encourages the intimacy between the two. With Clermont's revenge accomplished, the two unite in death, the welcoming world where they imagine they will find a suitable place. Rather than attempt reform, they act to satisfy only their idealistic integrity.

What remains when Clermont and the Guise have gone is a community of women: Tamyra, Charlotte, and the Countess close the play. The women, excluded from the bonds of love that link the men, must find their own way to forge community. Charlotte, the only woman who is pleased with Clermont's self-slaughter, initially proposes to follow him in Stoic fashion (V.v.200–4). Rather than turn back from her fate, Charlotte wants to move forward, to be transformed into another element. She who has attempted to embrace masculine prerogatives throughout the play still wants to join in the fellowship of men at the expense of her life.[59]

The Countess considers a similar course for a different reason: as the great lover of this play, she considers dying for love a fitting end: "He liv'd but in the Guise, / As I in him. O follow, life, mine eyes!" (V.v.206–7). Her words show most clearly both the competition between heterosexual and homosocial ties in the play, and the hierarchical nature of any relation of two in either context. Although Clermont has asserted the arbitrariness of high birth, he yet regards the Guise as his master, himself as the great man's creature (V.v.193). The Countess, recognizing the structure of their relationship, explicitly makes it the model for hers with Clermont.

Tamyra, however, has no specific relation to Clermont; neither sister nor mistress, she regards him principally as the brother and avenger of her dead lover. Throughout the play, she has lived with the knowledge of Bussy's death. Now, her evil husband dead, she urges resignation to Charlotte and the Countess: "To cloisters fly, / In penance pine! Too easy 'tis to die" (V.v.208–9). The cloister of the nunnery offers both a refuge and a penance; it could be understood either as a place of confinement and forced idolatry or as a place of female community. Charlotte's response evokes the sense of community, as well as implying that a woman's response to grief should be Christian, not Stoic and pagan (V.v.210–13). Charlotte suggests that rather than pursuing wholeness in themselves the women should turn their thoughts to Heaven. Thus, the most bloodthirsty avenger in the play, her object accomplished, reverts to an antithetical code of conduct; here, at least, there is reform. It seems as if Charlotte has been tamed by Clermont's death.

The Revenge of Bussy d'Ambois seems in many ways an antidote to the heroic *Bussy d'Ambois*. Although Clermont takes on the role of avenger as his brother would have, he explicitly rejects the roles his brother embraced: pursuer of honor, blunt soldier, great lover. Clermont remains indifferent to public acclaim; he seeks "To love nothing outward, / Or not within our own powers to command" (IV.v.4–5). His rejection of heterosexual love seems based on his wish to deny worldly appetites. By contrast, his brother's desire for honor seems degrading, especially in this corrupt court in which kings may ambush their closest counselors (V.v.139–43). Chapman uses the combat here to subvert its own mystique: Montsurry's death appears as a tragicomedy that exemplifies the rottenness of French society. The true object of the play is not Clermont's revenge but the mutual influence of Clermont and the Guise, two men whose stony regard for self-control results in the wonderment of the court rather than glory in a more traditional sense.[60]

Chapman and Shakespeare both regard the aristocratic concept of honor as problematic. Clearly noble figures use the expectations surrounding the combat to mask treachery or cowardice. In the context of these revenge tragedies, the corruption of society easily frays the fiber of aristocratic codes. Though scrupulous heroes may seek to use the duel for its redemptive power, it may easily be debased to a parody of itself. The duel appears in mangled form in both the contrary intentions of the combatants in *Hamlet*'s fencing match and the pathetic and anti-dramatic maneuvers of Montsurry in *The Revenge of Bussy d'Ambois*. Holleran points out about Shakespeare's plays, "When rituals are properly observed, they take place offstage and are simply reported. Onstage rituals break down" (65). The distorted rituals of the duel overtly comment on the corruption of the communities in which these combats occur, but that corruption does not correspond to the confused or deteriorating ethos that promoted the duel in English society. These staged duels result from more serious quarrels than those that instigated most duels in Tudor and Jacobean England, yet the combats go askew because only one participant holds the assumptions appropriate to the duel. The staged combat served more clearly to present a changing *mentalité* than to represent a current phenomenon. Yet the period's well-documented code of honor is not effaced from these tragedies: it surfaces in the homosocial ties inspired by the common devotion to these ideals. In both these staged combats, the loser acknowledges as he dies the wrongs he has committed; no matter what the circumstances, he forgives his opponent in a temporary accession of noble generosity.

By the play's end, the playwright has shaped the audience's perceptions so that we may regard the protagonist as a hero. Onlookers within the play, however, exhibit a different attitude. Their puzzlement is the playwright's final manifestation of the inchoate nature of reputation. Though the idea of honor was understood consistently by many members of the nobility and gentry, the playwrights' handling of the subject suggests that, among most members of London society, its essence and significance changed and fluctuated unpredictably.

CHAPTER 5

WHEN WOMEN FIGHT

The previous chapter presented dramatic and polemical texts that offer insight into conceptions of masculinity among early modern men of different social strata. In this chapter, I consider how female duellists were represented in the drama and what we can learn about cultural expectations from the dramatic convention of cross-dressed characters and their frequent use of the sword.[1] As Stephen Greenblatt has commented, "a culture's sexual discourse plays a critical role in the shaping of identity. It does so by helping to implant in each person a system of dispositions and orientations that governs individual improvisations" (*SN* 75). As a dramatic representation, I would argue, each instance of the cross-dressed duellist in these plays functions as both an individual improvisation and as part of a system of orientations.

It would be both facile and simplistic to say that women who used swords were viewed as monsters during the early modern period.[2] However, any woman who engaged in rapier fighting would have placed herself in the category of unwomanly women, unnatural women, or simply "man-maids." The figure of the man-woman included all of these.[3] Through an analysis of theological and historical texts, Phyllis Rackin has developed a thoughtful and persuasive argument that Renaissance thinking designated the body (or "flesh") as feminine, degraded, in contrast to the superior spirit, which was gendered masculine ("Foreign Country" 69, 76).

> Congruence between medical and theological discourse suggests a conception of gender difference just as coherent as our own although

> significantly different from it. Modern gender ideology [in contrast]....
> finds a prehistorical basis for masculine privilege in male physical
> strength. ("Foreign Country" 76)

Within the paradigm Rackin proposes, masculine women might be construed as elevated above their sex, transcending "both flesh and femininity" ("Foreign Country" 70). Spenser's Britomart and Belphoebe would both seem to be exemplars of this gender model. By contrast, Shakespeare's Queen Margaret in the first Henriad is characterized as unnatural, even monstrous in her masculinity.[4] In fact, both alternatives are evident in various Renaissance iconographies of the hermaphrodite, commonly linked with the masculine woman and with the female cross-dresser.

To understand the significance of the female duellist, it is necessary to acknowledge and to recognize her antecedents. The androgyne, perhaps the oldest category of blended sex traits, is described in Plato's *Symposium* as the third sex, "globular in shape...four arms and four legs, and two faces...and one head, with one face one side and one the other, and four ears, and two lots of privates, and all the other parts to match" (542–3).[5] The fable of the androgyne was extremely important to Florentine Neoplatonists such as Pico and Ficino, who read the androgyne as an allegory of the soul. The Neoplatonists strongly influenced English coterie writers, and images of the androgyne reappear frequently in love lyrics and in esoteric treatises on alchemy, astrology, and magic (Jerome Schwartz 121–3).[6] Another resonant idea of the man-woman derives from Ovid's account of Hermaphroditus, a beautiful boy whose name combined those of his parents, Hermes and Aphrodite. Overcome by desire for him when he swam in her fountain, the water nymph Salmacis seized and embraced the unwilling youth. As she prayed that they might never be separated, their bodies melded together so that they became a single being, neither male nor female but both at once. As Lauren Silberman points out, the experience of Hermaphroditus is both a return to the Platonic body of self-completion and "an unmistakable, if parodic, representation of sexual intercourse" (*Transforming Desire* 51).[7] The Renaissance interest in Ovid ensured that this story of the nymph and the beautiful boy was widely disseminated in translation and revision, and Renaissance readings of this myth offer many varied physiological, moral, and allegorical interpretations.[8]

Early modern response to the Amazons, the warrior women of classical legend, was still more ambivalent. The name "Amazon" was supposed to derive from *a-mazon*, without breast, from the reputed

Amazon practice of searing off one breast to enable the warriors to pull a bow more easily.[9] This practice was often perceived as symbolic of their ambiguous femininity. As Simon Shepherd explains, Renaissance uses of the legend suggest that the writers were both titillated and made uneasy by Amazons: "[Amazons] are ready to give up the credentials which make them sexually valued in a male world, that other breast, in order themselves to be manly. Their sexual fulfilment apparently depends on their capacity for brutality" (15). The Amazon often served as a figure for women who refused to submit to the authority of patriarchal institutions.[10]

By and large, literary versions of the man-woman, whether androgyne, hermaphrodite, or Amazon, were not too controversial, particularly if they were allegorical representations.[11] But various real-life forms of sex- or gender-combining were greeted with fear, disgust, or condemnation. Biological hermaphroditism was not socially permissible, as Laqueur explains in *Making Sex*.[12] The term "hermaphroditism" was often used to signify something that overturned perceived laws of nature, as in the unnatural combining of sexes in the body of the hermaphrodite. In the words of Jerome Schwartz, the image of the hermaphrodite represented "the figure not of inner harmony [as did the Platonic androgyne] but of grotesque, unnatural sexuality" (127).[13] For example, two different French authors used the term to express their revulsion at Henri III's transvestism and his sexual acts with young boys (Schwartz 125–6). In seventeenth-century England, Edward Denny used the word as a term of insult in his verse attack on Lady Mary Wroth.[14]

In England, cross-dressing, a practice that might be called sartorial hermaphroditism, was strongly condemned and frequently punished. Yet court and prison records, as well as sermons and pamphlets from this period, reveal that female-to-male cross-dressing was widely practiced.[15] Why was cross-dressing so popular? Constance Jordan's definition offers one answer; she calls it "a mode of behavior in which a person's sexual identity is not declared openly and his or her gendered character is deliberately registered as fluid or androgynous" (301). Cross-dressing may have been an attempt to recreate Plato's androgynous "third sex." Or perhaps the practice functioned as an intentional transgression of both class and gender boundaries (Howard, "Crossdressing" 424–5). The early modern pamphlet "Haec Vir" (1620), a somewhat revisionist defense of cross-dressing, offers an implicit recognition of the culturally determined nature of gender. In the dialogue between Haec Vir, the womanish man, and Hic Mulier, the Man-Woman, Hic Mulier says, "We are as freeborn as Men, have as free election and as free spirits; we are compounded of like parts and may with like liberty make benefit of our Creations" (in Henderson and McManus 284). But, according to Jordan, patriarchal institutions perceived this view as "the effacement of rank and hence an inevitable decline into anarchy" (302). The notion of gender as a continuum of masculine and feminine traits rather than a dualistic pair of opposites leveled not only gender distinctions but also distinctions of rank (Jordan 301).

Yet, in examining cross-dressing, we must be careful to avoid prematurely closing out possible explanations of an overdetermined practice. "Haec Vir" depicts cross-dressers as advocates of androgyny whose creation of an ambiguous gender challenges received assumptions of essential gender differences. But cross-dressing also served a much less radical purpose: not to challenge gender distinctions but simply to get around them. Cross-dressers might accept gender distinctions but wish to subvert them on an individual basis. Such revolutions were not political but personal. Literal female-to-male impersonation was not common during the period, but it was far from unheard-of. It is impossible to gain accurate records of it because, if successful, it went undetected.[16] Natalie Zemon Davis suggests that "[t]he usual stratagem for women who wanted to join an army or a navy in England, France, and the Netherlands was to hide their identity and cross-dress as a man" ("Women in Politics" 168). While cross-dressing could serve as a convenient front for lesbianism (Davis "Infractions, Transgressions, Rebellions" 441), for the most part it enabled women to cross both gender lines and the boundaries of social rank.[17] Thus, many women who passed for men by cross-dressing did so for practical reasons. The heroines of *Twelfth Night* and *Love's Cure* do so as well.

Playwrights, whose entire project of entertainment commonly met with hostility from the London city fathers, expected to address the underclass and the gentry and aristocracy more than the literate administrator. Given dramatists' goals and audiences, both different from those of the writers that Rackin considers, we should not be surprised that their sense of gender relations should also be different. This understanding, I would suggest, may be mapped out by analyzing representations of the cross-dressed duellist. This figure, which draws directly on the model of the Amazon as well as indirectly on those of the androgyne and the hermaphrodite, enables us to see how action is understood and staged by playwrights when it is performed by female rather than male characters.

The occasional portrayal of women as duellists in early modern English plays would seem to cast doubt on Howell's simplistic proverb "Women are wordes, Men are deedes" (D2r).[18] Although female duellists were almost entirely unknown (or at least undocumented) in the culture of early modern England, there are several notable female fighters in drama, the best known of which is *The Roaring Girl*'s Moll Cutpurse. To some extent, such characters do disprove the old proverb; more exactly, however, they demonstrate the inadequacy of the dichotomy it presents. Deeds and words are not the simple oppositions that the saying offers: they function as two poles on a continuum that might be called "action." (I have already suggested the usefulness of this model in the previous chapter.) The relation of word to deed complicates what is accomplished in the duel. Female characters who duel (or who come close to doing so) may engage in a masculine behavior, but they do so in uniquely feminine ways. Once we acknowledge the duel as the complex and meaning-bearing act that it is (a sort of inverse speech-act), we can recognize that female characters who enacted duels were performing a different act than were their male counterparts. Their modification of early modern and theatrical duelling practices is part of a subtle redefinition of what it meant to be a woman at that time.

Most consistently, female dramatic characters who engage in duels are represented neither as transcending their sex nor as violating its nature: instead they seem to accept the female role as a uniquely instructive one, using the combat as a didactic tool. Given the drama's emphasis on the spoken word, it is not surprising that many early modern plays granted to the duel of honor the significance of the judicial duel. In these cases, the statement that provokes the challenge to the duel serves as a predictive speech-act: I name you and proclaim you as traitor (or oath-breaker, liar, etc.). The challenge is both statement and promise: my hand will prove the truth of my refutation upon your body. In other words, both the challenge and the insult that precedes it propose truth-claims that the combat is supposed to prove. Men in the drama who fight for vengeance are doing something quite different.

Female characters in *The Maid's Tragedy, The Roaring Girl,* and *Love's Cure, or, The Martial Maid,* all seem to take their cue from Erasmus and Ascham, obliquely guiding their superiors through indirect discourse.[19] When Rackin links passion—especially (but not exclusively) sexual passion—with the feminine, her arguments suggest the likelihood of an association between intemperance and the female duellist. But in fact playwrights tended to use female duellists more to satirize or to show up masculine pretension than to demonstrate female irrationality. In different ways, each cross-dressed female duellist whom I discuss uses the duel to teach men to avoid acting on anger or sexual passion. Although some of these female characters are almost entirely free from "feminine" passions while others epitomize them, all pursue the same strategy in marked contrast both to their opponents and to their male counterparts in real life. Even when they are cross-dressed and carrying weapons, they do not imitate man "in action by pursuing revenge" (*Hic Mulier* 270) any more than women in real life generally did. Instead, they attempt the duel primarily as a didactic device. Their combats are not initiated by the circumstances that generally prompt male characters to fight; on the contrary, their motive is frequently the one that prompted duels among men in real life: perceived disrespect toward them or theirs. Unlike early modern male duellists, however, these female characters approach the duel as a possibility for rehabilitation rather than as an opportunity for punishment. The insults documented as the impetus to the early modern duel suggest that the ritual was often undertaken in order to humiliate or to penalize the addressee for bad behavior. In dramatic duels in which women play a part, the women want their opponents to learn to respect others—primarily, women. Female characters engage in the duel (if they do so at all) with much less braggadocio than male characters, often agreeing to keep their combat unknown. Their purpose is not to punish their opponent but to change his view of what is due to women.

I begin with a character type even more anomalous than the cross-dressed woman: the cross-dressed man. In *Swetnam the Woman-Hater Arraigned by Women*, the male lead disguises himself as a woman, Atlanta, to combat Misogynos (the character Joseph Swetnam). The anonymous author of this play follows Rackin's paradigm, using Lorenzo's disguise and duel to comment obliquely on the relation between *virtus*, the moral excellence that was generally considered exclusively male, and *eros*, the erotic energy that was often demonized or derogated by being defined as either feminine or effeminizing. After examining the ambivalence of *Swetnam*, an ostensibly protofeminist response to the historical Joseph Swetnam's *Arraignment of Lewd, idle, froward, and unconstant women*, I turn to four plays containing cross-dressed *female* duellists: Beaumont and Fletcher's *The Maid's Tragedy,* Heywood's *The Fair Maid of the West*, Middleton and Dekker's *The Roaring Girl*, and Beaumont and Fletcher's *Love's Cure, or The Martial Maid*. In these plays, women have many different objects in mind when they step up to the duel. But none are bloodthirsty, like so many male duellists in early modern drama, and almost none are egotistical, like the general run of duellists in England at that time. These dramatists destabilize the association between passion and *eros,* offering women a positive role within what we have traditionally assumed to be standard gender relations. What I am arguing may seem at first to resemble the old thesis of Clara Claiborne Park, who commented that cross-dressed stage heroines (who always return willingly to women's clothes at the end) may have been a gratifying spectacle to male audience members because these women seemed voluntarily to "tame" themselves in order to become suitable objects of matrimony (106–9). Dekker and van de Pol comment on a similar phenomenon in both popular balladry and real-life situations: "Cross-dressing could be permissible so long as the woman claimed no masculine prerogatives, maintained her feminine honour, was extremely successful as a man, and finally resumed life as a woman in the end" (88). But my point goes further: by presenting women who are, for the most part, accepting of their subordinate role, the playwrights actually liberate these characters by granting them a broader range of behavior within which they may function as women. Without challenging received norms, these dramatists posit a space within which woman may engage in duels, provided that the duels bear a different meaning than duels fought by men. To make sense of the portrayal of Besse Bridges and her sister duellists, we must acknowledge the assumption that so long as duels are not vengeful or a proof of one's word, they are not, in some substantial sense, "real." The sign of masculinity normally borne by the duel seems to derive not only from its active (or enactable) qualities: it also must be linked to the duellist's intentions—to the meaning carried by the challenge.

Swetnam the Woman-hater, an anonymous play licensed in 1619, is generally attributed to Heywood.[20] The play offers an inquiry into the value of female agency, presenting the question literally as a debate and as a combat between women's detractors and their advocates. Those on the side of misogyny attempt to create an autonomous male body with no need for women or for erotic motivation. Though this attempt is defeated, the play permits female agency to be demonized as the origin of uncontrollable erotic energy. At the end, the space that is made for women is merely the economic space of the marriage prize. In this play, the cross-dresser is a man who, disguised as an Amazon, loses the debate in defense of women but wins the duel against the misogynistic fencing-master, Joseph Swetnam. Although the play ostensibly parodies the historical Joseph Swetnam and his *Arraignment* (1615), it also takes part in the longstanding *querelle des femmes* "through the attitudes and actions of its characters," as Coryl Crandall says (15), and though Swetnam is mocked, female agency is undermined in the play as well. The plot, derived primarily from a novelette by the fifteenth-century writer Juan de Flores, combines traditional romance elements with contemporary topical interest.

When Leonida, Princess of Sicily, is discovered with her lover, Lisandro, Prince of Naples, the king's counselors assess the respective guilt of each lover by holding a public disputation on whether men or women are more guilty of offences in love.[21] Joseph Swetnam, author, misogynist, and swordsman, undertakes to defend men in the disputation. (He has been hounded out of England by that country's female population and has come to Sicily to start a fencing school.) Leonida's brother, returned from war and disguised as an Amazon, undertakes to defend women in the debate. Swetnam wins, and the princess is sentenced to death, though the prince saves his sister through a stratagem. Subsequently, Swetnam falls in love with the supposed Amazon; they meet again and engage in a duel. This time, the prince wins. He hands Swetnam over to the women of Sicily, who whip him out of the country.[22] Shortly afterward, Prince Lisandro unmasks the schemes of the corrupt counselor Nicanor and reveals himself to his father. All are reconciled.

The play's older male characters consistently depict the erotic aggression of women as a violent force that threatens to destroy both women and those around them. As a sort of counter-argument to this misogyny, the playwright offers an Amazon, Prince Lorenzo in disguise, who sets everything right. But constructing a male-to-female cross-dresser (no matter how benevolent) as a defense of women is a strategy bound to undermine its own premises. When Lorenzo/Atlanta defends women, he does so both as swordsman and as spokesperson, proving his physical superiority and silencing the biological women, who drop out of the action. The use of the Amazon fails adequately to solve the heavily stressed problem of the destructive potential of *eros*. The hermaphroditic figure of Lorenzo/Atlanta manifests only filial and fraternal affection. Though this character defends all women (and Leonida through them), his asexual nature does nothing to vindicate sexuality. Instead, Atlanta functions as a pedestrian *deus ex machina*. She stands in for women as a man who clearly champions the "weaker sex" because that sex has no effective social clout of its own. She rescues the lovers from an oppressive father figure, returning them for his blessing when he is ready to give it. Essentially, Atlanta facilitates the transfer of women from fathers to husbands through the economic medium of marriage. Passion is permitted in this play only in the subversive violence of the women who scapegoat the openly misogynistic Swetnam at the end. Although Swetnam is expelled, the play fails to acknowledge other masculine dangers, represented primarily by Nicanor, the corrupt counselor whom the king pardons.

Atlanta's verbal and literal duels are placed within the context of a misogynistic society and overtly attempt to combat these attitudes. Inherent in the community's misogyny is a barely concealed fear of *eros*. The play begins with a disturbing ascription of uncontrollable power to women. King Atticus of Sicily asks after his daughter, complaining, "The Girle is wanton, coy, and fickle too: / How many Princes hath the froward Elfe / Set at debate, desiring but her love? / What dangers may insue?" (I.i.162–65). From the first, an otherwise loving father expresses the view that the misogynist Swetnam will later propagate: that women's willfulness causes civil unrest.[23] Leonida's desire to choose her own mate is constructed as threatening to social stability. Later, Nicanor's perversion of Petrarchan rhetoric follows the king's lead:

> The Princesse is my Prisoner, I her Slave;
> I keepe her Body, but shee holds my Heart
> Inviron'd in a Chest of Adamant.
> *Scanfardo*: Is your Heart Iron?
> *Nicanor*:   Steele, I thinke it is;
> And like an Anvile hammerd by her words,
> It sparkles fire that never can bee quencht,
> But by the dew of her coelestiall breath. (I.i.183–91)

Prison, physical confinement, is defined as less significant than slavery, a spiritual subjugation. So long as Leonida holds Nicanor's heart, she controls him, although he furiously resents that control. Nicanor constructs men as victims of the disturbing power of female sexuality. He ascribes his feelings to Leonida's active subjugation of him, regarding her desirability as a weapon that she intentionally uses to control him. He looks forward to mastering her as she (in fact quite unawares) has mastered him. In his language, the courtly mistress–servant relation becomes that of master and slave, with harsh overtones of spiritual domination. Such terms intimate that the war between the sexes will shortly become literal.

The play opposes the power it ascribes to women with masculine attempts to cut women out of the sexual economy. If man could reproduce without women, the vagaries of erotic desire could also be eliminated. Swetnam himself expresses a desire for sexual autonomy from women; he complains because women are necessary for propagation:

> Happy were man, had woman never bin.
> Why did not Nature infuse the gift of Procreation
> In man alone, without the helpe of woman,
> Even as we see one seed, produce another? (I.ii.139–42)

He wants to eliminate women altogether, reproducing by some form of vegetable budding. During the debate, Swetnam asserts that women use female sexuality to control men—specifically, to destroy masculine autonomy.

In the public debate, the blame for Lisandro and Leonida's clandestine meetings is transformed into a new question: which sex is more responsible for initiating sexual activity? Leonida, who has shielded her lover by taking responsibility for their meeting, finds her case universalized by her spokesman, the misogynist Swetnam. This resourceful princess ironically loses her voice to a man who would refuse to believe that a woman could make the disinterested sacrifices that Leonida does. The defense of women (ostensibly Lisandro's side of the debate) is taken by the Amazon Atlanta. Though the larger reputation of women rides on Atlanta's performance, her victory would result in Lisandro's punishment and thus the defeat of Leonida's wishes.

The debate is characterized as a verbal combat: the speakers are called the champions of the lovers and the crowd critiques each speaker's "by-blows," "wards," "veneys," and "flourishes." These terms suggest a parallel between the real Swetnam's professional knowledge of fencing and his attack on women.[24] As the debate continues, its developing arguments favor Swetnam's agenda: desire is figured as an offence to civil society and, from the first, both debaters try to demonize the opposite sex by describing it as the one most afflicted by *eros*. The arguments of Lorenzo/Atlanta recall Nicanor's image of his metal heart:

> [Swetnam] doth charge
> The supple wax, the courteous-natur'd woman,
> As blamefull for receiving the impression
> Of Iron-hearted man, in whom is graven,
> With curious and deceiving Art, foule shapes
> And stamps of much abhord impietie. (III.iii.69–74)

This Aristotelian image makes a virtue of women's yielding but fails to challenge the negative perception of desire. Atlanta actually grants

Swetnam's assertion that "In all their passions women are impetuous, / And beyond men, ten times more violent" (III.iii. 92–3). Most of the debate considers "who begins the motion," men who tempt women to fall or women who inspire men's lust (a conventional question).[25] At no point is *eros* redeemed, and the chicken-and-egg controversy concludes when Atlanta starts screaming imprecations at her opponent, acting as the apparent embodiment of female intemperance.

Atlanta loses by playing the woman too far. She begins by asking the judges to look leniently on a woman's "small defects" and loses by becoming angry and shrewish. Coryl Crandall reads this loss of temper as the playwright's ironic attempt to show the theater audience that men, too, can scold and rage (13), but the resulting plot twists reflect ambiguously on the cross-dressed Lorenzo. Given early modern gender assumptions, should we assume that the loss was deliberate or inadvertent? Is Lorenzo simply a poor statesman? Doesn't the loss contradict the rhetorical power of the androgyne evident in such cross-dressed figures as Shakespeare's Rosalind and Portia? Lorenzo's cross-dressing apparently follows another model: as a hermaphroditic figure rather than an androgyne, he must mediate between two sexes instead of becoming a third.

But although Atlanta has lost the battle, she wins the war, for she conquers Misogynos in the war of love:

> *Swash*: Who, in the name of women, should this bee?
> ...Who, the Amazonian Dame, your Advocate,
> A Masculine Feminine?
> *Misogynos:*   I [Aye], *Swash,*
> She must be more then Female, has the power
> To mollifie the temper of my Love.
> Swash: Why, she's the greatest enemie you have.
> *Misogynos*: The greater is my glorie, *Swash,* in that
> That [sic] having vanquisht all, I attaine her. (IV.iii.61–70)

Yet in ideological terms this conquest simply reiterates Swetnam and Atticus's initial assumption: that women's desirability compels masculine lust. Swetnam's concept of marriage is the same as that of Nicanor: love as conquest and as subordination of another. In this situation, the misogynistic Swetnam's desire seems to have been aroused not by the Amazon's erotic charms, but by the erotic charge he gained from triumphing over her.[26] His desire also may be prompted by an intuitive recognition of Atlanta's true sex. The play's happy outcome results from Lorenzo's gender advantage as a male. Begged for a clandestine meeting, Atlanta complies, only to strike her would-be lover and challenge him to the duel. The Amazon conquers the misogynist—but only, it would seem, because "she" is a "he." The most threatening representation of female power follows, with the mob scene following Atlanta's conquest of Swetnam.

In its denouement, the play seems to offer two contradictory resolutions: one for men and one for women. If not for the epilogue, the message would carry an overt suggestion of man's superiority. When Lorenzo reveals Nicanor's perfidy at his father's court and then unmasks himself, both son and father magnanimously pardon Nicanor. To honor the moment of rediscovering his children, "this houre...sacred unto joy," Atticus shows mercy to a repentant villain (V.iii.207). His behavior merits praise for its manifestation of Christian charity, its example of Platonic rationality. But when Swetnam yields to Atlanta, "she" hands him over to a band of women (including the queen), who execute their own judgment on him. They bind him, poke him with pins, and subject him to a counter-arraignment, after which they muzzle him and send him out of Christian dominions. Their behavior reveals women not as inconstant but as dangerous. Their torture of Swetnam recalls the behavior of the wild Bacchae, whose power men ignored at their peril. Ultimately, the scene suggests that men have good reason to fear women's uncontrolled energy.[27]

An epilogue *does* follow the final scene, however, presenting an attempt to resolve the *querelle des femmes* more happily. The muzzled Swetnam is led onstage to be forgiven by Leonida, who urges, "Women are neither tyrannous, nor cruell, / Though you report us so" (11–12). Swetnam responds with praise and promises of future assistance: "Mercie and Beautie best doe sympathize: / And here forever I put off this shape / ...And vow to let no time or act escape, / In which my service may be shewne to you" (15–19). Although the Princess's voice is restored to her, the "service" promised by Swetnam reiterates the by-now mangled Petrarchism that has been consistently recast throughout the play. That "service" bears dark overtones of a Nietzschean slave mentality that may flip over into a harsh desire for mastery at any time. Leonida, ironically, seems reduced by her magnanimous gesture. The active enterprise that made her an engaging character has been replaced by the more acceptable propriety of a Mercilla.

Despite the happy ending, the expectations raised by the Amazon Atlanta/Lorenzo are, finally, disappointed. The intriguing twist of a male-to-female cross-dresser does not make good on the promise of social transformation that it initially seems to offer. That the androgyne may effect the metamorphosis that transforms and refines the community is something of a critical commonplace originating in Frye's *Anatomy of Criticism* (183). But in this case, Atlanta's strength reduces the social role that women are permitted. "Female" traits are demonized and then eradicated rather than integrated. In *Swetnam the Woman-hater*, the potential of the man-woman to integrate *eros* and *virtus* results simply in the eradication of *eros*.

Dramas with cross-dressed *female* duellists, however, are altogether different in kind. Few of these plays make the duel the climax of the action. Though these duels often serve as catalysts for a classical *peripateia*, they simply follow the consistent action of the play. In the drama, women who fight are under no necessity to transcend female limitations. In *The Maid's Tragedy*, for example, Aspatia, who is ruled by passion, overcomes the negative effects of her past weakness through a self-sacrificial duel. The combat recontextualizes Aspatia as an exemplar of an extreme type of feminine virtue, a marked contrast to her unpleasant, morally confused rival. In *The Roaring Girl*, Moll never loses her self-possession, but her behavior is so aberrant that many audience members probably read her as irrational, if not actually "mad." Despite the dubious rationality of these figures, they are not proscribed from engaging in a heroic act that consistently raises them in the estimation of the audience—all the more so as their motivations seem so generous, so free from the orgulous desire for vengeance or honor that prompts most dramatic duels.

To an ironic eye, the tragedy of *The Maid's Tragedy* is the lack of self-determination for women in patriarchal society. But the intended referent of the title was probably the death of Aspatia, seemingly a secondary character. As the play's only virgin, the sword-fighting Aspatia must, perforce, be the title figure, although she is not the female lead. The play opens in Rhodes with the wedding of Aspatia's former fiancé, Amintor, to Evadne; the king himself has made the match, having urged Amintor to break off his engagement with Aspatia. But as Amintor learns from his scornful bride on his wedding night, the king has urged this action to cover up his own liaison with Evadne. Humiliated, Amintor nonetheless feels he may not revenge himself on the monarch. Eventually, Evadne regains her sense of her own honor and kills her royal lover, but Amintor repudiates both her and her action. Meantime, Aspatia, heartbroken at Amintor's faithlessness to her, disguises herself as her own brother and forces Amintor into a duel. Once engaged in fighting, however, she remains passive, and Amintor gives her her death-wound.[28] As she dies, he discovers her identity and pledges his love once more; he then commits suicide, hoping to join her in death. Howard B. Norland, editor of the Nebraska edition of the play, reads the plot as an indictment of royal absolutism. Of the suicidal Aspatia, he says, "she represents the tragic implications of the king's abuse of his royal prerogative to serve his selfish ends" (xvii). But the moral action centers on Amintor, and I find Aspatia's duel central to his reeducation in appropriate values.

On the way to his nuptial bed, Amintor receives doleful congratulations from Aspatia. Alone, he tries to dismiss her grief and rationalize his change of affection: "My guilt is not so great / As mine own conscience, too sensible, / Would make me think; I only brake a promise, / And 'twas the king that forc'd me" (II.i.129–32).[29] Amintor refuses responsibility for his change of heart, though he grants, "[the king] had not my will in keeping" (II.i.127). Amintor remains similarly passive throughout the play. He does not force his wife to break off her affair, nor does he take revenge, resolving instead to live as a cuckold. He unintentionally aids Aspatia in her suicide as, almost despite himself, he finds himself engaged in the duel. Although Amintor characterizes his lack of initiative as submission to the king's overriding authority, his pliability throughout the play contrasts with other characters' decisiveness and reveals his rationale as an excuse for inaction.

Aspatia's behavior teaches Amintor, first of all, how to prosecute his own claims. Norland reads Aspatia's behavior as perverse; he calls it "the diseased picture of unrequited love" and refers to her "morbid, self-indulgent grief" (xvii). I disagree: this Ophelia-figure becomes the moral linchpin of the play. As the forsaken bride, she is the object of considerable audience sympathy. But she cannot derail her fiancé's wedding and she is socially proscribed from revenge. Given these parameters, Aspatia pursues her course of self-slaughter by means of an *acceptable* revenge. Posing as her brother (away on a military expedition), she challenges the righteousness of Amintor's behavior. Had her brother, the eldest able-bodied male of her family, been in Rhodes, he would almost have been obligated to challenge Amintor's faithlessness; posing as a male, she gains at least the opportunity to do so. To serve as her own champion is in itself not an inconsiderable assertion of will, since women were generally obliged to depend on male relatives to act on their behalf.

Aspatia's donning of masculine garb, her picking up of the sword, could easily have been interpreted as the immodest behavior of a loose woman, particularly since prostitutes were among the most common transgressors of sartorial gender boundaries in early modern England.[30] Aspatia's refusal to use the sword (logically, she would not have known how to wield it) ensured that she would retain audience sympathy. Although we may read her behavior as masochistic, we should not perceive it as a parallel to Amintor's passivity. Certainly, since she strikes wide of him but invites his blows, the duel is no contest. But Aspatia's primary purposes are to meet death and to make Amintor understand the results of his compliance—she has no wish to avenge his desertion of her by killing him. She is implicitly contrasted with Evadne, who reenters as Aspatia dies and urges Amintor to love her for killing the king. Evadne's regicide is immodest in its aggression, just like the immodesty of her earlier willingness to enter into the affair. Despite the king's corruption, Evadne's regicide is unforgivable. But because Aspatia has neither the intention nor the ability to win this duel, she retains her status as a modest maiden. Amintor shows how greatly he values that quality when, before he dies, he regrets his wrong to Aspatia more than his rejection of Evadne, though that too has resulted in a woman's suicide.

Aspatia's suicide does make her a morbid heroine. Her choice is difficult for us to read positively. But for a specifically Renaissance audience, it would have linked her with such heroic female suicides of Rome as Lucretia, whose suicide after her rape by Tarquin led to the founding of the Roman republic. At the very least, Aspatia's suicide is a form of self-determination. Despite the paucity of options available to her, Aspatia has not hesitated to pursue her desires as best she can. Until Amintor's marriage, she had tried to influence public opinion in her favor, hoping to sway Amintor by that means; afterward, she seeks death at his hands.

Aspatia instructs Amintor by making him understand that he cannot abdicate responsibility for his actions. She begins by challenging Amintor to the duel on the grounds of "[t]he baseness of the injuries [he] did her" (V.iii.58). Before the fight, Amintor acknowledges the justice of the charge, going so far as to say that he will not fight because his conduct has been indefensible (V.iii.83–5). But Aspatia urges him on, first striking and then kicking him. Finally, he accepts her challenge and proceeds to the combat. By forcing Amintor physically to kill her, Aspatia literalizes the plight in which his faithlessness had placed her. For a male courtier, breaking a promise at the ruler's behest may be justifiable. But the engagement between Aspatia and

Amintor had been a contract that designated her fate—in dissolving it, Amintor denies Aspatia any future in their society, since such a contract is all too close to a marriage. The broken engagement sharply limits any further possibility of another engagement for Aspatia, since it diminishes her value on the marriage market; more important, the engagement is clearly regarded by Aspatia as a marriage and as a commitment that defined her future. Without it, Aspatia feels that any possible future she can have is no future at all.

Once Amintor realizes the significance of his past actions and whom he has now killed, he realizes what he must do. With Aspatia's body in his arms, he chides himself: "I wrong / Myself, so long to lose her company. / Must I talk now?" (V.iii.242–4). With his love for Aspatia renewed, he sees a way both to withdraw from his dishonorable marriage and to rejoin the woman he loves without committing the sin of adultery. Immediately, he stabs himself to death. The heretofore malleable Amintor finally takes decisive and dramatic action, pursuing a course controversial both in his world and in that of the authors. At the end, Amintor takes an active role in deciding his fate.

Moll Cutpurse and Besse Bridges, heroines of *The Roaring Girl* and *The Fair Maid of the West* respectively, differ greatly from Aspatia. In broad terms, one could say that their dramas, like *Swetnam, the Woman-hater*, are part of the *querelle des femmes* tradition.[31] In *The Roaring Girl*, the duel of honor is a persistent theme as a truth-test throughout the first half. Although both plays interrogate women's potential (and even, perhaps, the potential of gender categories), they are also largely concerned with the relation between female reputation and female action. In these plays, men use language as a way to control women, whether directly through commands or indirectly through slander. While in reality unprotected women had little recourse if unrelated men attempted to establish intimacy through these means, both Besse and Moll resort to the sword to teach importunate men a lesson. When they fight, however, neither Moll nor Besse attempts to prove her worthiness. One heroine would hesitate to believe that feminine worth could be proven by such means; the other has already passed the point where community opinion affects her. Thus, neither one fights her opponent in a competitive spirit; instead, they fight for a reason that seems derived from that of the trial by combat—to reestablish truth. But neither one fights to disprove an accusation against her in particular, as one of the combatants necessarily would in the judicial duel. Instead, Besse and Moll fight to combat the problems that result when a man looks down on the female sex in general. As these two women are independent (though not necessarily subversive) figures, their combats serve as a significant part of their plays (though not as the main focus).

Besse Bridges, in *The Fair Maid of the West, Or, A Girle worth gold*, is undoubtedly a male fantasy on the order of patient Griselda. Besse waits faithfully for her Spencer to return from his voyage; when false news of his death reaches her, her only desire is to bring his body home to England. As she waits for Spencer, she establishes a thriving business; once she establishes her plan to find Spencer's body, she purchases a ship, hires old (disappointed) suitors as crew, and sails off to Fiall disguised as a man, fighting sea-battles with Spanish warships along the way. Yet Heywood's drama suggests that the great wonder of Besse is not her remarkable accomplishments but her fidelity to the man she loves. On two occasions, men who meet Besse confuse her with Queen Elizabeth, referred to as "the Virgin Queene" (V.i.101). Alluding to Besse's impending conquest of the King of Fesse's affections, the Chorus predicts,

> He sends for her onshore, how he receives her,
> How she and Spencer meet, must next succeed.
> Sit patient, then, when these are fully told,
> Some may hap say, I [aye], there's a Girle worth gold. (IV.xii.16–19)[32]

What renders Besse a prototypically biblical "virtuous woman" (with reverence to Proverbs 31: 10–31) are not her considerable abilities but her chaste nature and charity toward others.

Besse's greatest challenge throughout the play is not so much to attain her goals as to maintain her reputation. From the first, Besse's status is in question; though two captains describe her as sweet, modest, and honest, the unfortunate Caroll comments incredulously, "Honest, and live there? / What, in a publike Taverne, where's such confluence / Of lusty and brave Gallants?" (I.i.32–4). Directly after she becomes Spencer's fiancée, she is insulted by Caroll, who insinuates to Spencer when he finds the two sitting together, "She would draw [no wine] to us, / Perhaps she keepes a Rundlet for your taste, / Which none but you must pierce" (I.vii.26–8). When Spencer tells him to mind his manners and says that Besse is worthy to sit with them, Caroll gives him the lie, leading to a duel in which Caroll is slain. Spencer must flee the country, and Besse feels guilty over the death: "My innocence / Hath beene the cause of blood, and I am now, / Purpled with murder, though not within compasse / Of the Lawes severe censure" (I.xi.2–5). Besse's virtue is always clear to us, the audience; it is the male characters whose false assumptions must be repeatedly corrected by Besse's actions.[33]

Besse relocates to an inn in Foy that Spencer has given to her. There, as mistress of the establishment, she must still endure the insults of Roughman, a roarer who tells his friend Forset that he must "know of what burden this vessell is.... and til then, I cannot report her for a woman of good carriage" (II.ii.3–6). As he himself says, his domineering words are both a test of Besse and a strategy to subordinate her to him. When Roughman blusters, "I tell thee maid, wife, or what e'er thou beest, / No man may enter here but by my leave. / Come, let's be more familiar" (II.ii.75–8), Besse shrewdly suspects that his bluster conceals cowardice. After an encounter in which she repeatedly pacifies his choler, she secretly resolves to challenge him. Dressed as her own (fictional) brother, she puts on a sword and challenges Roughman to a duel late at night: "You are a villain, a Coward, and you lie" (II.vii.18). More to our surprise than that of Besse, Roughman submits himself immediately, and at her command he gives up his sword, ties her shoe, and lets her stride over his prone body. Still in the guise of her own brother, she agrees to spare his life but warns him not to attempt to domineer in Besse's house or threaten her guests, "Which if I ever shall hereafter heare, / Thou art but a dead man" (II.vii.59–60). Yet, believing the encounter unknown to anyone in Foy, Roughman returns to Besse's household and continues his behavior. Finally, Besse shames him publicly: "You base white-lyver'd slave, it was this shooe / That thou stoopt to untie: untrust these points: And like a beastly coward lay lang / Til I stridd over thee. Speake, was't not so?" (III.v.39–42).

Besse follows up this public humiliation with the threat of further violence. Oddly enough, her threat seems to acknowledge the unfitness of a duel for one in women's garb: "Give me that Rapier: I will make thee sweare, / Thou shalt redeeme this scorne thou hast incurr'd, / Or in this woman shape Ile cudgell thee, / And beate thee through the streets" (III.v.45–8). When Besse treats Roughman in a literally man-to-man fashion, he reveals himself as a coward. So she promises to enact traditionally female violence—man-beating—if he fails to redeem his cowardice, not by attempting to bully her, but by finding a truer model of manhood.

Besse thus uses three different disciplinary devices and, though her aims vary, not one is employed to seek vengeance. The initial challenge to combat is a test; revelation of it is a disciplinary device; and the final threat is a didactic device, a sort of Skinnerian negative reinforcement of cowardice.[34] Besse knows from the first that the mastery Roughman attempts to gain over her servants is an oblique strategy toward controlling Besse herself. She does not want to punish him for it but to teach him to give up the attempt. The type of masculine privilege that he appropriates is not one that belongs to all men, only to the man she regards as her husband: Spencer. Roughman tries to win Besse by acting as though she is his; to disprove his act, she appears as her own male protector. But when Roughman refuses to admit absent authority as legitimate, Besse humiliates him—actually forcing him to confess to his cowardice so that she may, from then on, dominate him. If Roughman cannot be dissuaded from wooing her, he must be emasculated. But Besse uses the combat itself as a warning, not a castration; only when Roughman refuses to change his ways does she use public shame to control him (and further threats in order to redeem him). Although she wins the duel before it begins, she needs to follow up with a public recital of it to bring it home to her opponent. Besse even states that her original intention is to correct, not punish: as "Besse Bridges brother," she urges, "Roughman thou art blest / This day thy life is sav'd, looke to the rest" (2.7.48–9). This correction of manners eventually is supplemented by her correction of fact, which brings him not only to feel shame but also to recognize the respect owed to the woman he patronized before, as the further threat makes him recognize what his mistaken notions of manliness have deserved.

Combat is a symbolic theme in *The Roaring Girl*. When Sebastian's father attempts to manipulate him by complaining of him to friends, the young man regards the ploy as an oblique attack in a game of fence: "How finely, like a fencer, / My father fetches his by-blows to hit me! / But if I beat you not at your own weapon / Of subtilty—" (I.i.232–5).[35] Sebastian has a strategy in mind, one even more subtle than his father's. But when Sir Alexander refers to Moll as a "naughty pack," suggesting her sexual promiscuity, the rhetorical combat threatens to become literalized: "I say, that tongue / That dares speak so, but yours, sticks in the throat / Of a rank villain: set yourself aside / .... Any here else had lied" (I.i.262–6). The code of a gentleman forbids Sebastian to challenge his own father's words, but he seems to have lost his self-control entirely. Perhaps the effect may be lessened, however, by his aside before the outburst: "Now is my cue to bristle" (I.i.257). His father responds more to Sebastian's concealed comment than to his open threat: "I'll pierce you deeper yet" (I.i.268). To conceal his desire for Sebastian to make a mercenary match, Sir Alexander plays the part of the neglected father of an unfilial son; to conceal his more serious interest in gentle Mary Fitzallard, Sebastian pretends to a serious love for the cross-dressed Moll. No combat erupts, because neither one is deceived by the other as yet; both play instead to the community opinion of Sir Alexander's dinner guests, the local gentry. Neither Sebastian nor Sir Alexander speaks truth, since both wish to affect the opinion of their community, the lever with which each hopes to budge the stance of the other. At that point, the implied challenge fades away, suggesting early on that the regard for truth or for honor in this society is not very great.

Trivial causes for anger erupt in this society. A quarrel is hinted at but is effeminately turned aside:

> *Goshawk*: Thou hast the cowardliest trick.... I could find in my heart to make a quarrel in earnest.
> *Laxton*: Pox, and thou dost—thou knowest I never use to fight with my friends—thou'lt but lose thy labour in't. (II.ii.96–100)

Into this effete and gossipy society comes Moll, wearing a man's jerkin and a woman's riding skirt, Hic Mulier incarnate. Moll has received a great deal of critical attention in the last twenty years. Many readers have interpreted her as subversive of the established social order, based on the estimate of her community, which responds primarily to her adoption of men's clothes and secondarily to her free speech: "This wench ... strays so from her kind, / Nature repents she made her" (I.i.339–40); "Some will not stick to say she is a man. And some, both man and woman" (II.i.217–18); "a monster with two trinkets" (II.ii.81); "that bold masculine ramp" (V.ii.14).[36] If we listened solely to the play's citizens, we would believe that no women in early modern London had ever considered combining masculine and feminine raiment. But as Deborah Jacobs comments,

> At every point in the play where there is a potential debasing of the social order, the figure of Moll Cutpurse, as an instrument of the state ... deflates these challenges. The play may, in fact, be staging some sort of resistance, but it is not written on Moll's body, and it certainly does not triumph. (78)

Aside from the challenge to received mores accomplished by her clothing choice, Moll enforces rather than subverts traditional society. She plays the part of Plautus's clever servant, aiding Sebastian and Mary Fitzallard in their thwarting of the blocking father figure. She saves a spendthrift from false arrest and forces two petty criminals to confess their tricks to the gentlemen in her company. As Jean Howard comments, "it is not always perfectly clear that [Moll] embodies a consistent social philosophy or class-gender position" ("Crossdressing" 438).

But Moll *is* interested in improving the lot of other women. Although she tosses off a neat couplet on her willingness to aid gentlemen in scrivener's bands (set down for debt), her primary concern is to lessen society's misogyny. On four different occasions, she speaks of the peculiar wrongs of woman in London society, saving her greatest exasperation for male gossips who ruin the reputations of chaste women: "How many are whores in small ruffs and still looks! / How many chaste whose names fill Slander's books! ... a fencer may be called a coward; is he so for that?" (5.1.356–67). Moll's point is that gossip feeds on falsehood.[37] To trust it is to be deceived; to spread it is to be a liar. Gossip is particularly pernicious because it seems not to originate with any single person and therefore cannot be stopped. But Moll warns her acquaintance not to trust gossip, which wrongs more people than it characterizes truly. For women, as she points out, gossip is particularly harmful because rumors of inchastity may ruin a woman's life. Moll herself is another story: "Perhaps for my mad going some reprove me; / I please myself, and care not else who love me" (V.i.360–1).

Moll's duel is prompted by the arrogant and sexist assumptions of Laxton, the gallant who, on making her acquaintance, attempts to buy sex from her. His apparent delicacy enables her to avoid the use of falsehood when she plans to teach him a lesson. He begs, "Let's meet," and Moll accedes: "'Tis hard but we shall meet, sir" (II.i.297–8). Laxton, however, expects to meet for purposes of fornication; Moll intends to meet for combat. Upon their meeting, Laxton does not recognize her; she is dressed as a man. Moll responds to his amazement with a promise: "I'll swear you did not [know me]; but you shall know me now" (III.i.57). Moll's triple pun plays on Laxton's continued failure to understand Moll's virtuous character. As she agrees that he has not recognized her, he understands her to mean that he shall gain carnal knowledge of her; in fact, her intention is to teach him more about what kind of person she is.[38]

When Moll offers to match Laxton's prostitute's fee in a wager as to who will win their combat, she also explains her intentions: "To teach thy base thoughts manners: thou'rt one of those / That thinks each woman thy fond flexible whore; / If she but cast a liberal eye upon thee" (III.i.72–4). In a lengthy speech, Moll strongly condemns men who assume that a friendly woman is a loose one; she criticizes men who make their reputations by telling other men about fictional conquests of real women. Equally, she condemns those who seduce virtuous women in financial straits, women who feel they cannot afford to deny their seducers. She challenges Laxton to justify his assumption that he could buy her favors and tells him, "In thee I defy all men, their worst hates / And their best flatteries" (III.i.93–4). In this play, in which the secondary plot depicts a war of merchant wives and gallants against merchant husbands, Moll's duel brings word and deed together. But though Moll threatens to "write so much / Upon thy breast, 'cause thou shalt bear't in mind ... I scorn to prostitute myself to a man," she does not actually do so (III.i.109–12). Instead, she uses the duel to teach Laxton a lesson *by means of* her conquest. On Laxton's submission, Moll threatens to kill him, forcing him to try various formulae to assuage her wrath:

"I do repent me; hold!" (III.i.117)
"I ask thee pardon." (III.i.121)
"I yield both purse and body." (III.i.122)
"Spare my life!" (III.i.125)

When Laxton begs for his life, taking Moll as seriously as he would a man, she treats him according to the code between gentlemen.[39] When he appeals to her mercy, on the other hand, she shows none. Moll's intention is to return Laxton to true dealing. Their combat, as she says, gives Laxton a "true" knowledge of her. Indeed, their fight is (for her, at least) a return to the truth, since she brings him to the duelling field through subterfuge.

Clara, the heroine of Beaumont and Fletcher's comedy *Love's Cure, or, The Martial Maid*, seems at first not to fit the paradigm of the woman who duels with a didactic purpose. Initially Clara approaches fighting with a masculine appetite for the sport; certainly, she gives it up reluctantly. Like Aspatia in *The Maid's Tragedy*, Clara actually proposes to enact the duel as a means of self-slaughter. But although these facts seem likely to subvert the challenge to the social order that modern readers may desire from cross-dressed characters, in fact *Love's Cure* subverts gender constructions of the period more effectively than even *The Roaring Girl*. In threatening the enactment of a duel, Clara forces on the men in the play a new perception of their roles as representatives of their families. Of the female duellists I discuss here, Clara is the figure whose action most clearly alters the community's understanding of gender. By bringing together *virtus* and *eros*, Clara suggests the possibility of a more flexible role for both sexes. Cross-dressed from childhood, Clara first appears as a Britomart figure who fights with her suitor rather than searching for him (as Britomart does). But Clara becomes most powerful when she exchanges her male clothing for skirts, uniting what the playwrights characterize as masculine force and feminine gentleness.

As the play begins, the noble Clara, raised as a boy in the Spanish camps of the Eighty Years' War, returns with her father, Don Alvarez, to their native Seville. Their presence completes the household of her mother Eugenia and her younger brother Lucio, who has been raised in Seville as a girl in order to protect him from the family's enemies. After a joyful reunion, the parents pledge to restore both children to a proper sense of gender. Comic complications occur when Clara falls in love with the family's enemy, Vitelli, a man both attracted and repelled by her skill at swordsmanship; her brother Lucio eventually becomes infatuated with this man's sister.

Although Don Alvarez and his elder child are discussed in the play's opening, they do not appear onstage until Scene iii. Clara's entrance at that point is clearly meant to disorient the audience. Wearing male attire, she is addressed by her father: "My loved Clara ... Lucio is a name thou must forget / With Lucio's bold behaviour" (I.iii.257–9).[40] While Clara has now resumed her female name, she has not yet returned to female clothing. A brawl with Vitelli breaks out before Don Alvarez and his wife have exchanged more than a few words, and Clara and her father both draw their swords to fight. Only when the victory is won does Don Alvarez have the opportunity to present this swordsman to his wife. He urges Eugenia, "to increase thy comfort, know, this young man ... / Is not what he appears, but such a one / As thou with joy wilt bless—thy daughter Clara" (I.iii.395–8). Perplexity among audience members would be understandable, to say the least.

Clara causes gender confusion entirely different from that of cross-dressed figures such as Middleton and Dekker's Moll Cutpurse. Although Moll is described as a monster, she is supposed to be easily recognized as a female character.[41] Moll fashionably combines men's and women's clothing (like the women at whom *Hic Mulier* is aimed). Clara's disguise is meant to be complete: she effectively impersonates a man. Unlike Moll, Clara has no wish to confuse others by dressing or acting anomalously; with her father's endorsement, she has dressed and acted as a man for sixteen years. Clara accepts the ideology that keeps the sexes separate; she simply wants to continue passing as a man. As the action moves inevitably toward a showdown between Vitelli and a member of the Alvarez family, the play pointedly asks how Clara can return to a womanly self-presentation and still continue to defend her family.

Clara's initial problem with womanhood becomes apparent only gradually: a man's social rank, his bearing and standing in the world, are much more fluid than that of his female counterpart. Raised as a male in a battlecamp, Clara has become a soldier. Despite her one impassioned speech about gentlemen's honor, Clara comprehends her masculine role in a way that was becoming increasingly outdated in Jacobean society.[42] She is bluff, outspoken, distrustful of courtiers, and constantly mindful of the battlefield. Her behavior makes her a fine companion among men, but fits her for no corresponding female role. When she reverts to women's costume, she also must learn to behave appropriately to her rank. Born not only a woman but a *lady,* she finds that her soldierly habits translate to a lack of gentility when she aspires to womanhood.

Clara's love for Vitelli enables her to find an appropriate mode of behavior. The use of Petrarchan rhetoric throughout the play serves as an index to the changing merits of *eros* and *virtus*. When Vitelli anticipates the return of Alvarez and his child, he imagines his hatred of the family as a hawk that slept while no male Alvarez lived in Seville:

> But now, since there are quarries worth her sight…
> I'll boldly cast her off, and gorge her full
> With both their hearts. (I.i.124–7)

The image mimics the Petrarchan trope of love's quarry. Vitelli literalizes the trope of love as pursuit, turning it into a literal hunt with the intent to wound or kill. The imagery is undercut by parody in the next scene, which opens with Lucio's concern for his mother's poultry. Yet the violence of Vitelli's appetites cannot be tamed by Lucio's domesticity; in this society, male and female are polarized to such dangerous extremes that Clara and Lucio may be recognized early on as *pharmakoi* that cure the community. The danger is evident in the pleasure that the servant Bobadilla takes in threatening the girlish Lucio with his Toledo blade: "If he were a wench now, as he seems, what an advantage had I, drawing two toledos" (I.ii.174–5). Lucio's feminine helplessness provokes both sadistic *and* erotic impulses. In this play, violence and sex are conjoined in the masculine sphere and need tempering by the feminine.

Clara eventually develops a playful Petrarchism that metaphorizes her former life on the field of battle, and she consciously develops both feminine rhetorical skill and a new concept of honor. But at first she also literalizes Petrarchan tropes, though she regards *eros* as a weakness, something to be treated with contempt. Her evident satisfaction at being the inflicter of wounds is comical, especially when her too literal account of her experiences causes Lucio to remonstrate at her language:

> *Clara*: [W]ith that [sword], and this well-mounted, skirred
> A horse troop through and through, like swift desire,
> And seen poor rogues retire all gore, and gashed
> Like bleeding shads.
> *Lucio*:   Bless us, sister Clara.
> How desperately you talk. (II.ii.751–5)

Clara conceives of herself as being as speedy and overpowering as desire, love's arrow. She effeminizes the enemy, gashing them open to bleed like fish on a hook. Lucio, already feminized, finds these images frightening: they suggest men with a lack, an absence—their power gone.

When Clara first enters, her expressions of discomfort at court manner seem to echo those of Shakespeare's Hotspur. Here are Clara's opening words:

> I had rather meet ten enemies in the field,
> All sworn to fetch my head, than be brought on
> To change an hour's discourse with one of these
> Smooth city fools or tissue cavaliers. (I.iii.251–4)

Hers seems the contempt of the old military aristocrat for the new man, like bluff Lord Willoughby's unease with the more socially adept courtiers of Elizabeth's court. Alvarez's response indicates the problem that will result: "My loved Clara ... though thy breeding / I' the camp may plead something in the excuse / Of thy rough manners, custom having changed, / Though not thy sex, the softness of thy nature ... / Yet now [Fortune] smiles" (I.iii.257–67). Though a gentleman may behave boldly, harshly, even roughly without impropriety, a woman who does so is judged unwomanly, and in so doing she loses caste.[43]

Social rank is the unspoken concern of the play. Alvarez's wife is named Eugenia, from the Greek words meaning "well-born"; Bobadilla rejoices that the homecoming that restores Lucio's original gender raises him, Bobadilla, to the higher rank of steward. Before Vitelli's sister, Genevora, is introduced, the young woman who serves as an implicit contrast to Clara is Malroda, Vitelli's mistress, whom Vitelli seduced when she was his mother's waiting-woman. Malroda repeatedly charges Vitelli with having taken not her virginity but her respectability. Although the axis of gender is foregrounded, rank inflects the various representations of gender.

When Clara is still dressed in masculine garb, she shows a confident understanding of social codes. Explaining to her astonished father and his friend why she must fight on Vitelli's side if he is outnumbered, she thinks as a man and a warrior. "Are you men?" she asks. Manhood and honor are synonymous to her, as she has been taught, and she appeals to her teachers to remember their code. She makes an organized, eloquent plea for more appropriate behavior, making outlandish suppositions about her father's motives to demonstrate his lack of a valid warrant for his actions. But as a woman Clara acts in ways that consistently misplace her on the scale of social rank. Dressed in women's attire, she hums a martial air, casually proposes to fence with her brother, complains of her confining skirts, and permits without reproof Bobadilla's crude joke about women's buttocks. When Bobadilla echoes her disdain for overly formal courtiers, we must acknowledge that her socialization seems more in keeping with that of her servant than with her own standing as a gentlewoman. When she loses her temper with Bobadilla, she addresses him as "You dogskin-faced rogue, pilcher, you poor John, / Which I will beat to stockfish" (II.ii.732–3). These piscatory terms of opprobrium are common in Shakespeare's scenes of servant- and tavern-life. Compare them to Malroda's entirely womanly and high-styled rage:

> Leave your betraying smiles,
> And change the tunes of your inticing tongue
> To penitential prayers; for I am great
> In labour even with anger, big with child
> Of woman's rage, bigger than when my womb
> Was pregnant by thee. (III.iii.1161–6)

Malroda's anger, like Clara's, manifests a clear sense of gendered power relations, but her choice of words shows her drawing on a source of woman's strength—the womb—to convey with dignity her elemental anger at the inequity of their positions. Clara's language, in contrast, is ridiculous without her possession of the phallus (represented by the sword) that is implicitly compared with a lack on the part of the addressee (represented by fishiness, which in slang terms frequently represents the vagina). Malroda rails in a way appropriate to a lady of high rank; Clara, in a way common to men who own nothing beyond the power of the phallus. The contrast indicates that Clara needs not a phallus, but a better understanding of linguistic codes.

When Clara falls in love, she recognizes intuitively that she must play a game both like and unlike that of war: "I begin to find / I am a woman, and must learn to fight / A softer, sweeter battle, than with swords" (II.ii.875–7). Vitelli first responds to Clara's swordsmanship with admiration for her as a woman: "Oh you the fairest soldier I e'er saw; / Each of whose eyes, like a bright beamy shield / Conquers without blows, the contentious" (II.ii.801–3). As Malroda later explains, Vitelli is an experienced seducer. Clara can hardly win him with threats of force; yet her rhetorical power is insufficient to sway him from his intention to kill her male relatives. Ruefully, Vitelli warns her of his intentions: "[H]e, whose tongue thus gratifies the daughter / And sister of his enemy, wears a sword / To rip the father and the brother up" (II.ii.814–16). Clara refuses the traditional women's role to which he would assign her; when he begs for a token to remember her by, she urges their triviality:

> *Vitelli*: A ribbon or a glove.
> *Clara*: Nay, those are tokens for a waiting maid
>   To trim the butler with.
> *Vitelli*: Your feather.
> *Clara*: Fie; the wenches give them to their serving men. (2.2.839–42)

Clara's gift refigures both Vitelli's Petrarchan rhetoric and his urges to phallic violence. She gives him her much-prized sword, urging him to recognize the implications of receiving this gift as a love-token:

> Oh, this favour I bequeath you, which I tie
> In a love-knot, fast, ne'er to hurt my friends;
> Yet be it fortunate 'gainst all your foes…
> As e'er it was to me. I have kept it long,
> And value it, next my virginity. (2.2.860–5)

When Clara realizes what gift would be appropriate, she speaks lovingly but with authority; at this point she combines and redefines *eros* and *virtus,* using Vitelli's desire for a favor to bridge the gulf between them. Rather than hoping to overcome his wish for vengeance with physical or rhetorical force, she takes the opportunity to set up a counter-custom with meanings that must reverse his plan to murder her father. This initial maneuver is successful. Vitelli responds, "I'll not infringe an article of breath / My vow has offered to ye" (II.ii.870–1).

In giving Vitelli her sword, Clara both literally and symbolically divests herself of violence and phallic power. Handing over her manhood to Vitelli, Clara transforms it from a killing weapon to a love-token, forcing Vitelli to redefine what he may do as a man if he wants to enact the role of lover. From this point, Clara moves steadily toward revising less the notion of femininity (as she has before) than the notion of masculinity. In so doing, she satisfies society by conforming to accepted notions of womanhood; at the same time, she weakens the link between violence and masculinity derived from the military elite culture of late medieval feudalism.

When Clara and Vitelli next meet, Clara has just witnessed the attempted robbery of Vitelli by Malroda and Malroda's new lover. After chasing them away, Clara speaks with consummate tact: she apologizes "[f]or pressing thus beyond a virgin's bounds / Upon [his] privacies" (IV.ii.1559–60). This done, the two frankly negotiate the question of marriage. Vitelli explains his fear of being mastered by Clara, at which point she gives up more than her sword:

> from this hour
> I here abjure all actions of a man,
> And will esteem it happiness from you
> To suffer like a woman. ...
> I will show strength in nothing but my duty
> And glad desire to please you. (IV.ii.1587–95)

With her pledge of subordination, Vitelli capitulates as well, whimsically sealing their vows with a kiss and a comment on Clara's hermaphroditic qualities: "Madam, though you have / A soldier's arm, your lips appear as if / They were a lady's" (IV.ii.1601–3).

Clara's capitulation may seem to modern readers an unnecessary lowering of herself. But if we accept the play's presentation of Vitelli as inherently desirable, we must recognize why Clara must renounce her martial skills and masculine ways.[44] Clara unsettles Vitelli's gender assumptions but cannot entirely overturn them. When Malroda loses her temper, curses Vitelli, and threatens to pistol him, he shows none of the admiration that he had for Clara's swordsmanship. Instead, he threatens to have her placed in a house for Magdalens and warns her that his willingness to maintain her financially depends on her docility: "I ne'er promised you marriage, nor have vowed, / But said I loved you, long as you remained / The woman I expected, or you swore, / And how you have failed of that, sweetheart, you know" (III.iii.1226–9). Vitelli places Malroda in a double-bind: he has promised to love her only so long as she remains subordinate to his wishes. For her to complain of his treatment, even with just cause, is to break her bond and forfeit his regard. According to his definition, she has no recourse at all in case of ill-treatment. Although she may make some headway with the grandeur of her angry speech, any threat of real violence from her is unacceptable. Clara is potentially much more dangerous: Malroda's threat of physical violence is laughable, whereas Clara could indeed carry out some violent act. Although Clara's charm for Vitelli is in her Amazonian quality, her hermaphroditic blending of masculine and feminine, he fears to take on any role toward her but that of conquering Theseus.

Even after her new vow, however, Clara never perceives herself as a subjugated warrior. Aware that love is a "softer, sweeter battle" than war, she works within her self-imposed constraints to master Vitelli without resorting to the superior swordsmanship that would shame him to acknowledge. The play comes to a climax with the showdown between the noble houses of Alvarez and Vitelli. Now an enemy to bloodshed, Clara must dissuade her father, brother, and lover from killing one another. When the king's proclamation authorizes a duel to settle the two families' feud for good, Clara develops a strategy that seeks to redefine manhood and honor. In this plan, Clara is aided by Genevora, Vitelli's sister, whose traditional femininity has inspired Clara's effeminate brother to discover traditionally masculine traits within himself.

Simon Shepherd has argued that, in contrast to Clara's more serious problems, "Lucio's training into manhood is comic and grotesque" (88). This is, I think, untrue. As Clara has been the avatar of manhood at the play's opening, Lucio assumes that mantle by the play's end. The representation of his initial feminine manner is, indeed, comic; there is no suggestion that his behavior manifests "positive civilized virtues," as Jonathan Dollimore suggests (73).

Lucio's experience of lust aids him in the understanding and development of a sense of masculinity: "My poor womanish soul, which hitherto hath governed / This coward flesh, I feel departing from me; / And in me by [Genevora's] beauty is inspired / A new and masculine one, instructing me / What's fit to do or suffer" (IV.iv.1798–1802). The result is that he, not Clara, fights a duel.

He seeks out Lamorall, his rival, who has threatened him and taken Genevora's glove from him, and challenges him for possession of it. In the process of the duel, he also wins Lamorall's sword, so symbolic of manhood that Lamorall begs him to take his life as well. In response, Lucio offers his own sword as a token of friendship. He takes only the favor in sign of victory, asking merely to be regarded as an equal.

Genevora's influence over Lucio's masculinity is most salutary in its effect on his understanding of honor. After winning the duel, Lucio condemns the widespread custom of publicly proclaiming his own victory: "I have no tongue to trumpet mine own praise / To your dishonour: 'tis a bastard courage / That seeks a name out that way, no true born one" (V.i.1888–90). The trope of true-born versus bastard courage recalls Clara's earlier differentiation between lawful honor won in war and bastard honor won in mortal combat on the street. By promising not to publicize his own triumph, Lucio trumps Lamorall a second time. His decision creates a new definition of manhood that places private merit above reputation. In doing so, he redefines masculinity according to the model of provided by *The Courtiers Academie* rather than according to the old military ideal. This very consonance with the courtly ideal, however, could be read as a masculine mode already modified by feminine values because of its devaluation of public opinion. But whatever the significance of these new ideals, they are vanquished as soon as Lucio's father acknowledges him and suggests that they stand together in a public duel. Family allegiance gains priority over newer conceptions of masculine honor.

The protocols of the duel are, surprisingly, viewed as negative by most of Alvarez's former comrades-in-arms. His friend Sayavedra perceives the legal duel as lowering men to the level of beasts; he calls it "[b]eyond the bounds of Christianity" (V.iii.2046). Clara, too, regards this practice as more bloodthirsty than honorable.

Clara's initial address to the men relocates the issue of social construction by applying it to the tradition of the duel. Who better than Clara can recognize that social practice does not offer universal rules? She urges that if she could discard the male clothing she had grown accustomed to, then Vitelli too could overcome the urgings of custom and lay aside his vendetta for her sake. Arguing that "[c]ustom, that wrought so cunningly on nature / In me, that I forgot my sex... you did unweave" (V.iii.2097–100), she reaches the conclusions of the witty pamphlet character Hic Mulier, who said that "[c]ustom is an idiot." Reinforcing Clara's argument, Genevora attempts to recast valor as moral courage: "he is most valiant / That herein yields first"

(V.iii.2148–9). Clara recalls Vitelli's oath to return her sword to her when she requests it; she asks for it now. Each maiden, finally, calls on Fortune to punish her brother for being untrue to vows to his beloved; they urgently pray for their brothers' deaths and their lovers' survival. To no avail: the men stand firm in their decision to duel.

Finally, the assistant asks, "Are you men or stone?," to which Alvarez replies, "Men, and we'll prove it with our swords" (V.iii.2179–80). Men, as opposed to stones, have feelings, may respond to reason, and may answer appeals. What aspect of manhood does Alvarez plan to prove? Swordsmanship proves the capacity of men to inflict pain, to conquer, to subdue others.

To alter the course of events, the *women* must subordinate their menfolk. Yet the method must avoid brute force, despite the fact that Clara may be the best swordsman of either family. Were she physically to subdue the men, she would inspire such unease in Vitelli that she might lose his affections. Her solution must conquer the men without resorting to physical means.

Following Clara's plan, Genevora resorts to their final strategy: she promises, "The first blow given betwixt you, sheathes these swords / In one another's bosoms" (V.iii.2184–5). The two women stand poised, each with a rapier pointed at the other. This tableau stops the proceedings short. Dollimore asserts that the strategy succeeds because it short-circuits the homosocial uses that the men have been making of the women:

> the currents of sexuality and violence, circulating between the men and sustaining sexual difference between male and female, are suddenly switched off. ... If [the women] die the most necessary spectators and objects of masculine performance disappear. Also ... men become redundant as the women threaten to perform phallic violence on themselves in order to forestall male violence. (74)

I offer a different interpretation: far from making men redundant, the women's pledge to kill one another holds up to the men a mirror of their senseless violence, showing its failure to make good on several of the premises underlying it. First, the men's decision to fight has been based on the assumption that the duel will bring honor to the winners and shame to the losers. In contrast, the women's suicide pact promises that both parties will die, thereby transforming "loss" into honorable martyrdom. Yet the pointlessness of the pact makes it monstrous, just as the pointlessness of the duel makes it barbaric. In forming the pact, the women also criticize the men's desire for honor, recalling Lucio's comment two scenes earlier that " 'tis a bastard courage / That seeks a name out that way" (V.i.1889–90). Moreover, the women's pact undermines the notion that the men can prove their manhood through enacting the duel. As the women demonstrate, the willingness to risk death is not an exclusively male prerogative. If women too die in "combat," how can that combat define or indicate one's masculinity?

Finally, the women's pledge reminds the men of the aspect of honor that they have neglected: protection of the family. Their strategy places the men in a domestic rather than a public context and redefines manhood as a regard for one's relatives. If Vitelli causes his sister's death in order to avenge his uncle, what has he gained? The proof of manhood is rooted in defense of the family, on which this vendetta and the proposed duel are based. If the duel results in the destruction of the family, then it no longer serves its intended purpose. Once the family refuses to be defended on these terms, the men must discard the concept of honor that has compelled them to ignore reason, break promises, and disregard the appeals of those they love best. Although the women's gesture may be called masochistic in that they promise to turn their violence upon themselves rather than on their men, the gesture is never put to the test. It remains rhetorical, a manipulative device whose certain success means that they will never have to perform what they have pledged. After considering their options, the menfolk give up the combat and own themselves beaten by people more resolute than themselves. In Alvarez's words, "These devilish women / Can make men friends and enemies when they list" (V.iii.2191–2). Clara's strategy has succeeded, and *eros* has been wedded to *virtus* at last.

In all but one of the plays I have discussed, the female duellist instructs her antagonist by offering to become his opponent. From our vantage point, of course, the opponent is generally a representative of the larger system to which these women are responding—and this reading may not be anachronistic. Because of its ritual qualities, the duel could never serve merely as a fight on formal terms. It always bore some larger significance, offering a subtle commentary on the character of those who engaged in it. Significantly, the play that purports to be a defense of women, *Swetnam, the Woman-hater*, twice breaks down in that project at crucial points in the action. In contrast, plays with a less overt agenda seem consistently to present a different picture of fighting women. Having acknowledged these plays' implications about gender, we may recognize that these dramas offer new insight into the meaning of the duel as well. As I said in opening the chapter, intention *does* matter: if enacted for benevolent purposes, the duel ceases to serve as a sign of masculinity. For us, indeed, it may signify the existence during the early modern period of a slightly less restricted view of woman's role. By their very lack of innovation in their portrayal of women, these plays restructure the negative portrayal of gender fluidity found in *Hic Mulier* and *Haec Vir,* and in doing so they offer an alternative to the extreme polarization of the sexes evident in those and many other popular documents of the period. But they also indicate that the duel was so closely bound up with masculine self-assertion that a duel lacking this element was scarcely a duel at all. The duel, was, of course, a symbolic act—a speech-act in reverse, as I have said. If the cultural meaning of the duel was altered, so was the relationship between duelling and masculinity. Lacking the element that brought the two together, the duel was much less subversive of institutional order. It was a practice *almost* fit for women—so long as it gained for them none of the prerogatives that men hoped to gain when *they* engaged in the practice.

Conclusion

I began this book with Thomas Greene's explanation of the potential that humanists saw in self-fashioning: "the surpassing of natural human limitations, undoing the constraints of the incomplete, the contingent, and the mortal" (250). Though humanism and the courtly ethos were opposed in significant ways, it is clear that elements of the one leaked into the other, giving new meaning to fairly traditional forms of ritual violence.[1] What is fascinating about the literary and cultural phenomenon of the early modern duel is that a *practice*, rather than study, application, thought, or conversation, should be perceived as possessing transformative potential. I have, for the most part, avoided discussion of the ritualistic aspect of the duel, but its power in some contexts clearly approaches the magical: by enacting this ritual, one can ascertain the truth of a specific matter. For our purposes, however, the ritualistic transformation that the duel offers the participants rather than the community may be more significant. This aspect of the duel may be best conceived today in terms of cultural acquisition rather than magic—as one of the "normative criteria for elite identity" that Frank Whigham discusses (33). Whigham asserts that "the ostentatious practice of symbolic behavior [is] taken to typify aristocratic being. The gentleman is presumed to act in certain ways; the limiting case would have it that only a gentleman *can* act in those ways" (33). To some early modern subjects, the duel represented aristocratic bearing; to others, a masculine bearing; and to some, the opportunity to gain both.

Although the literary texts in this study range from plays in which the ideology of heroism reigns unchallenged to others in which different values take priority, I do not claim a "development" from one mind-set to another. Manhood and masculinity were complex phenomena, and even the most dominant ideas about them could not achieve hegemony. Instead, manhood was understood in complex ways and along several different axes. Masculinity could be represented by any of the following dualities: gentlemanliness as opposed to commonness, manliness as opposed to womanliness, maturity as opposed to boyishness, family representation as opposed to unaffiliated individualism, or victory as opposed to failure. It could be defined in spatial terms, social terms, or developmental terms—and most of these bore some relation to violence. Masculinity was not a monolithic concept. It functioned differently even for the same people in different contexts. If it has a single element, it is its association with the conquest of others; if a single social relation, its need for a second person to oppose and to define it relationally. Although the early modern English understanding of manhood is not illusory, it could not exist without a variety of antonymic constructions that defined its position.

The construction of the heroic mode of masculinity exemplifies the recent critical tenet that literature may affect the culture just as the culture does literature. As custom and the romance narrative combined to create the courtly ethos, the Renaissance construction of aristocratic masculinity drew on literary as well as historical antecedents. The duel, as an aspect of this construction, gave men a way of asserting their elite status by linking essentially transgressive violence with more culturally acceptable forms. The actual practice of the duel was shaped in part by the texts that provided early modern Englishmen with models of manhood; in turn, those real-life duels provided Renaissance playwrights with fertile material for satirical treatment, valorization, and further exploration of what exactly it meant to be a man in the rapidly changing social world of early modern England.

Notes

Introduction

1. Fencing-masters wrote manuals about their trade, often with sections discussing the ethics or mechanics of the duel itself. Clergymen and others wrote anti-duelling pamphlets; the subject was mentioned in the ubiquitous books of honor written or translated by such prominent figures as William Segar and John Kepers. Duels were mentioned in the popular character books of the day, and playwrights frequently used the challenge or the ritual of the duel as a dramatic device.
2. The relation between humanism and violence has long been debated by scholars; critics as old as Robert P. Adams (*The Better Part of Valor: More, Erasmus, Colet, and Vives on Humanism, War, and Peace 1496–1535*, 1962) and as new as Robin Headlam Wells (*Shakespeare on Masculinity*, 2000) have argued that the humanistic tradition is specifically anti-militaristic. But while such writers as More and Erasmus responded negatively to the medieval culture of violence, their pacifism must not prevent us from acknowledging the support of bellicosity evident, for example, in the educational philosophies that they and their fellow-humanists developed. In Book I of *The Governor* (1531), Elyot frequently refers positively to the development of courage in pupils as one of education's goals (Ong 117). Ong points out that, influenced by those who employed private tutors, Renaissance education often linked the period's cult of glory with the epic poem,

   > together with the typical Renaissance view that such a poem is the highest creation of the human mind.... By the same token there develops, under the concurrent influence of Plato's *Republic*, a keen interest in courage ... as an express objective in the education of boys. (Ong 113–14)

   As Hans Baron points out, the Florentine humanists developed a concept of education that involved training men for citizenship, for involvement in the community and its affairs (I:13). After 1400, many humanists such as Leonardo Bruni began to defend the emotion of anger (Baron I:29–30). Baron mentions Matteo Palmieri as well as

Cristoforo Landino, who wrote in *De Vera Nobilitate* "that nature puts the emotion of anger into the soul of brave men not in order to shut out the light of reason but to serve the growth of bravery" (I:30). The desire for glory is also mentioned specifically by such figures as Francesco da Fiano, a curial humanist who argued that we would not possess the great writings of the Church Fathers if the authors "'had not been fired by ardent longing for praise and glory among men'" (*Contra oblocutores et detractores poetarum,* qtd. in Baron I:31). *The Courtier,* too, is far from anti-militaristic, presenting performance in war as one of many measures of the good courtier.

The humanist tradition is significant in a larger context because its influence pervaded society, and because humanist ideals affected broad areas of thinking. As Ruth Kelso points out, the ideals of the Italian humanists were "grafted onto the soldier ideal" (*Gentleman* 116). I do not suggest that most English humanists supported the duel (though they often characterized their debates as verbal duels) but that strong and evident elements of humanistic ideals contributed to the mentality that helped to popularize the practice of duelling.

3. G. F. is far from unique in making use of Michael's character as a militarist. In *The Blazon of Gentrie* (1586), John Ferne asserts that

> knighthood (if you will beleve me) is more ancient than lawes: yea then the laws of nature, written in the hart of the first man: for *Michael* an archangel, the first Knight, and now the patrone of that order, was provost and general, in the army of those holy spirits, that fought against *Lucifer* and his adherents. (35–6)

4. Ruth Kelso asserts, in fact, that "the whole theory of the law of honor and the duel is a part of the individualistic tendencies of the renaissance" (*Gentleman* 104).
5. Knighthood, initially defined by military obligation to the Crown, became defined by the amount of one's annual estate revenues (Stone, *CA* 71; T. Smith 43). At the same time, the financial holdings of peers fell overall by about 25 percent between 1558 and 1602. At the end of that period, significantly fewer older families held a great deal of land (Stone, *CA* 156–7). In fact, there was more movement up and down the social ladder for men of rank at this time than in any preceding period.

The legal power of the aristocracy was diminishing over time as well. The Acts of Henry VII had asserted "that the prime loyalty of every subject was to the Crown, and only secondly to his 'good lord'" (Stone, *CA* 202). The Crown strove to impose and enforce laws that applied even to the nobility. According to Stone, sovereigns purposely reduced the power of the peerage by permitting individual peers to engage themselves in a net of debts and, in addition, noblemen became dependent on the sovereign for advancement in the form of gifts, offices, and honors (*CA* 268).

By the end of the sixteenth century, the Tudors had substantially reduced the number of "great" (and influential) landholding families in England (Stone, *CA* 263–4, 269). By the time of the English Revolution, having local influence had become less important than having the support of the crown. Correspondingly, the influence of the nobility on their tenants and neighboring gentry decreased because so many members of the aristocracy had begun to spend substantial amounts of time at court or in London. The aristocracy was forced to submit to the laws of the sovereign and the mores of the court. With these changes, even the more established aristocracy evinced anxiety about how to redefine the social roles of aristocrat and gentleman.

6. See Sydney Anglo's excellent book on monarchic uses of pageantry, *Spectacle, Pageantry, and Early Tudor Policy* (Oxford: Clarendon, 1969).
7. Frank Whigham's book *Ambition and Privilege: The Social Tropes of Elizabethan Courtesy Theory*, on courtesy theory and conduct books, deals extensively with issues of social rank but avoids almost any discussion of drama or gender issues.
8. Recent scholars, among them Jonas Barish, Stephen Orgel, and Laura Levine, have foregrounded certain assumptions and broadened the significance of London theatrical practice by examining the arguments of antitheatricalists for indications of gender assumptions. Orgel's discussion of transvestite theater also includes a summary of Maclean's and Laqueur's work on medical treatises, which suggest that "the line between the sexes was blurred, often frighteningly so" (Orgel, "Nobody's Perfect" 13). Basing his argument on dramas and philosophical tracts, Orgel asserts that

> the love of women threatens the integrity of the perilously achieved male identity. The fear of effeminization is a central element in all discussions of what constitutes a "real man" in the period, and the fantasy of the reversal of the natural transition from woman to man underlies it. ("Nobody's Perfect" 14–15)

While these readings of the culture agree on the perceived danger of putting on the clothes of the opposite sex, they disagree as to what exactly it is that cross-dressing threatens. Jonas Barish suggests that there was some notion of essential identity, of which clothing was perceived as a part. In contrast, Laura Levine suggests that notions of gender were based on behaviors that needed constant reenactment in order to erase cultural anxieties about the potential slippage of such constructs. The evidence is mixed, as summarized by Gail Kern Paster in the opening of her book *The Body Embarrassed: Drama and the Disciplines of Shame in Early Modern England* (1–22). If we, like Orgel, accept the existence of eccentric or pathological views ("Nobody's Perfect" 17), we ought, perhaps, to acknowledge that there may not be a central view of gender, that the cultural viewpoint on this subject is fractured rather than monolithic.

9. Discussing Merleau-Ponty's assertion that a body is both an historical idea and a set of possibilities, Butler explains,

> In claiming that the body is an historical idea, Merleau-Ponty means that it gains its meaning through a concrete and historically mediated expression in the world. That the body is a set of possibilities signifies... that its appearance in the world, for perception, is not predetermined by some manner of interior essence.... These possibilities are necessarily constrained by available historical conventions. ("Performing Feminisms" 272)

This approach, as she herself says, "seeks to explain the mundane way in which social agents *constitute* social reality through language, gesture, and all manner of symbolic social sign" ("Performing Feminisms" 270). When Butler refers to performativity, she is in fact drawing upon a centuries-old tradition whose assumptions surface in texts like *Duell-Ease*.

10. Such historians as Norbert Elias, *The History of Manners* (1939) and Philippe Aries and Georges Duby, eds., *A History of Private Life*, Vol. 3, *Passions of the Renaissance*, as well as such theorists as Mikhail Bakhtin, *Rabelais and His World*, and Mary Douglas, *Natural Symbols: Explorations in Cosmology*, have brought us to a consideration of the body as such. Other critics and theorists such as Francis Barker, Peter Stallybrass, and Elaine Scarry have treated the body with what I consider a greater degree of abstraction and less particularity about physical, fleshly attributes.

11. As Sydney Anglo points out, the lists of professions and psychological types delineated in such books as Overbury's *Characters* can reveal how far the change had gone: none of the character books in the seventeenth century present a knight as Llull or, even, as the romances of the late medieval period would have done (*Chivalry in the Renaissance* xii).

12. Those who expected to fight with the sword wore armor if they could (some countries forbade the use of armor in the case of trial by combat [Neilson]). Fighters usually alternated a blow with a posture of defense, usually in counterpoint to their opponent. Such combats were extremely tiring, especially in full armor; as Turner and Soper explain, "true heavy swordfights quickly wound down, leaving two gasping, straining knights attempting desperate single blows" (109). The combatant with the greatest strength and endurance generally won.

13. Sieveking 391; Turner and Soper 10.

14. One hand only is needed to hold the weapon, while the other may ward off blows or hold a dagger; the thrust is emphasized, by some teachers almost to the exclusion of the slashing blow.

Chapter 1   The Duellist as Hero

1. Saviolo's book actually has a chapter entitled "Whether the subjecte ought to obey his Soveraigne, being by him forbidden to Combat." The answer: if obedience would violate the subject's honor, then engage in the duel even at the cost of disobeying the monarch.
2. Lea comments that when Irish Celts were first described in histories, their customs included the judicial duel, complete with fixed regulations. In this he cites Senchus Mor, a code claimed to have been compiled under the supervision of Saint Patrick (Lea 109). Trial by combat is mentioned in the law codes of many early Germanic peoples (Bartlett 103; Bryson, *Italian Duel* xii); in fact, it appears in the Germanic revisions of Salic law, put into their final form by Dagobert I in 630 (Lea 112–3).
3. See Bartlett 104 and Kiernan 33.
4. According to the Ancient Laws of England (i. 489), "an Englishman accused by a Norman of perjury, murder, homicide, or open robbery could defend himself as he preferred—by the ordeal of carrying the hot iron [trial by ordeal] or by the duel [trial by combat]" (Neilson 31). Normans had the same option, but while "an accused Englishman who [would] not fight [had to] go to the ordeal," if a Norman was accused by an Englishman who would not fight, the Norman could clear himself by oath (Neilson 32).
5. See Neilson 36, Lea 146, Bartlett 108.
6. According to Lea, "It was an appeal to the highest court.... Enlightened law-givers... were also disposed to regard the duel with favor as the most practical remedy for the crime of false swearing which was everywhere prevalent" (117–18).
7. For a detailed discussion of how the judicial duel functions in *Richard II* and *1 Henry IV*, see my article "'Those Proud Titles Thou Hast Won': Sovereignty, Power, and Combat in Shakespeare's Second Tetralogy," in *Comparative Drama* 34.3 (2000): 269–90.
8. One could argue that the convergence of violence and the law in trial by combat exposed the extent to which government institutions depended on force and custom to impose laws on a submissive majority. But the increasingly elaborate ceremonies that aligned this secular ritual with ecclesiastical ones mystified the connection between law and *puissance*.
9. Certain groups were legally or culturally prohibited from combat; members of these groups—usually women and ecclesiastics—hired a champion to fight for them in the case of a judicial duel. Cf. Bartlett's discussion of these matters (112).
10. See Keen 16 and Ferguson, *The Chivalric Tradition* 142–3 for a fuller discussion of the chivalric tradition. Jousts were typically "set-piece encounters between pairs of opponents, coming forward *seriatim* from opposite ends of the lists, and charging one another before the spectators" (Keen 87).

When a spectacle was physically bounded, as the joust was by the lists, it was easier to observe and, hence, probably, more entertaining for spectators than the freely ranging tournament. Critics today believe that the popularity of the judicial duel may have aided the joust's rise in popularity over the *melée*. The physical boundaries also helped to set off the joust as play, distinguishing it from purposeful aggression. Huizinga asserts that

> All play moves and has its being within a playground marked off beforehand either materially or ideally, deliberately or as a matter of course. Just as there is no formal difference between play and ritual, so the "consecrated spot" cannot be formally distinguished from the play-ground.... temporary worlds within the ordinary world, dedicated to the performance of an act apart. (10)

11. See also Kiernan 37–43 on the social needs served by the violence of the tournament and the joust in medieval Europe.
12. The Tudors often used ceremonies celebrating royal births, royal marriages, coronations, and military victories consciously to "establish and consolidate the Tudor dynasty" (Bornstein 110). Their festive ceremonies often involved tournaments.
13. See McCoy and Billacois for a discussion of these issues.
14. During the Tudor era, the joust developed into several forms: the tilt, a charge on horseback with spears; the barriers, a combat on foot with swords; and the extremely elaborate *pas d'armes*, a stylized recreation of a classic military scenario in which one or two men hold a narrow area (the "pass") against all comers (Wickham I:17). Many tournaments involved a loose dramatic narrative like that of the masque; the loosely structured story offered an explanation for the jousts or the *pas d'armes* that remained the central part of the entertainment.

    In the *Pas d'Armes de la Sauvaige Dame*, for example, Claude de Vaudray enacted the role of "Le Compaignon de la Joyeuse Queste," a knight who, after a duel in a strange country, is saved by a hermit and a native wild woman. After the pair have nursed him back to health, the knight offers, in gratitude, to perform some feat of arms for the lady. This feat is the *pas d'armes* combat, which de Vaudray performed. The story was presented first by a proclamation, which told the first part of the tale; a procession in which all the characters appear, emerging from an artificial mountain; and the combat itself in which the knight defended the mountain, which served as the *pas* (Wickham I:24–5; I:42–3). The Accession Day tilts of Elizabeth's reign became opportunities for the Queen's favorites to compliment her or to beg for the continuation of her goodwill. For example, the Accession Day tournament of 1582 featured the allegorical pageant of the Four Foster Children of Desire (Sidney, Fulke Greville, Lord Windsor, and the Earl of Arundel), who laid siege to the Fortresse of Perfect Beautie, which was the queen's balcony overlooking the tiltyard.

The stage-designs of the tilts also resembled that of the masque, using elaborate chariots and stage-pieces something like parade floats. Writers were employed to write parts of the tournaments, just as they were for masques. George Peele wrote the verses for a tilt in 1590; Jonson provided speeches for "A Challenge at Tilt" in 1613; Shakespeare and Burbage collaborated on creating an impresa for the Duke of Rutland (Wickham II:i:230–1). As poorer youths were squeezed out of the competition altogether, artifice and invention were prized on a par with valor.

15. Diane Bornstein cites the courtesy books of the period as indications of the importance of ritual to life at court (83).
16. See also Bornstein 125.
17. Paraphrasing Muzio and Piccolomini, authors of Italian fencing manuals, Ruth Kelso explains,

    The better sort fought from the desire for honor, and the fear of dishonor.... The worst sort fought from contempt of others and desire not to have a superior in anything, as Piccolomini analyzed it, which is after all only a perverted notion of what honor consists in. (*Gentleman* 101)

18. See Saviolo's condemnation of cowards (V2v) in ironical contrast to Marozzo's comment that few knights act in accordance with their professed assertion that they would rather die with honor than live with shame (123v, cited in Bryson, *The Point of Honor* 13).
19. The joust was sportive in its very disinterestedness: while personal hostilities might be carried onto the tilting field, the combat was traditionally enacted for the love of the glory that could be won. (It seems only fair, however, to offer Huizinga's view that the participants in any ritual take seriously the symbolic connection between the actions of the ritual and the conditions of the real world [15–27].) Ostensibly, the duel's purpose was to prove one's opponent a liar, a goal that could be satisfied by other outcomes than death—admission of a lie, recantation of an insult, or just drawing blood rather than killing. It seems possible from the many duels aborted by the combatants or by the interference of friends that one purpose was to enact a ritualistic show of hostility. Yet many duellists stated at the outset that killing their opponents was their goal, and while not all duels resulted in death, both participants knew that they were risking their lives.
20. Though the weapons used for these two types of combat diverged considerably (as did the ways of using them), a letter written by Sir Philip Sidney raises the possibility of cross-training. In 1580, referring to fencing practice, Sidney urged his brother Robert Sidney to practice the slash as well as the thrust, saying, "It is good in itself; and besides increaseth your breath and strength and will make you a strong man at the tourney and barriers" (Letter, Oct. 18, 1580, Arber

reprints [1877], 1:309; qtd. in Kelso, *Gentleman* 153). Given the date of the letter, it is possible that Robert Sidney was being trained by an English Master of Defence who might not even have taught use of the rapier; on the other hand, the Sidney family may have hired a French or Italian master after Philip Sidney's experiences on the Continent—in which case, Philip Sidney may have perceived some correspondences between rapier fencing and broadsword fight.

21. Cf. Billacois 29.
22. See also Stone, *CA* 692. Stone notes that "[f]ive overlapping cultural ideals, those of the man of war, the man of learning, the statesman, the polished cavalier, and the virtuoso all demanded educational training abroad" (*CA* 693). Yet the English view of Italy was ambivalent. Stoye comments that English dramatists revealed contradictory attitudes towards Italy in their plays, fluctuating violently from attraction to repulsion (71). Among the gentry and aristocracy, however, the fascination is evident in the numbers of translators and editions of Italian works (Javitch, "Rival Arts" 178–83). Since visits to Italy or France were considered the best method of becoming proficient in riding, dancing, and fencing, we should not be surprised that several illustrious fencing-masters from Italy were welcomed when they came to England and were patronized by English nobles who received them as fencing tutors.
23. As the sixteenth century wore on, even jousting became an increasingly uncommon as a form of aristocratic entertainment. Dennis Brailsford comments that "the direct physical combat of noble men gave way to the sight of rustics tilting at a quintain" (27). When jousts did occur, the weaponry was modified to render the contests more sportive, less deadly. "Lances had lost their sharp points and become blunt poles; sword and buckler contests now employed swords deprived of both sharp edge and point, and with the lunge debarred" (Brailsford 27).
24. Cf. Brailsford 29. Though some English Masters of Defence eventually included the rapier among the weapons with which they professed skill (Berry 55, 81), those who could afford to pay foreign fencing masters preferred to do so, believing that they were more expert (Castle 31, 127, 264–5; Aylward 26). Many members of the gentry, in fact, preferred to study fencing during their travels on the Continent, where they could choose from among the experts of several different countries—specifically Italy, Spain, or France. Only three Italian fencers are documented as teaching the art of fencing in England: Rocco Bonetti, who came to London around 1569; Jeronimo, referred to by the English swordsman George Silver as Bonetti's "boy" (either a son or an assistant); and Vincentio Saviolo, a Paduan trained in both the Italian and Spanish styles of fencing, who came to England in 1590. Bonetti, who initially came to England as an emissary of Càtherine dei' Medici, taught fencing primarily at the school he set up

in a hall in the Blackfriars that he had purchased from John Lyly, but both Jeronimo and Saviolo traveled to the country houses of the gentry to give private lessons (Aylward 40–1, 52).

Why no more came is a mystery. Castle suggests that the hostility of the English Masters of Defence prevented many foreigners from infringing upon their monopoly (264), but Aylward suggests instead that the financial difficulties and general xenophobia that these three experienced may have been a warning to others; he also comments that "the Court craze for the Italianate was passing with the great Queen," although the popularity of the duel was not (61). Caused in part by the scarcity of foreign masters in England, their mystique gave the impression of far greater knowledge, described in such texts as Florio's *Second Frutes* and satirized in such passages as the descriptions of Tybalt in *Romeo and Juliet* (cf. Joan Ozark Holmer, " 'Draw, if you be men': Saviolo's Significance for *Romeo and Juliet*").

25. As Brailsford explains,

> Indeed, with the advent of the rapier it became increasingly necessary for anyone who was likely to find himself in a quarrel to have the skills of parry and thrust, especially in view of the vicious nature of the new weapon. The English even won for themselves abroad a reputation for rashness in entering into affairs of honour. (29)

26. In *The Blazon of Gentrie*, John Ferne praises *Ludus Gladiatorius*, "the skill how to use any weapon, either for the defence of our selves, or the offence of our enemies," and *Ludus Torneamentie*, "the game and play of Turney, a most warlike and millitarie exercise, befitting chiefly the practise of Gentlemen" (75). Yet he scorns what he calls "common fencers," arguing that "[i]f [matches] be playd for the cause of gaine, to move laughter and sport to the people, such playes be reprobate, and not onely worthy of dispraise, but rather to be accounted infamous" (76).
27. See David Kuchta's argument in his article "The Semiotics of Masculinity in Renaissance England" (233–46).
28. For the connection between courtliness and effeminacy, see Kuchta; for the connection between poetry and the court, Javitch, *Poetry and Courtliness* 50–75; and for the connection between vice and the court, Javitch, *Poetry and Courtliness* 107–40.
29. Certainly the Cult of Elizabeth had many devoted followers, but even the best known—Ralegh, Sidney, Essex—had moments of rebellion. All three of these men followed to the end the ideal of the aristocratic warrior, despite the evidence that the usefulness of that model had come to an end. The conflict between warrior and courtier may be perceived as embodied in the challenges that these men offered to their rivals.
30. Kiernan discusses the influence of Italian humanism and of chivalric ideals on aristocratic Elizabethan notions of honor and nobility,

showing how these notions both shaped and were shaped by the social custom of the duel (48–54).

31. Enacting the duel impinged on the government's sanctioned monopoly on punishment; moreover, its practice exposed the similarity between punishment and revenge. The connection was recognized as one that held dangerous implications for revolutionary elements, insofar as it could suggest that even the sovereign's power to impose his will derived from his *puissance,* and not the other way around. Bacon recognized the anarchistic threat inherent in revenge, arguing "Revenge is a kind of wild justice which the more man's nature runs to, the more ought law to weed it out: for as for the first wrong, it does but offend the law; but the revenge of that wrong putteth the law out of office" (52–3). In these terms, the phenomenon of the duel increased the power of male aristocrats at the expense of the monarch's.

32. Cf. Sydney Anglo, Diane Bornstein, Arthur Ferguson, and Maurice Keen.

33. For example, in Erasmus's *Enchiridion militis christiani,* the kinds of virtues endorsed indicate that the life of a Christian knight is not one that only a tiny elite may aspire to; on the contrary, many can hope to follow this path. Of course, Erasmus's native country differed from most of Western Europe in both its political and its economic system; his notion of knighthood seems drawn from the virtues of small craftsmen, farmers, and shopkeepers (cf. Bolgar's discussion of Erasmus 134–7).

    Later romances such as *Morte D'Arthur* demonstrate an overriding concern for the structure of the state: good knights subordinate their aggression to serve the needs of the state and the commands of the king. Rather than focusing on Lancelot, Malory's tale presents the story of a king who "had dedicated his life to a noble conception and who saw that conception and his kingdom fall in ruins around him" (Bolgar 129). Such civic notions held little appeal for most of those attracted to duelling.

34. In Tasso's *Discorso della virtu eroica e della carita,* the author shows his willingness to differentiate between types of virtue. Mazzoni, writing in 1688, saw the difference in terms of philosophical and poetic notions of heroic virtue—and to him the two were incompatible. Whereas one involved a purification of the soul, the other "consist[ed] entirely in military *fortezza*.... and frequently harm[ed] instead of benefiting mankind" (Mazzoni 280–5; qtd. in Steadman 7). Rene Le Bossu found a contradiction between the conception of heroic virtue extolled in Aristotle's *Ethics* and that expounded in the *Poetics:*

    [T]here is nothing in common between the two species of hero. The one should be raised above other men through his virtue; the other should not even be in the rank of the most perfect men. (Le Bossu 41; qtd. in Steadman 7)

35. Gordon Braden points out that Greek tragedy did not become available in Italy until the fourteenth century, whereas Seneca's plays were fairly well known in the previous century (101).
36. Braden comments, "the aristocratic code in Homer is a code of excellence in the transitive sense.... one's achievement has meaning in comparison to someone else's loss" (10).
37. Cf. Cedric H. Whitman and Seth L. Schein. Whitman asserts that self-destructiveness is an element of heroism: discussing Achilles, he says that "the self-destructiveness of the hero hinges upon a certain excess, an ability to outdo not only everyone else, but especially himself" (62). Schein refers to the tragic contradiction "that a hero achieves greatness and meaning in life only through the destruction of other would-be heroes and through his own destruction" (90). The classic example is Achilles' choice to remain at Troy and gain glory in death rather than to enjoy a long and peaceful life.
38. Braden discusses the complex nature of this development:

> Classical terms do not usually challenge the feudal heritage on this point [honorific categories], but blend in with it or supplement it; Roman modes of self-regard become part of a powerful continuity of medieval aristocratic values.... the real event in cultural history is the persistence of essentially chivalric standards as their content alters or even disappears. (77)

39. Billacois asserts that "[t]he judicial duel may not have remained alive in practice, but it remained so ... in the collective consciousness" (27). Alluding to early modern historical narratives and history plays, he comments, "Such things would have led people to think of the ritual duel before judges as a normal procedure and would have prevented recognition of the value of a duel which rolls judge, litigant, witness, sentence, and execution into one" (27).
40. For a different reading of the play, see Carol Cook's excellent article "'The Sign and Semblance of Her Honor': Reading Gender Difference in *Much Ado about Nothing*" (186–202).
41. Cf. Naunton's account of Sir John Perrot 65–7.
42. See also Mark Thornton Burnett 2–5 and John Hajnal 449–94.
43. All quotations of Shakespeare's works are from William Shakespeare, *The Riverside Shakespeare,* ed. G. Blakemore Evans (Boston: Houghton Mifflin, 1974), unless otherwise noted.
44. I am indebted for these references to Paul A. Jorgensen, *Shakespeare's Military World* 252–7.
45. See, for example, Hays 80–1 and Barton 328.
46. See Barton 328 and Cook.
47. This is, in fact, the kind of manipulation that Stephen Greenblatt describes in his well-known analysis of Iago (*RS* 232–54).
48. As Patricia Parker points, out, during this period women were considered the talkative sex; in fact, the figure *Garrulitas* is gendered female in emblem books such as Alciati's and Whitney's (see Parker,

Fat Ladies 27). Although this figure diverged from the "silent, chaste, and obedient" ideal of womanhood, she was a type as familiar in the theater as in the marketplace. Although her statements were not granted the legitimacy of male speech, her license to speak was generally accepted.

49. In fact, the proverb sought to contain such monstrosities as the horrifying (but common) talkative man, who might even have been considered "womanish" or effeminate.
50. See Greenblatt, *RS* 222–54, and Maus, *Inwardness* 35–71.
51. For a thoughtful discussion of several instances of this occurrence in the play, see Mark Taylor's article "Presence and Absence in *Much Ado about Nothing*" (1–12).
52. His reference to drizzling rain and the drunkard's loquacity links his confession to womanishness (cf. Paster, *The Body Embarrassed* 23–63).
53. When Leonato responds by asking, "What do you mean?," the question is manifold: not only, "What are your intentions toward my daughter?" but, "How do you expect us to regard the author of this monstrous impudence?" "In what context should we take this sudden change of attitude?" "Can you possibly intend for us to take this charge seriously?" All these are encompassed in the "meaning" Leonato asks to have elucidated. Claudio's words seem so far from reality that Leonato does not know how to take them.
54. Dogberry's intuitive recognition of criminal proceedings has always troubled critics: Jean Howard argues that the members of the Watch "perform a sentimental, utopian function" (*Stage* 64); Krieger complains that they never threaten society's values or the play's power relations (61). But Anne Barton wisely notes their generic function: they "reassure the theatre audience that comedy remains in control of the action, even when the potential for tragedy seems greatest" (Introduction 330).
55. Cf. Bloom 4–8.

Chapter 2   The Art of Fence and the Sense of Masculine Space

1. Spicer notes in contrast the rarity of the hand-on-hip pose for female pictorial subjects during this period except for women "of princely status... or a female warrior such as Juno or Athena" (100).
2. Bryson reads " 'gentlemanly' extravagance in conduct" as an inversion of the accepted hierarchy of manners. Noting a counterpressure against modesty and discipline, she suggests that "the assertion of freedom in demeanour and gesture could be an assertion of status, despite the principle that the superior man was he who exercised an exemplary self-control" (152).
3. For the influence of Foucault on Vigarello's article, see Part Three of *Discipline and Punish: The Birth of the Prison,* particularly Chapters One and Two, 135–94.

4. Of the three English fencing manuals that I examine here, two are (at least in part) translations of earlier Italian volumes. Giacomo di Grassi's *His True Arte of Defence* was translated into English by one J. G. and published in London in 1594. It was originally published in 1570 in Venice as "Ragioni di adoprar sicuramente l'arme" (Jackson v, Castle 67). Vincentio Saviolo's *His Practice* was published in 1595; the second half, *Of Honor and Honorable Quarrels,* is an adaptation of Muzio's *Il Duello.* Only George Silver's *Paradoxes of Defence* (1599) is entirely English.

Silver discusses the Italian masters in London in a note appended to his volume, referring to "three Italian Teachers of Offence in my time": Rocco, Jeronimo, and Vincentio (64). Vincentio (Saviolo), he said, "taught Rapier-fight at the Court, at London, and in the countrey, by the space of seaven or eight yeares" (66). Florio refers to Saviolo in the Seventh Dialogue of his *Second Frutes* as Master V. S., "[t]hat Italian that looks like Mars himself" (qtd. in Aylward 55). As for Silver, he refers to himself in his title page as a gentleman, a detail corroborated by his 1579–80 marriage license from the Bishop of London (cited in Aylward 63).

François Billacois, a twentieth-century historian, comments that until 1600, English manuals of fencing per se were all Italian, but by 1640 "it was to the French academies that the English nobility were sending their sons to learn the use of arms" (28).

5. Opposing the understanding of Renaissance gender ideology produced by such theorists as Thomas Laqueur and Stephen Greenblatt, Phyllis Rackin proposed that "although Renaissance gender ideology, like our own, was conflicted and contradictory, it was not incoherent... instead, it was constructed on different principles and within different discourses" ("Foreign Country" 69). My work had its genesis in an attempt to balance the views of Stephen Orgel and Laura Levine, whose work on gender and theatricality developed the notion that during the early modern period "the line between the sexes was blurred, often frighteningly so" (Orgel 13). In this chapter, I strive to develop an analysis of masculine spatial assumptions as one of the "different principles" to which Rackin refers above.

6. I should acknowledge the debt I owe in developing these ideas to Marcel Mauss's concept of *habitus*—effective and traditional physical actions that "vary... between societies, educations, proprieties and fashions, prestiges" and are in some way shaped by these institutions (73). My consideration of bodily subjectivity has also been shaped by Gail Kern Paster's discussion of "the subjective experience of being-in-the-body," particularly by her assertion that "we need to conceptualize an equally formable, if not equally visible, *internal* habitus" (*The Body Embarrassed* 3, 4).

7. In other passages, however, Walker shows an awareness that the meaning of body language may vary from place to place. His comment on

the unusually high value Italians place on ceremony and civility suggests a surprising degree of cultural relativism: "though in this Countrey of great freedome and litle jealousy ... they are unnecessary, or also unfitting; yet it may be fitting to know how to entertain a Stranger; or how we are entertained by him" (219).

8. Each of these aspects of physical subjectivity has been examined by anthropologists. For example, Erving Goffman's noted work *Relations in Public: Microstudies of the Public Order* analyzes the communicative aspects of the body. Goffman speaks of the messages unintentionally given by a subject, broadcast to others by body language. Goffman uses the term "externalization" to characterize "the process whereby an individual pointedly uses over-all body gesture to make otherwise unavailable facts about his situation gleanable" (11). Goffman's focus on interpreting the body parallels the work of Edward T. Hall, who investigates the ways the body interprets its environment. In *The Hidden Dimension,* a text for the general reader that summarizes numerous technical articles, Hall analyzes the subjective experience of space that characterizes different cultures and subgroups. Hall developed the term "proxemics" to refer to the study of the structuring and perception of space. His work and that of his followers attempts to define physical experience "as it is perceived through [different sets] of culturally patterned sensory screens" (2).

9. It should be clear, in fact, that the name of the sport called fencing is derived from the word "defense." The word "fence" as it refers to an artificial barrier used as a boundary marker or a means of confinement possesses the same etymology; the barrier itself was first conceived as a means of protection, of defense against attack.

10. In di Grassi's words, "Wards and weapons are such sites, positions or placings which withstand the enemies blowes" (c4r). Saviolo's rapier wards often involve a simultaneous counterattack.

11. Unlike the readiness of the Stoic, which is a preparation for all eventualities, the readiness of the fencer or duellist is partly physical: it is a protective stance coupled with a mental alertness that prepares for attack. "Readiness" must involve a conscious preparation to protect the boundaries of one's personal space. Hamlet's comment "the readiness is all," which comes soon before his fatal fencing exhibition, could be read as a joking allusion to the fencer's readiness, since the comment is so clearly placed in a Stoic context ("If it be now, 'tis not to come; if it be not to come, it will be now; if it be not now, yet it will come") (V.ii.220–2). Hamlet's ethos as a duellist is discussed more fully in chapter 4.

12. Turner and Soper discuss the sense of the space needed for defensive purposes as one that the well-trained swordsman develops; they point out that the sport of kendo, practiced today, "also places great stress on this idea of a buffer zone (known as *ma* or *mai-ai*)" (86). This

sense of space obviously plays a part in structuring the development of a sense of personal space. However, Turner and Soper never consider how a change in weaponry and in protective means may alter the use of this space or the way the combatant will experience it.
13. For the length of the rapier, see Baldick 40, Turner and Soper 85, and John Smythe (1590). For an attempt to regulate the length of rapiers, see Hughes and Larkin, *Tudor Royal Proclamations* 2:462, Proclamation 646:

> A branch of a proclamation published the 12th of February in the eighth year of the Queen's majesty's reign concerning swords, daggers, rapiers, and bucklers.... Item, her majesty ordereth and also commandeth that no person shall wear any sword, rapier, or suchlike weapon that shall pass the length of one yard and half-a-quarter of the blade at the uttermost, nor any dagger above the length of 12 inches in blade at the most.

14. With certain modifications, I would consider applying to this relationship Foucault's explanation of the soldier's relation to his rifle:

> Over the whole surface of contact between the body and the object it handles, power is introduced, fastening them to one another. It constitutes a body-weapon, body-tool, body-machine complex.... Thus disciplinary power appears to have the function not so much of deduction as of synthesis, not so much of exploitation of the product as of coercive link with the apparatus of production. (*Discipline and Punish* 153)

15. The physical closeness resembles the distance commonly observed by partners in courtly dancing, although our understanding of fencing may be more enhanced by a comparison with rustic dances. True, the dances of the court, like fencing, feature the elite classical body: elongated, separate, balanced. Skiles Howard notes that this kind of dancing forms "near parallels and harmonious diagonals ... yet the dancers are patently isolated from each other" (337). But for the most part, partners move in unison (S. Howard 330). But popular country dances like the bergomask are both more intimate and more improvisational (S. Howard 336). Analyzing Theodore de Bry's early modern engraving "Court and Country Dancers," Skiles Howard points out that the county dance's "irregularity of form ... suggests spontaneity of movement," in contrast to the clearly rehearsed poses of the dancing courtiers (339). Although the proxemic intimacy of fencers resembles that of courtly dancers, the reciprocal and spontaneous movement of paired county dancing offers a significant parallel to fencing.
16. The domination that may be established in situations of physical intimacy may be perceived in the distinction Howard draws between merely joining a round dance and selecting a partner, inviting her to the dance, and leading her to the floor. As Howard says, discussing the directives given to men in an early modern dance manual, the man "establishes his dominance in a gesture that dictates its response" (335).

17. Saviolo warns his readers not to engage in casual fencing matches since friends may have ulterior motives in proposing them, and even a purely friendly match may change its character if a participant becomes incensed.
18. Neither Saviolo nor di Grassi respond in such a doctrinaire way; instead, each offers strategic reasons for his recommendations. Di Grassi, in discussing the swordfight, places such faith in the defensive ward that he urges against any withdrawal. Having the enemy close at hand is a mutual disadvantage: neither combatant can attack with the farthest part of the sword "in which it beareth most force" (D4v). But by using an effective ward, a swordsman can repel his opponent long enough to decide how best to attack at these close quarters. Thus, di Grassi states that the good swordsman "ought to settle and repose himself in his ward, therein deliberating upon some new devise, or expecting when his enemie will minister occasion to enter upon him" (C4r).
19. These physiological responses result from the heightened secretion of adrenaline that occurs when members of a non-contact species find themselves approached too closely by others (see Hall 10–12, 110–13, 121).
20. Turner and Soper refer to these maneuvers as "voiding procedures with the body" or "the body void" and regard them as a way of parrying an attack (86, 97).
21. Frequently Saviolo suggests some imitative move:

    > I will beate the pointe of his swoorde with my dagger toward my lefte side, and so make a direct thrust to his head: then the scholler must step with his right foote in the place of my lefte. (*2v–*3r)

    > You shall come with your right foot, to the place where your maisters right foote was, and shal give him a thrust in the belly or in the face. (I2v)

22. The "Letters patent...for the establishment of the Royal Academy of Dance for the City of Paris, March 1662" officially stated that dance was

    > recognized as one of the most decent and necessary for forming the body, and giving it the first and most natural dispositions for all sorts of exercises, and among others for the exercise of arms. ("Letters patent...for the establishment of the Royal Academy of Dance for the City of Paris, March 1662," trans. Franko 176)

    English court customs were heavily influenced by those of the French, as Gordon Kipling discusses in *The Triumph of Honour: Burgundian Origins of the Elizabethan Renaissance*. Skiles Howard, who builds on Vigarello's work in her examination of social codes in English dancing, asserts, "During the sixteenth century, royal entertainments in England increasingly emulated the customs of the Continental courts, one of which was dancing that reinforced distinctions of rank and gender" (338–9).

Vigarello's material (and that of his successors) offers useful parallels between the social function of dance and that of fencing. Both courtly accomplishments offered male aristocrats the opportunity to compete with one another for the approbation of their peers (cf. Skiles Howard and Mark Franko). Though the courtly dance pairs men and women while the fencing match pairs two men, in both cases the men involved are actuated by competitive principles and by the desire to impress others.

Furthermore, both courtly dancing and fencing involve issues of gender and dominance. In dancing, male courtiers use the woman as a foil and as a means to address their prowess to other men; in fencing, men compete more directly, though they still address watchers the figure who loses the match loses both social and masculine status. Both kinds of contest create a seeded hierarchy derived from consistent challenges and their outcomes throughout the community. Skill in these particular pastimes becomes equated with masculine honor, newly conceived; success in both these kinds of contest stands in for sexual accomplishment, valued in turn because of an assumed equation with martial skill.

23. On the rise of rapier-fencing in England, see Stone, *CA* 243–7 and Aylward 26–7. The public response to this phenomenon, however, is far from positive.

24. Many condemned the related practice of duelling, perceived alternately as an aristocrat's prerogative and as an affront to monarchic authority. Silver opens his publication with "An Admonition to the noble, ancient, victorious, valiant, and most brave nation of Englishmen" to cast off "these Italianated, weake, fantasticall, and most divellish and imperfect fights" (1). *A Discourse concerning Duels* (1687), by T. C. D. D., argues that engaging in duels, customarily fought at that time with rapiers accompanied by a secondary implement such as dagger or cloak, affronted the king, the laws, and the government. But William Segar endorses the duel in *The Booke of Honor an Armes,* linking the custom of duelling not with Continental traditions but with the late medieval English trial by combat (22–3) and with jousts and tournaments (28–9). John Selden, in *The Duello, or Single Combat* (1610), makes a similar connection to the trial by combat, even referring to the weapons used several hundred years before the advent of the rapier (48–50).

In circles where fencing was valued, skill in its performance was linked to honor; the chivalric ideal underlay the implication that duelling was a necessary skill for military men because their honor was so valuable to them. The connection between duelling and honor is the subject of part two of Vincentio Saviolo's *His Practice;* honor and combats are discussed in Chapters Three and Four of John Kepers's translation of Haniball Romei's treatise *The Courtiers Academie.* The historian Fredrick R. Bryson discusses at length the connection between honor and the duel in *The Sixteenth-Century Italian Duel: A Study in Renaissance Social History*, xx–xxviii and 3–23. For duelling and honor among military men, see Middleton and Rowley, *A Fair Quarrel*, III.i.6–8.

25. For primary texts, see T. C. D. D., *A Discourse of Duels*; G. F., *Duell-Ease*; Anon., *Antiduello*; William Wiseman, *The Christian Knight*; Francis Bacon, *The Charge of Sir Francis Bacon Knight, His Majesties Attourney Generall, touching Duells*; and James I, *A Publication of his Majesties Edict, and Severe Censure against Private Combats and Combatants*. See François Billacois for the cult of honor in France and for information on English views. For English views, see again Stone, *CA* 242–50.

26. In eighteenth-century France, the "projects of docility" (in Foucault's term) no longer had as their object "the signifying elements of behaviour or the language of the body, but the economy, the efficiency of movements, their internal organization" (*Discipline and Punish* 137). Yet Vigarello emphasizes the importance of performance in the production of the upright body (188–9).

27. In *The Duel: Its Rise and Fall in Early Modern France*, the social historian François Billacois supports this view. He comments, "Italian fencing worked on speed, surprise and the suppleness of bodies that it rendered imponderable, bodies that slipped away in the moment they exposed themselves. It drew balletic figures, which were at once effaced and substituted by others" (67).

28. Phyllis Rackin points out that in Nashe's *Pierce Penniless his Supplication to the Divell* (1592), the author conflates "Englishness with masculinity and both with a lost historic past ... oppos[ing] the masculine domain of English history to the degenerate, effeminate world of present-day English experience in order to defend theatrical performance as an inspiration to civic virtue and heroic patriotism" ("Foreign Country" 79).

29. Richard Foster Jones has documented comparisons among sixteenth-century English rhetoricians of their language to "plain, serviceable, honest, and unadorned clothing," which Jones considers an expression of a distrust of rhetoric (19, 31). Later writers valued the English language for its strength, simplicity, and antiquity (Jones 235, 262, 291). The seventeenth-century estate poem frequently reiterates the importance of the lord's working knowledge of his estate, as in Herrick's approving comments on Endymion Porter in "The Country Life, To the Honored Mr. Endymion Porter, Groom of the Bedchamber to His Majesty." When effete courtiers are portrayed in literature, they are almost invariably contaminated by foreign customs. Jonson's English gull Sir Politic Would-be is Porter's antithesis: he lives in Venice and asserts that a wise man should call the whole world his native land.

Given this context, we can more easily understand the reactionary George Silver who, despite his status as a gentleman, evinces his faith in the virtues of the common English laborer so much that he seems to equate English nativity and literal association with the soil, each as a positive trait. Silver perceives something innately English in the ploughman, and his association of fencers, foreigners, and aristocrats indicates his sense that the English aristocracy has been vitiated by contact with Europeans:

> Our ploughmen have mightily prevailed against them, as also against Masters of Defence both in Schooles and countries, that have taken upon them to stand upon Schooletrickes and jugling gambals: whereby it grew to a common speech among the countrie-men, Bring me to a Fencer, I will bring him out of his fence trickes with good downe right blowes. (2)

His words associate fencing with both the tricks and deceptions of travelling vagabonds—members of the underclass—and the seductive but empty shows of Continental courtiers. The common element is indeed that of performance—amusing deceit, false because insubstantial. Silver opposes concrete physical phenomena—blows—to the false appearances of the fencer's showy skills. In his formulation, fencing skills are against nature, constructed by an oversubtle civilization. He considers the art of fence not only overrated but also artificial and ineffective in its techniques of defense and offense.

30. George Silver's stories about the many challenges Saviolo received from English swordsmen reveal that swordsmen were very likely to engage in the boorish behaviors to which Anna Bryson refers. The skilled fencer (in contrast to the wielder of the broadsword) seems unlikely to act like a boor; one clear constraint imposed on the would-be duellist is the ritualism of the challenge, which calls for a very cool head.

31. Early modern pamphlet writer J. Cocke calls the theatrical player "*a daily Counterfeit*...a Motley...a shifting companion" (qtd. in Barish 106). Jonas Barish, in his examination of Renaissance views of theatricality, describes mimicry as "the power to become, or to pretend to become, what one is not" (96). He asserts that not only did antitheatricalists distrust such behavior, but that playwrights, through their depictions of Machiavellian villains, indicated a similar distrust (96–106).

32. This association with the unique and individualistic contrasts with Foucault's view of "discipline" as a leveling strategy. In discussing French eighteenth-century military discipline, Foucault says,

> Disciplinary control...imposes the best relation between a gesture and the overall position of the body, which is its condition of efficiency and speed. In the correct use of the body, everything must be called upon to form the support of the art required. (*Discipline and Punish* 152)

Superficially this passage seems to describe the training in fencing that the Anglo-Italian manuals detail. But while these elements are present in fencing drill, they are the basics from which improvisational skills develop. Foucault's "discipline" imagines a mass of men functioning under the command of a leader; fencing, a very different "discipline," emphasizes the strategic responses of two interactive opposing partners.

33. Vigarello is clearly indebted to Foucault's discussion of France's eighteenth-century military system. Discussing military training, Foucault says,

> The individual body becomes an element that may be placed, moved, articulated on others. Its bravery or its strength are no longer the principal variables that define it; but the place it occupies, the interval it covers, the regularity.... The soldier is above all a fragment of mobile space, before he is courage or honor. (164)

It may be possible that such terms could be applied to those trained in fencing at a French *military academy*; however, it should be clear that this terminology is antithetical to many of the tenets of the training and understanding of the art of fence as that art was practiced in England.

34. While the standard of excellence in French fencing manuals, according to Vigarello, is "less and less one of strength, and increasingly one of elegance" (179), Saviolo describes what is utilitarian:

> [When] the scholler hath received his Rapier into his hand, let him make his hand free and at lyberty, not by force of the arme, but by the nimble and ready moving of the ioynt of the wriste of the hand, so that his hand be free and at libertie from his body. (D3v)

Saviolo recommends that the muscles be relaxed and that the fencer consciously rely on the wrist joint. Such movement comes less naturally than that which relies on the elbow joint, but creates much less fatigue and enables the fencer to maneuver the rapier more quickly, easily, and accurately. The hand should be able to move independently of the body instead of being locked in place.

35. In some cases, in fact, training was identical. Stephen Orgel has pointed out in *Impersonations* that many actors held memberships in professional guilds (64–8); records of the Company of the Masters of Defense of London indicate that Richard Tarlton earned the rank of master of the art of fence under Henry Naylor on October 23, 1587 (Sloane MS. 2530, p. 6; rpt. in *The Noble Science* 53). The use of this skill in his profession as actor is obvious, apart from any other uses he had for it; however, it is questionable whether any actor would have had the wherewithal to train in the use of the *rapier*.

36. See, for example, Jonas Barish, *The Anti-theatrical Prejudice* (1981); Suzanne Gossett, "'Man-maid, Begone!': Women in Masques" (1988); Jean E. Howard, "Crossdressing, The Theatre, and Gender Struggle in Early Modern England" (1988); Laura Levine, "Men in Women's Clothing: Anti-theatricality and Effeminization from 1579 to 1642" (1986), later reprinted in *Men in Women's*

Clothing: Anti-theatricality and Effeminization, 1579–1642 (1994); Katharine Eisaman Maus, "'Playhouse Flesh and Blood': Sexual Ideology and the Restoration Actress" (1979); Stephen Orgel, "Nobody's Perfect: Or Why Did the English Stage Take Boys for Women?" (1989), later reprinted in *Impersonations: The Performance of Gender in Shakespeare's England* (1996); Phyllis Rackin, "Androgyny, Mimesis, and the Marriage of the Boy Heroine on the English Renaissance Stage" (1987); Peter Stallybrass, "Transvestism and the 'Body Beneath': Speculating on the Boy Actor" (1992); and Sophie Tomlinson, "She That Plays the King: Henrietta Maria and the Threat of the Actress in Caroline Culture" (1992).

37. Such a special emphasis also would have been created by self-contained mimetic elements within the framework of the action: plays-within-a-play, masques, puppet shows, and set competitions such as duels, fencing exhibitions, and wrestling matches (to name a few).

38. Roach argues that the early modern stage-player's understanding of realism was closely tied to beliefs about the relation between the passions and humoral psychology; such ideas go all the way back to Quintilian. But Roach points out that ideas of acting also were influenced by early modern developments in scientific method. He cited John Bulwer's *Chirologia: Or the Natural Language of the Hand* (1644) as a text detailing outward signs that the author considered universal, much as some scientists today have detailed similar facial expressions that signify the same emotion in widely differing cultures.

39. All quotations from this play are from Ben Jonson, *The Alchemist*. In *Ben Jonson*, C. H. Herford and Percy Simpson, eds. Oxford: Clarendon, 1937. 10 vols. 5:283–408.

CHAPTER 3   SEXUAL STATUS AND THE COMBAT

1. Training in the art of fence was available to anyone with ready money, since the only qualification needed to take lessons was the ability to pay for them. However, Silver points out that when the Italian fencing-master Signior Rocco founded his fencing school in London, "[h]e taught none commonly under twentie, fortie, fifty, or an hundred pounds" (64).

2. Many apparently contradictory instances of women attempting to gain notice can be understood as occasions that ultimately redounded to the credit of their husbands or their families—conspicuous consumption in finery, for example.

3. See also Thomas Fuller's account of "The Constant Virgin" in *The Holy State and the Profane State*, 1:35–7.

4. Richard Weste's *The Booke of Demeanor* makes the same points to young boys serving at table: "Stand straight upright, and both thy feet / together closely standing, / Be sure on't, ever let thine eye / be still at thy commanding" (209). In *Of Education, Especially of*

Young Gentlemen, Obadiah Walker says, "A *slow pace* is proper to delicate and effeminate persons, an hasty one to mad men; strutting is affectation, wadling is for the slothful and lazy, and in measure to dancers" (216).

5. The art historian Joaneath Spicer asserts that feminine virtues such as containment had their own body language and, in fact, women painted in assertive poses often connoted negative traits, as in allegories of Pride or Vanity (100).
6. See also Stone *FSM* 195 and Henderson and McManus 79. In her discussion of Shakespeare's "The Rape of Lucrece," Georgiana Ziegler says,

> From [Lucrece's] point of view... her body is private and intimate, a "quiet cabinet" or a "weak hive" into which "a wand'ring wasp hath crept / And sucked the honey which thy chaste bee kept" (442, 839–40). The cabinet and the hive both have housewifely associations and just as the good wife was expected to keep safe her husband's possessions, so Lucrece sees herself as the keeper of Collatine's honour in her chastity, "that dear jewel I have lost" (1191). (80–1)

By these metaphors, Lucrece objectifies herself; the imagery suggests that, like the cabinet and the hive, she has no power to block the invader, to arrest the unnatural intruder.

7. In practice, some women chose to defy convention by returning the physical attacks of such aggressors as abusive husbands (Hair, *Before the Bawdy Court* 244; qtd. in Henderson and McManus 80). Such women endured considerable censure from their communities (cf. Underdown).
8. Vives held dancing in unqualified disapproval, and the evangelical minister Eustorg de Beaulieu urged his niece to avoid dances (qtd. in Kelso, *Lady* 52).
9. Cf. Austern.
10. Kelso explains Bruni's view that

> it is wholly inappropriate for women to study delivery, the proper place to throw out an arm or vigorously raise the voice, or any part of the craft of public address in debates or court trials or controversies of any sort, which belong to men. (69)

11. Of the English humanists, only Richard Mulcaster argued in favor of exercise for women, suggesting that activity benefitted the health "of both sortes, *male* and *female*, young *boyes* and young *maidens*" (138; cited in Semenza, "Recovering the 'Two Sorts of Sport,'" 18–19). Gregory M. Colon Semenza's ongoing archival research indicates that, despite the dicta of the conduct-books, women did participate in sports on occasion. However, the degree of vigor differed according to the type of sport involved, and this in turn was regulated by rank. Noblewomen seldom engaged in activities more energetic than walking or riding, while women in agricultural settings often played

ball or took part in foot races (Semenza, *Sport, Politics, and Literature in the English Renaissance*, forthcoming).
12. Cf. Rowson.
13. See also Gary Spear:

> [E]ffeminacy was considered the result of inordinate sexual appetite and was associated with a range of sexual practices that ran counter to the increasingly intense proscriptions defining sexual intercourse as solely a means of reproduction within the confines of heterosexual marriage. (417)

14. See Trexler 12–37, particularly the analysis of the ancient Cretan practice of homosexual rape (27–30).
15. Athenians during the classical era actually accepted homosexuality as part of a man's sex life, though reciprocal desire between men of the same age was virtually unknown (Dover 1–17). In early modern England, the situation was more ambiguous. Discussing the prosecution of Meredith Davy, a laborer who had had occasional sex with his master's apprentice (a twelve-year-old with whom he shared a bed), the gender studies historian Alan Bray comments,

> The young apprentice would have had a lower standing in the household than Davy, who was an adult; and it was presumably this which encouraged [Davy]—wrongly, as it turned out—to think that he could take advantage of the boy. (48)

Bray offers a detailed analysis of several social contexts in which man/boy sexual contact, while censured, was nonetheless accepted (48–57). These contexts include "the household, the educational system, homosexual prostitution and the like" (74). As Bray points out, "so long as homosexual activity did not disturb the peace or the social order, and in particular so long as it was consistent with patriarchal mores, it was largely in practice ignored" (74). What violated these mores was in fact sex between adult men, which was taken much more seriously than relations between a man and a boy. A notable exception, James I's liaison with Buckingham, would probably have provoked even more comment had it not involved a significant difference in status that both parties acknowledged, even referring to one another in correspondence as "dad" and "dear child" (cf. G. P. V. Akrigg, *The Letters of King James VI and I* and, for a selection of Buckingham's letters, David M. Bergeron, *King James and Letters of Homoerotic Desire,* pp. 179–219). In fact, aristocratic patronage is a context that Bray probably should have discussed, since that system provided status inequities that, like age differences, would have rendered sex between adult men more acceptable.

16. Here Laqueur summarizes the findings of several scholars in the vanguard of gender studies, including Maud Gleason, David J. Cohen, and David Halperin. Their work deals with imperial Rome as well as classical Athens.

17. In support of this comment, Orgel refers to Shakespeare's Rosalind reminding Orlando that "in matters of love the two are all but identical" (51); to the fact that handsome boys in England at this time were praised "by saying that they looked like women" (51); to many situations in which boys "were, like women—but unlike [adult] men—acknowledged objects of sexual attraction for men" (70). However, I should point out that Orgel makes this claim in opposition to Jonathan Goldberg who, in *Sodometries*, specifically argues *against* perceiving male/male sexual involvement solely in terms of a dominant/submissive axis that (in Goldberg's view) turns homosexual acts into "heterosexual simulation."

18. In support of her argument about the intended purpose of taunting, Vermeule discusses the double meanings of certain words commonly used in this context—*meignumi*, meaning to mingle in battle or in sex; and *damazo* or *damnemi*, terms that can refer variously to taming (as with an animal), raping (as with a woman), or killing (as with an opponent) (101).

19. All quotations from this play are from Anon., *Swetnam the Woman-hater Arraigned by Women*, in *Swetnam the Woman-hater: The Controversy and the Play*, ed. Coryl Crandall (Purdue, IN: Purdue University Studies, 1969), 53–140.

20. Judith Haber notes a similar joke in *The Duchess of Malfi*. In *Duchess*, the title character addresses her husband/lover Antonio, saying, "I ent'red you into my heart / Before you would vouchsafe to call for the keys" (3.2.61–2). Here "enter" refers to account-book entries similar to those of Swetnam's roll-book, but, as Haber notes, since this account-book remains within the Duchess herself, the comment implies that the Duchess's "integrity as subject consists not in remaining impenetrable but in choosing who may 'enter' her" (140). Haber uses the term "enter" in a sexual sense; however, in the play, the word is actually uttered as the speaker's extended personal space is violently penetrated: in the middle of the Duchess's sentence, her brother Ferdinand furtively enters her room with his poniard drawn. Thus, all three meanings of the term recur in Webster's play.

21. All quotations from this play are from Philip Massinger, *The Unnatural Combat*, in *The Plays and Poems of Philip Massinger*, eds. Philip Edwards and Colin Gibson (Oxford: Clarendon, 1976), 2: 195–272.

22. The mechanisms I discuss here actually parallel those operating in Aufidius's taunt of "Boy" to Coriolanus, an insult that Adelman briefly discusses in "Anger's my Meat."

23. As Valerie Traub points out, Hotspur provides "the equation of sexuality to violence ... that will later designate Hal's assumption of the masculine role" (466).

24. Valerie Traub says of the world of *Henry V*, "[t]o be masculine ... is to be the active subject of a sexualized violence and a violent sexuality. It is never clear which is cause and which effect" (473). Traub argues that the question of causation is unanswerable because of "the circuitous interdependency of subjectivity, sexuality, and gender" (473).

25. Fleming inserted this information into the 1587 edition of Holinshed's *Chronicles* (III:34).
26. Whether the Welshwomen were in fact "dependents" of the men is questionable; sixteenth-century English historians recorded that the women of Wales actually fought as warriors.
27. Offering a contrary view, Phyllis Rackin argues that the Douglas's damaged testicle serves as a symbolic castration neither in Holinshed nor in Shakespeare. Because of his valor, she believes both authors imply, the Douglas "is honored as a noble man, a status unaffected by the genital wound" ("Foreign Country" 83). I would assert, however, that Douglas, freed but impotent, may be a better sign of Lancastrian hegemony than an imprisoned Douglas who could be canonized as a martyr by fellow Scots.
28. For earlier interpretations that characterize Hal as a boy beloved by men, see (among others) Empson 41–4 and 98–105, Findlay 229–38, and Goldberg 145–75.
29. Goldberg reads these insults very differently; he comments that Hal's "thinness, in these charges ... carries the accusation of 'genital emaciation'" and that "Falstaff points to the phallus Hal lacks" (*Sodometries* 174). While I acknowledge Falstaff's derision, on which Goldberg's reading depends, I think that there's more going on in those lines than Falstaff himself is aware of, and that these elements are reinforced by many other allusions within the play.
30. As Gerard H. Cox points out,

    After Hotspur contemptuously asks the whereabouts of the "nimble-footed madcap Prince of Wales," Vernon replies in terms that create a world of figures as well as the form of what Hotspur–and we–should attend. (139)

    One might be tempted to characterize Hal's self-assessments as *eironeia*—in G. C. Sedgewick's words, "a pervasive mode of behaviour, a constant pretence of self-depression, of which understatement is only one manifestation" (10, qtd. in Saccone 58).
31. Valerie Traub perceives this speech as a reference to a "bloody birth fantasy": "Cleansed in a battle both martial and natal, the newborn babe will become simultaneously his father's son and his nation's hero" (465–6). Her reading underscores my point that manhood could be conceived in terms of a maturity/immaturity dichotomy. Hal's desire to be reborn figures the battle as a rite of passage that initiates the prince into the adult world of male warriors.
32. In the words of Jonathan Goldberg,

    the masculinity that Hal achieves by killing and robbing Hotspur of his accomplishments is one that secures itself as proper male/male admiration, an incipient heterosexuality, a homo-narcissism that guards against any possibility that Hal's relations with men—with Falstaff—might be sexual. Killing Hotspur, Hal has become a real man, a man's man. ... From Hotspur, Hal acquires what criticism will come to see as his heterosexual credentials, a way to view male/male relations as the escape from the danger of effeminization, and a way to regard male/male sexual relations *as* effeminizing. (*Sodometries* 169)

Unlike the critics to whom Goldberg later refers, I do *not* see Hal's emulation of Hotspur as "that mirror of male/male admiration supposedly free of the taint of sodomy" (*Sodometries* 170).

33. I owe this point to a conversation I had about staging some years ago with Alexandra G. Bennett.

CHAPTER 4 MISPERCEIVING MASCULINITY, MISREADING THE DUEL

1. For discussions of the king/subjects and father/dependents analogy, see, for example, Stone, *FSM* 152–6 and Rackin 76–7.
2. According to Stone,

> It was customary for [children] when at home to kneel before their parents to ask their blessing every morning, and even as adults on arrival at and departure from the home.... Even when grown up, sons were expected to keep their hats off in their parents' presence, while daughters were expected to remain kneeling or standing in their mother's presence. "Gentlemen of thirty and forty years old," recalled Aubrey, "were to stand like mutes and fools bareheaded before their parents." (*FSM* 171)

3. Cf. Stone, *FSM* 197–9, Jardine 37–67.
4. Mervyn James says, "For [Sir John Townley] and his like, gentility was a matter of traditional standing and local opinion, which needed no prying inquiry on the part of a king's herald" (338).
5. Alice Shalvi asserts that the term "honor" generally "during the sixteenth century... ceased to be used primarily in the Aristotelian sense of an external good awarded by others, but was extended to cover also the behavior and moral quality of the person honoured" (61). Watson supports Shalvi's view with this quotation from La Primaudaye:

> [T]he ancient Romans built two Temples joined together, the one being dedicated to Vertue, and the other to Honor: but yet in such sort, that no man could enter into that of Honor, except that he passed through the other of Vertue. (Watson 94).

6. For women, however, "honor" and "virtue" were synonymous with chastity—that is, with maintaining virginity until marriage and monogamy afterward (Watson 159, Kelso, *Lady* 98). Curtis Brown Watson points out that while "woman's honor was almost exclusively a question of sexual purity, the moralists stressed the same incentives as in their discussion of a man's honor" (159). As I point out in the next chapter, the virtue of Besse in *The Fair Maid of the West* is characterized less as a consequence of her extraordinary valor and enterprise than as a derivation of her extraordinary fidelity to the person and the memory of her fiancé.

Kelso insightfully comments, "Honor for both men and women was something external, a good name, for men a reputation for excellency in many things, for women only in one thing, chastity" (*Lady* 98). Significantly, as she points out, chastity is rarely mentioned as a masculine virtue at all. She further notes that the duel gave men an option for avenging imputations to their honor, whereas a woman had no redress unless a man was willing to champion her and challenge the insult as a lie. Linda Woodbridge has commented that "the male values were so action-oriented, the female values so passive and abstemious.... the contrast tells us something about masculinity" (private correspondence).

7. If Stone is correct in saying that early modern men were suspicious and unable to form intimate bonds (*FSM* 194–5), women's talkativeness may be a sign of greater intimacy in the female household community.
8. See Barish 80–131 and Levine for the antitheatrical tract-writers' belief that drama could alter the audience's morals or affect their volition.
9. Readers will recognize Montaigne's strategy from "Of Sumptuarie Lawes" in which Montaigne argues that the best way to moderate excessive spending on apparel is to make a statute "That no man or woman, of what qualitie soever, shall, upon paine of great forfeitures, weare any maner of silke, of skarlet, or any gold-smiths worke, except only Enterlude-players, Harlots, and Curtizans" (233).
10. See also Anna Bryson.
11. See Goldberg, *James I and the Politics of Literature* 1–54 for James I's desire to control his subjects' thoughts.
12. At the same time, the values of the Christian hero became less and less important. C. L. Barber points out that during the seventeenth century, "the behaviour demanded by honour came to overlap less with Christian virtue; greater emphasis was placed on revenge and duelling; 'reflected' reputation was accorded greater importance" (*The Idea of Honour* 283).
13. All quotations from this play are from Thomas Middleton and William Rowley, *A Fair Quarrel*, ed. George R. Price (Lincoln: University of Nebraska Press, 1976).
14. Moreover, the metaphor of words as coin was current (pun intended) in the work of several writers of the period; it appears in Hobbes, in Jonson's *Discoveries,* and in a reference that More makes to Quintilian.
15. An understanding of the authors' stance on duelling is even more relevant than for most dramas: the play's title-page states that the play was not only performed publicly but was also "Acted before the King" (Price xi). Since James had published an edict four years before, detailing specific punishments for those who engaged in challenges and private combats, his willingness to see the play is an important aspect of its reception, especially as James and Middleton were later

associated in the production of an anti-duelling pamphlet entitled "The Peace-Maker." Cf. Dunlap.

16. Of all other critics, the one who comes closest to my view is George E. Rowe, Jr., who says that Middleton "suggests... that the idealized code of honor which forms the basis of [Ager's and the Colonel's] actions is as incapable of dealing with the complexities of existence as the comic ideals examined in Middleton's earlier plays" (154–5). Rowe, however, makes this point only briefly, in a discussion of Middleton and comedy; the issue is worthy of examination in part because the play seems so open to very contradictory views. Bowers asserts that "[t]he nub of the play is unquestionably Captain Ager's refusal to fight in a wrong cause, for with this situation the dramatists could condemn a practise and yet uphold the theory" ("Duelling Code" 64). David Holmes, similarly, says that Middleton endorses Ager's "readiness to fight for truth" as well as "the idea that in certain circumstances a man of conscience is justified in engaging in a duel" (117). One critic alludes to "the absolute purity of Ager's code of conduct"; yet, in contrast, A. L. and M. K. Kistner assert that through the play the authors show that such values as the male code of honor "are false values, the only true ones being the Christian virtues of love, peace, chastity, and material abnegation" (31), and they further argue that Ager, "whose golden calf is his honor or reputation," "follows false ideals" (33). Heinemann, too, says that the play "turns on the folly of duelling, and of the aristocratic code" of honor (114). Most recently, Brian Parker has summed up Ager as an illustration of the contradiction between the two books of Saviola's *Practise*: cold- bloodedly scrupulous about cause... but with an aggressive drive for personal honour underlying all his decisions, which Saviola condemns even when a cause is "just," a quarrel "fair" (72).

    Given this plethora of views, I turn back to David Holmes's allusion to Middleton's use of "indirect and intimative modes of theatrical expression" (194) and try to tease out the implications of the play myself.

17. However, Segar argues in *The Booke of Honor and Armes* that illegitimate birth may be redeemed: although

    > men so borne, cannot maintane themselves to be Gentlemen by birth, and therefore directlie must not claim such title, or enter the trial of Armes, and therefore in that respect may be repulsed, not as infamous, but as ignoble... [this] defect either by valorous indevour in Armes, or vertuous studie in learning may be supplied. (32–3)

18. We may note the vainglorious tone of the correspondence between Lords Bruce and Sackvile, for example, as in Sackvile's reply to Bruce: "soe will I allwaies be readie to meete any that desire to make triall of my valor by soe faire a course as you requier" (Folger MS. 1054.4. x.d. 165). Because of the threat to civil order inherent in this attitude, even the few writers who endorsed the combat attempted to restrict the practice of duelling. A combat, all manuals sternly specify, should

only be the last resort: if at all possible, a quarrel should be settled by verbal satisfaction or in civil trial. In his adaptation of Girolamo Muzio's *Il Duello,* Vincentio Saviolo argues cogently that the challenger's motives must avoid all baseness:

> [H]owbeit the cause of their quarrell be just, yet they combate not justly, that is, not in respect onely of justice and equitie, but either for hatred, or for desire of revenge... whence it commeth to passe, that many howbeit they have the right on their sides, yet come to be overthrown.... Wherefore, no man ought to presume to punish another. (Y4r)

19. For an alternative and equally valid interpretation of this scene, see Levin 226–7. Levin argues that the roaring scenes parody "the duelling code—or rather, the abuse of this code exemplified in the main plot by the Colonel.... the outward forms of what is supposed to be a code of honor" (226). Brian Parker argues that even Chough's "Cornish passion for wrestling, with its insistence on 'fair play' and a 'fair fall' and use of specialized jargon, provides a comically non-aristocratic version of the duelling of the main plot" (66).
20. See also Clark 297.
21. We can find support for this impression of protobourgeois attitudes in other plays by Middleton as well. In *The Phoenix,* Falso and Tangle engage in a parodic verbal duel with law-terms.
22. As Brian Parker comments,

    > [Middleton's] status as a professional writer... placed him at the very edge of social respectability. Not surprisingly, his drama as a whole reflects an acute and painfully ironic sense of class conflict and of what the gentry of the early seventeenth century considered socially acceptable. (54)

23. Romei carefully considers the arguments that analogize combat and battle, swordsmans' strategies and military strategies, but in response to these arguments he finds that the most basic parallels were those existing between the duel and the law:

    > As for the persons that enter into combate, who can deny that the termes of assailant & defendant (as we have said) be not properly belonging to Lawiers?... in Combate injuries are debated, which be opprobrious, and which not: And who can better distinguish of this then the Lawier, who hath justice for his proper object... and consequently of injuries, which bee the principall part of injustice?... In combate the lie is discussed, and question mooved, which is a prevalent lie, and which none: & this apperteineth to the lawier; for the magistrate punisheth lying, and especially that which to another mans losse and reproach, is tolde. (158–9)

    Ager's attempts at reconciliation could be viewed as a further degree on the continuum that would include his internal debate on the justice of his cause. But to his soldier friends, Ager's reasoning seems overly nice, and entirely opposed to the military ideal of action as virtuous. Thus, when Ager tries to make peace with the Colonel, his

second comments, "Stay, let me but run him through the tongue a little; / There's lawyer's blood in't" (III.i.61–2).
24. For an alternative explanation of this scene, see A. L. and M. K. Kistner 37–8.
25. Brian Parker (70–1) and Kistner and Kistner (39–41) oppose one another in their interpretation of the morality of the Colonel's response to Ager's victory.
26. In *The Elementary Structures of Kinship,* Levi-Strauss asserts that women served as counters to facilitate, bind, and organize relationships among men (61). Gayle Rubin's article "The Traffic in Women: Notes on the 'Political Economy' of Sex" further examines the ramifications of this idea. Ironically, my reading of this scene accords quite closely with that of Richard Levin, one of the earliest critics of this play after Bowers (1971). Levin asserts that "the real equivalent in this action to the embrace of Jane and Fitzallen is not Ager's betrothal to this woman ... but the climactic moment ... when he falls headlong into the Colonel's waiting arms" (230–1). Levin comments only briefly on the implications and the sexual politics inherent in this parallel, implicitly accepting the male friendship at face value.
27. René Girard argues that Hamlet "needs, in order to stir up his vengeful spirit, ... a revenge theater more convincing than his own" (287). Among the plot elements that Girard perceives as revenge theater are the players' performance of Hecuba's murder, Fortinbras's attack on Poland, and Laertes' own performance of mourning. This last, he argues, is what determines Hamlet to act (288–90).
28. Girard offers a different and very intriguing perspective; he argues that

> Claudius and the old Hamlet are not blood brothers first and enemies second; they are brothers in murder and revenge. In the myths and legends from which most tragedies are drawn, brotherhood is almost invariably associated with the reciprocity of revenge. ... [T]he status of a brother can become a mark of undifferentiation ... the sign paradoxically that there are no more signs and that a warring confusion tends to prevail everywhere. (284)

29. See Bowers, *Elizabethan Revenge Tragedy* 184–202 for the prevalence of this convention.
30. C. L. Barber refers to Hamlet as "a prince who encounters and must redeem the buried majesty of an ideal royal father" (190). Barber also insightfully describes this play, along with *Julius Caesar* and *Macbeth,* as "tragic struggles to take over heritage and male identity by destroying paternal figures of authority, attempts to destroy them so as to become them—only to find self-destruction in the process" ("The Family in Shakespeare" 191).
31. Cf. Maus, *Inwardness* 1–6.
32. Cf. Paster, "Leaky Vessels" 211–33, Jardine 103–40.
33. It is convenient to cite Ernest Jones's *Hamlet and Oedipus* (1949) as the beginning of the body of psychoanalytic criticism of *Hamlet.* C. S. Lewis, however, names Schlegel (1815), Hazlitt (1815), Hallam

(1837–9), Coleridge (1856), Sievers (1866), Raleigh (1907), and Clutton-Brock (1922) as critics who analyze Hamlet's psychology (cited in Lewis 140–1). Maus (1995) has recently addressed the issues of theatricality and deceit in her excellent discussion of "seeming" in *Hamlet* (*Inwardness* 1–5).

34. See Saxo *Inwardness* Grammaticus.
35. Although by Shakespeare's time the judicial duel was something of an anachronism, it was still practiced in Europe at the time the play was set. However, Shakespeare probably thought less about historical consistency than about evoking a generally medieval world (cf. Calderwood and Rackin).
36. In *Elizabethan Drama and the Viewer's Eye,* Alan C. Dessen suggests that the poisoned sword of the false fencing match functions as an emblem of the corrupt poison spreading from Claudius throughout the kingdom (103–7) and that "the duel metaphor aptly describes the battle of wits and stratagems waged since act 2" (103). Astutely, Dessen comments,

> The plot of *Hamlet* is replete with feints, thrusts, parries, and counterattacks. … Laertes represents Claudius's final weapon, while Hamlet's bated sword may serve as a comment upon his "almost blunted purpose." In a summary statement immediately preceding the fencing match that serves as dramatic climax, Shakespeare has given his audience a suggestive analogy between the duel and the central conflict of the tragedy. (103)

37. Although Hamlet is notoriously inattentive to courtesy throughout the play, we have Ophelia's word for his former self as

> The courtier's, soldier's, scholar's, eye, tongue, sword,
> Th' expectation and rose of the fair state,
> The glass of fashion and the mould of form. (III.i.151–3)

38. As far as the anachronistic nature of the fencing match is concerned, such a performative event does not seem to have been common in England even during the period when Shakespeare was writing. As Joan Ozark Holmer points out, the fencing match in Shakespeare's version of *Hamlet* was his own innovation. Holmer suggests that

> Shakespeare's sophisticated addition of the fencing match … is not so strange as it is ingenious and relevant for an Elizabethan audience directly concerned with rapier play and actual duels as well as the code of honor attendant upon such gentlemanly activity. ("Shakespeare's Duello Rhetoric" 18)

Holmer's comment explains why Shakespeare might have invented such an entertainment for the play's final scene. I suspect that Shakespeare was combining a variety of courtly practices like the joust, for example, when he invents this conclusion to the play. He also may have known that displays of skill with sword and buckler were common entertainments in Anglo-Saxon days. But the custom did not carry over to rapier-fights among gentlemen-though the records of the English Masters of Arms indicate that on two occasions their members were summoned to give displays at Greenwich. As I explained in Chapter One, fencing-masters discouraged their pupils from engaging in "friendly" bouts, particularly outside of the fencing school, and though a few pupils probably did so anyway, their purpose would have been sport or practice, not the entertainment of others. There is no record that fencing exhibitions like the one in *Hamlet* were ever performed as courtly entertainments during the Tudor or Stuart reigns. Given that such performative displays of skill were associated with those whose social status was below that of the gentleman, it seems unlikely that such performances as Laertes and Hamlet's occurred in Renaissance England.

39. For discussion of Claudius's use of the performative fencing display as concealment for the assassination of Prince Hamlet, see Holleran 67 and Alexander 23 and 174–5.
40. I should acknowledge the debt that this point owes to Johan Huizinga.
41. My perceptions of closure in *Hamlet* have been greatly shaped by a conversation with Nicholas Pullin at the 1999 Text and Presentation Conference at the University of Florida. Indeed, our conversation eventually brought me to reverse the earlier position that I detailed in "Manhood and the Duel: Enacting Masculinity in *Hamlet*," *The Centennial Review* 43.3 (1999): 501–12.
42. James W. Stone argues,

> This feminine in [Hamlet] bonds homosocially with the same element in Horatio, Hamlet's soulmate.... Horatio displaces Ophelia as Hamlet's bosom bondman because he is safely desexualized. He is feminine insofar as he represents the allegorized rational soul, but he has excised the (feminizing) madness and passion of sexual desire. (80)

43. See Adelman on Gertrude, Holleran on Ophelia.
44. As Eugene Waith points out, *Bussy D'Ambois* was written for one of the private theaters and its themes were probably shaped by Chapman's desire to address that more sophisticated audience (110–11). Richard S. Ide argues that playwrights were likely to perceive Robert Devereux, Earl of Essex, as the prototypical model for the soldier in conflict with society; Ide also reads Chapman's dedication of his 1598 translation of *The Iliad* to Essex as a sign of admiration and sympathy (*Possessed by Greatness* 3–5). Even though Waith and Ide differ as to how contemporary culture shaped these plays, they agree that Chapman consciously responded to his society in the creation of the dramatic figure of Bussy.

45. Cf. Ornstein 51–2, Ide, *Possessed by Greatness* 78, Kistler 143.
46. Boas and Parrott linked Chapman with Stoicism in their editions of the two plays; see also Schoell 118, Wieler, Smith 340, Hallett and Hallett 269, and Bement 345–57.
47. Ennis Rees suggests that Chapman conceives of two heroic types based on Homeric models: the Achilles type, of which Bussy would be an example, and the Odysseus type, exemplified by Clermont. In the dedication to his translation of *The Odyssey,* Chapman characterized each of Homer's epics as essentially different:

> In one, Predominant Perturbation; in the other, over-ruling Wisedome: in one, the Bodie's fervour and fashion of outward Fortitude to all possible height of heroicall Action; in the other, the Mind's inward, constant and unconquered Empire, unbroken, unaltered with any most insolent and tyrannous infliction. (*Chapman's Homer* II:5)

> On this basis, Rees abstracts a dichotomy of heroism to Chapman's plays (30). MacClure follows Rees on this issue (109). Although I find the analogy overly simplistic, I believe Rees and MacClure are wise to recognize other classical models for Renaissance notions of heroism besides that offered in the *Poetics.*

48. See MacClure (113, 125) and Tricomi for a similar view.
49. Kistler argues that reading the play as an apologia for Stoicism is false to Chapman's intentions; she asserts that "[i]n Clermont, the playwright has carefully drawn a pedantic philosopher who is destroyed because he is unable to translate his abstract ideals into daily reality" (131). Responding to several critics including Kistler, Ide argues in "Exploiting the Tradition: The Elizabethan Revenger as Chapman's 'Complete Man'" that Stoicism is neither "a monolithic ideal governing Clermont's behavior … [nor] the norm by which to judge his actions" (160). In Ide's view, Clermont becomes a complete man by reconciling through his behavior the contradictions between Stoicism and "an aristocratic code of heroic conduct" (161).
50. Ide asserts that

> The psychological context of the imagery is the association of the element of fire with Mars, with choler, and with the passion of anger. But in its grandeur the imagery is associated with the Olympian fire of Zeus the Conqueror, as Hesiod's *Theogony* depicts him (lines 617–719), with the godlike spirit of Homer's epic warriors, and with Achilles' heroic wrath in particular. This crucial epic evocation testifies that Bussy's spirit, like that of Achilles … is fueled by Olympian fire, not by the earthly counterfeit. … One is aware, however, that the fire imagery … of *The Iliad* conveys not only the grandeur but the danger of such a divine gift. (*Possessed by Greatness* 82–3)

51. Waddington remarks that "Bussy's stature in the duel is enhanced by the description of his opponent's death" (24). Waith remarks on the context in which Chapman enlarges on the action through metaphor.

> In contrast to Marlowe, whose imagery presents the hero's situation concretely, Chapman uses imagery to
>
>> make some thought about the hero concrete—the sea of his energy, which is both wild and yet contained within bounds—the fire of his spirit, which has the various qualities of a torch borne in the wind, a beacon, a falling star, a thunderbolt, and which, after death, returns to a world of fire. Marlowe's images keep the hero himself before our eyes; Chapman's focus the mind's eye on a problem of the heroic nature. (111)

52. Ide suggests that Chapman did not intend the audience to be distracted but consciously attempted to "elicit an ambivalent response from the audience" (*Possessed by Greatness* 84). Ide believes that Chapman's intentions were inflected by the mixed views of Essex after the rebellion (*Possessed by Greatness* 83–4).
53. Lever points out how Chapman eventually indicates the hero's limitations in staging the manner of his death: "Bussy is killed by gunpowder, the first weapon of the modern state, which strikes out of reach of his sword, and is indifferent to human valour" (47). This ignominious death shows the conquest of Bussy's magnanimous spirit by the low-born but pragmatic assassin with no particular ideals.
54. All quotations from this play are from George Chapman, *The Revenge of Bussy D'Ambois*, in *The Plays of George Chapman*, ed. Thomas Marc Parrott (New York: Russell and Russell, 1961), 75–148.
55. Parrott, however, asserts that while Montsurry is a poltroon in the sequel, in the original play he "commands in a measure, at least, our respect for his faith in his wife, his horror at the discovery of her guilt, and his resolute determination to have revenge at any cost" (II, 576).
56. Cf. Lordi 27. As Lordi points out, Baligny says that it would be "hellish" "[t]o live depriv'd of our King's grace and countenance" (II.i.60–1). The play predates James's edict against duelling—but it anticipates echoes James's wording.
57. Leggatt suggests that Chapman may have intended to caricature the Stoic philosophy of passive acceptance "when Montsurry lies down and refuses to fight" (526). Lever, offering an alternative view, asserts that Chapman purposely uses several parodic elements in this scene "to isolate the revenge theme and make it evident to the audience that sympathetic identification is not called for.... Chapman suggests the partial and inadequate nature of the attitudes to life presented so far on *both* levels of his play" (53). Lever argues that Chapman creates this effect in order to show Clermont as a complete human being at the end of the play (53–4). However, other critics (including myself) perceive Clermont as a unified character who remains what he is through the end of the play.
58. Kistler argues that the focus of the play is not the revenge itself but Clermont's change from Stoic to cerebral avenger who "must eventually betray his own principles" (131–2). In contrast, Hallett and

Hallett assert that there are two plots—the revenge plot and the plot in which Clermont acts as the king's subject, a plot that attempts to consider "how...a good man [can] be the loyal subject of a corrupt ruler" (271). Lordi also suggests that the play unites two plots—"the revenge plot and the intrigue plot"—but he perceives in the play a "unity of design" that focuses "on the contrast between the nobility and honor of [the] ideal hero as opposed to the ignobility and treachery of nearly every other character in the play" (14).

59. Lordi perceives Charlotte's sense of honor as

> limited to the primitive code of an eye-for-an-eye and excessive pride in family ... reminiscent of the private, divisive, dangerous kind of wild justice and pride ... which ends in hatred, the blood feud, and the destruction of society. (31)

Lordi considers her view a contrast to Clermont's "more balanced concept of honor" (31).

60. As Kistler points out, "The final irony of *The Revenge* is the same as that in *Bussy:* Clermont's existence, like Bussy's, has no impact whatsoever on political reality. The corrupt court system continues unaffected by their lives or deaths" (143).

Chapter 5   When Women Fight

1. Linda Woodbridge sees an early modern anxiety about gender roles reflected in the practice of cross-dressing and the convention of the cross-dressed stage heroine.

   > All through these years, literature maintained a steady interest in female mannishness, male effeminacy, and the whole question of the "nature" of men and women, often suggesting that traditional sex roles were undergoing pronounced mutation in the modern world. The most obvious literary vehicle for exploring such issues was transvestite disguise in the drama. (*Women and the English Renaissance* 153)

2. Antitheatrical tract-writers such as Phillip Stubbes refer to cross-dressed men as "monsters, of both kindes, half women, half men" (F5V). Almost any behavior that went contrary to cultural norms of gender might be demonized in this way. I would like to define the nature of that monstrosity and to consider other significant, related ways of regarding gender hermaphroditism.

3. I use the early modern terms "man-maid" and "man-woman" as blanket expressions encompassing various forms of gender blending; Suzanne Gossett, however, suggests that the term "man-maid" was conventionally used to refer to Pallas Athene (from my point of view, a prototypical martial maid) (109–10).

4. Theodora Jankowski discusses Margaret and much of the recent criticism regarding her in *Women in Power in the Early Modern Drama* (89–102).

5. Steve Brown argues that many recent studies of theatrical cross-dressing have been marred by what he deems an overreliance on such works as Carolyn G. Heilbrun's *Toward a Recognition of Androgyny* (1973) and June Singer's *Androgyny: Toward a New Theory of Sexuality* (1976). To apply the ideas of these works to the early modern period, Brown argues, is anachronistic; he comments that " 'androgyny,' as promoted by Heilbrun and Singer, is scarcely the ancient, transhistorical philosophy...it may seem" (260). Brown points out that the term "androgyne" in sixteenth-century England was used to refer to effeminate men, eunuchs, and biological hermaphrodites; the Neoplatonic use of the term was strictly as a kind of trope (260).

For the sake of ease, I shall refer to the Platonic notion of the manmaid as an "androgyne" and the corpus of traits derived from the myth of Hermaphroditus as the "hermaphrodite." I am well aware, however, that during the early modern period the word hermaphrodite, like androgyne, referred less to classical myth than to the monstrousness of gender- or sex-combining. In *Ganymede in the Renaissance: Homosexuality in Art and Society*, James M. Saslow explains,

> The terms *hermaphrodite* and *androgyne* (man-woman) were used interchangeably by Greek and Latin Writers. Patristic Greek also used the word [androgynos] to mean "effeminate," leading to early conflation of the concepts of hermaphroditism, effeminacy, and homosexuality.... The word *hermaphroditus* continued to signify homosexual during the Middle Ages.... The same complex of associations continued to link the hermaphrodite with sexuality, particularly homosexuality, throughout the Renaissance. (78)

But the myth of Hermaphroditus was used during the English Renaissance as a figure for certain interesting gender relations. Douglas Bush briefly notes Spenser's use of the myth in Book III of *The Faerie Queene* (142). Lauren Silberman offers an incisive and extremely convincing analysis of the myth's influence on gender construction on different planes of *The Faerie Queene* (*Transforming Desire* 49–70). Although the term "hermaphrodite" had negative connotations of monstrousness, literary uses of the myth functioned in entirely different ways.

6. According to Jerome Schwartz, androgyny represented in this tradition "a dreamlike idealism in which sexuality is the means of achieving some transcendent state of mystical union with the Godhead" (123). In an earlier article, Rackin relates androgyny to the potential of the individual: "an image of transcendance...of breaking through the constraints that material existence imposes on spiritual aspiration or the personal restrictions that define our roles in society" ("Androgyny" 29). In contrast, Grace Tiffany explains the use of androgyny as "the effort to create interpersonal relationships, and

thus to reconstitute the original healthy hermaphroditic organism" (31). All of these meanings do appear in different contexts.
7. Not only can this interpretation be found in the sequence of events but also in Ovid's word-choice. As Silberman says,

> The potential double meaning of words such as "perstat" [stands firm], "mollita" [soft], and "mollescat" [became soft or effeminate] points up the gap between Hermaphroditus' understanding of his own experience and what his story can signify.... Although Hermaphroditus gives an implicitly moral interpretation to his physical transformation—he has become weak and effeminate—the physical suggestions of postcoital flaccidity indicate a physiological interpretation of his experience. (*Transforming Desire* 51)

8. Writers such as John of Garland, Giovanni del Virgilio, and Boccaccio view the story as an allegory for how the sex of a fetus develops, arguing that the fountain of Salmacis represents the womb; others read the boy and the nymph as symbols representing "the true self and those impulses and influences unworthy of that self" ("Mythographic Transformations" 645–6). Yet others identify Salmacis as the love of sensual pleasures, while one writer, Bersuire, reads the fable as "an allegory of the incarnation" ("Mythographic Transformations 646–7).
9. See Heywood, *Gunaikeion: or, Nine Bookes of Various History Concerning Women* (1624) 223, for one version of the story.
10. For example, in *The First Blast of the Trumpet against the Monstrous Regiment of Women* (1558), a diatribe against Mary Tudor, John Knox refers to Amazons, calling them "monstrous women, that could not abide the regiment of men and therefore killed their husbands" (10). His allusion indicates a logical progression: autonomous women violate the laws of nature, and therefore they are monstrous; monsters commit monstrous acts, like murder of one's husband (petty treason according to English common law). This type of murder both confirms Amazons as monsters and demonstrates how the subversion of anatomy (in Knox's terms) leads to the overthrow of civil law and the structures that form the basis of civil society.
11. For allegorical uses of the man-maid figure (indiscriminately referred to as *both* androgyne and hermaphrodite), see Geoffrey Fenton's *Monophylo* (1572), Elyot's *The Boke named The Governour,* and, most famously, Spenser's *The Faerie Queene.*
12. As Laqueur explains, during the early modern period those who possessed the genitalia of both sexes were examined to determine "to which gender the architecture of their bodies most readily lent itself" in order to "[maintain] clear social boundaries, [maintain] the categories of gender" (135).
13. See also Nancy Hayles, *The Ambivalent Ideal: The Concept of Androgyny in English Renaissance Literature*. R. Valerie Lucas points out that the terms "monster," "hermaphrodite," and "Amazon" were all applied to female transvestites by their critics (68). A most useful

text on the subject of literary uses of the man-maid figure is Grace Tiffany's *Erotic Beasts and Social Monsters: Shakespeare, Jonson, and Comic Androgyny*; Tiffany rightly, I think, divides representations of the man-maid into positive androgyny or "mythic hermaphroditism," meaning a representation drawing on Neoplatonic ideas of the androgyne, and negative androgyny or "satiric hermaphroditism," meaning representations that depict the man-maid as transgressive, foolish, or monstrous (11–20). However, Tiffany makes little or no use of Ovid, an omission that I try here to rectify.

14. This verse letter, "To Pamphilia from the father-in-law of Seralius," is reprinted in *The Poems of Lady Mary Wroth*, ed. Josephine Roberts. The letter was brought to my attention by Ann Rosalind Jones and Peter Stallybrass's article "Fetishizing Gender: Constructing the Hermaphrodite in Renaissance Europe."

15. For a discussion of the references to cross-dressing in the records of the Repertories of the Alderman's Court in the London City Record Office and the Bridewell Court Minute Books, see the work of R. Mark Benbow, cited by Howard in her "Crossdressing" article.

16. The historians Rudolf M. Dekker and Lotte C. van de Pol found 119 cases mentioned in seventeenth- and eighteenth-century Netherlandish documents, and fifty cases in Great Britain during the same period; they consider these cases "the tip of the iceberg" (1, 3). Dekker and van de Pol's study is a fascinating and valuable account of female transvestism during the period. They record that the tradition of female transvestism existed throughout Europe but was strongest in England, Germany, and the Netherlands (2). It was acceptable for women to wear men's clothing for certain restricted periods, as during festivities, often when they were traveling, and sometimes when they were hunting (8). The commonest professions for documented cross-dressed women were that of soldiers and sailors. The women were probably discovered because the close quarters in which soldiers and sailors lived prevented them from concealing their sex forever. It is difficult to tell whether these careers were popular among cross-dressed women or whether they are the ones in which cross-dressers were most frequently discovered (9–10). Unlike Jean Howard and her source, the historian R. Mark Benbow, Dekker and van de Pol are able to say with certainty, "practically all our disguised women came from the lower classes" (11). Many of these women found that it was easier to get work commonly allotted to adolescent boys than to men because their feminine appearance made them look much younger than men of their own age (15). Most were single and alone in the world, and they found more and better economic opportunities disguised as men than they did as women (32–5).

17. In her *Cité des Dames*, Christine de Pizan records two stories of virgin women who dressed as men in order to become monks.

The cross-dressing enabled them both to join masculine society and to escape that society's restriction of female self-assertion. (Lucas offers a useful discussion of transvestism in female saints in "*Hic Mulier:* The Female Transvestite in Early Modern England" [75].) Montaigne recounts the story of several young women from a village who decided "to dress up as males and thus continue their life in the world" (5). As Stephen Greenblatt points out,

> A man in Renaissance society had symbolic and material advantages that no woman could hope to attain.... All other significant differential indices of individual existence ... could, at least in imagination, be stripped away, only to reveal the underlying natural fact of sexual difference. (*SN* 76)

When Shakespeare's Rosalind and her cousin Celia leave Duke Frederick's court, Celia suggests that they disguise their gentility to avoid harassment and assault; Rosalind proposes to cross-dress: "Because that I am more than common tall, / ... We'll have a swashing and a martial outside, / As many other mannish cowards have / That do outface it with their semblances" (I.iii.115–22). Her "semblance" is compared, by implied analogy, to her disguised rank. Both disguises increase the women's safety in the anarchic world they fear they will find outside of court. Jean Howard posits that "if citizen wives of the Jacobean period assumed men's clothes as a sign of their wealth and independence, lower-class women may well have assumed them from a sense of vulnerability" ("Crossdressing" 421).

18. A variant of this aphorism is still, in fact, a state motto for one of the mid-Atlantic states of the United States (!).
19. See the work of Barbara Correll for an insightful discussion of the role of the social inferior and his (or her) ability to influence superiors through indirection.
20. For the probable authorship of *Swetnam the Woman-hater,* see Coryl Crandall's Introduction, 28–30, and Woodbridge 320–1.
21. This disputation probably recalls Ovid's story of the debate between Jupiter and Juno about whether men or women enjoy more pleasure in sexual intercourse (told in the story of Tiresias, who was the umpire of their debate). In this case, we can easily recognize the shift from pleasure, an unquestionable positive in classical Roman culture, to the offenses done to others and to society through the manipulation of desire, a negative.
22. Woodbridge comments that this scapegoating of the misogynist is common in early modern dramas that give prominence to women. She suggests that discrediting the misogynist or casting him out is intended to eliminate any anxiety and to clear the way for a happy ending (*Women and the English Renaissance* 289–90).
23. This is, in fact, a conventional argument that appears in texts such as Robert Vaughan's *A Dyalogue defensyve for women, agaynst malycyous detractours* (1542).

24. As well as writing *The Arraignment of Lewd, idle, froward, and unconstant women* (1615), the historical Joseph Swetnam also wrote *The Schoole of The Noble and Worthy Science of Defence* two years later.
25. Linda Woodbridge offers a history of such debates in her landmark study *Women and the English Renaissance: Literature and the Nature of Womankind, 1540–1620*.
26. It would be reasonable to recognize here an echo of the story of Penthesilea, the Amazon queen. Fighting in Troy against the Greeks, she was killed by Achilles, who fell in love with her when, as Jeanne Addison Roberts says, "she [was] safely dead and no longer threatening" (129).
27. Interestingly, Simon Shepherd offers a very different reading of this scene. In his view, the women's actions are liberatory:

> That [the women] should act as a *group* is one of the important political gestures of the play: Swetnam had sought to privatise women as individuals, to use the terror of gossip to isolate and confine.... The women of the play, anticipating the Leveller petitioners, are happy to share their evil name together, and the play supports them.... The duel of the Amazon and woman-hater has to be followed by the irruption of women from outside. (216–17)

28. This plot twist, which appears in this 1610–11 play, also appears in Sir Philip Sidney's *The New Arcadia* in the story of Parthenia, who disguises herself as the Knight of the Tomb and goes to seek death at the hand of Amphialus, who has killed her husband Argalus in combat (395–9).
29. All quotations from this play are from Francis Beaumont and John Fletcher, *The Maid's Tragedy*, ed. Howard B. Norland (Lincoln, NE: University of Nebraska Press, 1968).
30. Cf. Howard "Crossdressing."
31. In *Women and the English Renaissance: Literature and the Nature of Womankind, 1540–1620,* Linda Woodbridge seeks "the impact of the formal [*querelles des femmes*] controversy on other genres" (114) and notes that "[t]he literature exactly contemporary with the height of the controversy over women in male attire ... from about 1610 to about 1620, ... rejoices in assertive women" (244), but warns that "the connection between literature and life in the Renaissance was oblique rather than direct" (265). I suggest here a rather classic New Historicist move: that these two heroines appeared in plays written and enjoyed partly because they both present and contain dangerous energies. Other critics have noted that Moll Cutpurse seems rather purer than her real-life counterpart, and Besse, despite considerable ability, is entirely submissive to the patriarchal order. The creation of Besse and Moll seems to me to revise earlier stereotypes of the shrew. As Simon Shepherd asserts in *Amazons and Warrior Women: Varieties of Feminism in Seventeenth-Century Drama,* the presentation of such characters suggests that assertive women may still be rendered "safe."

32. All quotations from this play are from Thomas Heywood, *The Fair Maid of the West, Or, A Girle worth gold* in *Heywood's Dramatic Works* (New York: Russell and Russell, 1874, rpt. 1964), 2:255–331.
33. As Jean Howard points out, "As long as Bess inhabits the tavern world her chastity remains a subject of wonder and doubt" ("An English Lass amid the Moors" 103). Bess's difficulty is, in fact, the barmaid's dilemma: to keep her customers, she must make the place pleasant to them. The demands of her job guarantee that men will often try to force greater intimacy upon her than she is willing to grant. Bess actually manifests a fair degree of rhetorical skill in her ability to keep most men at a distance while making them feel welcome to the inn, but Heywood's plot places more emphasis on the two over-aggressive men with whom Bess's careful rhetoric fails.
34. Jean Howard's comment on the incident is very telling. She argues that "as a crossdresser who knows how to wear and use a sword, Bess *could* be that threatening figure from the masculine imagination: the castrating woman who turns the world upside down" ("An English Lass amid the Moors" 105). My point, of course, is that none of the female duellists I discuss turn out to be the castrating woman at all. Howard further argues that Bess' strategy is enacted "to teach a man to be more manly" (105). The validity of this point depends on how one believes that Heywood defines manliness.
35. All quotations from this play are from Thomas Middleton (and Thomas Dekker)'s *The Roaring Girl* in *The Works of Thomas Middleton*, ed. A. H. Bullen (New York: AMS, 1964), 4.1–152.
36. See, for example, Viviana Comensoli's discussion of Moll's "boldly unconventional nature" (258–60); Mary Beth Rose's assertion that Moll is "an embodiment of female independence boldly challenging established social and sexual values and, by the fact of her existence, requiring evaluation and response" (368); Jonathan Dollimore's argument that "the representation of gender inversion generates an interrogation of both the sexual metaphysic and the social order" (65); and Jean Howard's comment that the play is "traversed by discourses of social protest not found in most of the plays I have so far examined" ("Crossdressing" 436).
37. In his Introduction to *The Roaring Girl*, the editor Paul Mulholland touches briefly on this point (29–30).
38. Mary Beth Rose notes the first two of these three meanings (381).
39. See Mulholland's brief discussion of this scene and its relation to a parallel incident in the anonymous jest-biography *Long Meg of Westminster* (15–16).
40. All quotations from this play are from Francis Beaumont and John Fletcher, *Love's Cure Or The Martial Maid*, ed. Marea Mitchell (Nottingham, UK: Nottingham Drama Texts, 1992).
41. Both Mary Beth Rose (367) and Jean Howard ("Crossdressing" 436) make much of this aspect of *The Roaring Girl*. While it is true that

there are a number of disguised women in early modern drama, the fact that Clara would prefer to continue her life as a man indefinitely suggests to me that the playwrights actually characterize her not even as a man-woman or hermaphrodite but as a woman who has *crossed over* into masculinity—a cultural transsexual, if you will. I would argue that this aspect of Clara's identity renders her portrayal even more subversive than Moll's.

42. Rather amusingly, this element of the plot rings changes on a stage convention commonly used in the depiction of *male* soldiers. In her chapter on the stage misogynist, Woodbridge comments on "a figure from the debate about changing sex roles in peacetime—the soldier who returns to find his martial masculinity inappropriate in a civilian world where women's tastes and values prevail" (*Women and the English Renaissance* 278–9).

43. Jardine points out that the popularity of humanist education for gentry and noblewomen may perhaps be explained by its use to indoctrinate women to the values of obedience, modesty, and chastity (*Daughters* 51–7). Nearly all scolds who were publicly shamed belonged to small towns and wood-pasture villages (Underdown 119–26). There is some indication that gentlewomen and noblewomen were more carefully trained in subordination than were women of lower rank, who also had a greater measure of economic independence from men.

44. Lucas rightly, I think, suggests that Clara's promise recalls a scene in *The Life and Pranks of Long Meg of Westminster* (1582) when Long Meg submits to her new husband's beating rather than choosing to fight with him. Both scenes "allay ... the anxieties about the bellicose female transvestite who attacks men" (79).

Conclusion

1. When I refer to the opposition between humanism and the courtly ethos, I refer specifically to humanists' attacks on chivalry as a mode of being that conceals beneath its glamor the brutality of war. Dominic Baker-Smith examines the works written by More and Erasmus between 1513 and 1518—specifically Erasmus's *Institutio Principis Christiani* (1516) and his *Dulce bellum inexpertis* (1514), and the part of More's *Utopia* that deals with war—to show how both writers seemed to respond to Henry VII's desire for military glory with a condemnation of chivalric ideas. Assessing their role in European politics at that time, Baker-Smith comments, "in a Europe poised for international conflict the cult of honour seemed to them to be a baneful influence" (144).

BIBLIOGRAPHY

Adelman, Janet. *Suffocating Mothers: Fantasies of Maternal Origin in Shakespeare's Plays,* Hamlet *to* The Tempest. New York: Routledge, 1992.
———. "Anger's My Meat: Feeding, Dependency, and Aggression in *Coriolanus.*" In *Representing Shakespeare: New Psychoanalytic Essays.* Eds. Murray M. Schwartz and Coppelia Kahn. Baltimore: Hopkins University Press, 1980. 129–49.
Akrigg, G. P. V. *Jacobean Pageant, Or the Court of King James I.* Cambridge: Harvard University Press, 1962. Rpt. New York: Atheneum, 1967.
———, ed. *The Letters of James VI and I.* Berkeley: University of California Press, 1984.
Alexander, Nigel. *Poison, Play, and Duel.* Lincoln: University of Nebraska Press, 1971.
Andrewes, Lancelot. *The Morall Law Expounded.* London: Sparke, Milbourne, Cotes, and Crooke, 1642.
Anglo, Sydney, ed. *Chivalry in the Renaissance.* Woodbridge, UK: Boydell, 1990.
———. Introduction. *Chivalry in the Renaissance.* Ed. Sydney Anglo. Woodbridge, UK: Boydell, 1990. xi–xvi.
———. *Spectacle, Pageantry, and Early Tudor Policy.* Oxford: Clarendon, 1969.
Anon. "Hic Mulier" and "Haec Vir." In *Half Humankind: Contexts and Texts of the Controversy about Women in England, 1540–1640.* Eds. Katherine Usher Henderson and Barbara F. McManus. Urbana: University of Illinois Press, 1985. 264–76; 277–89.
Anon. *The Life of Long Meg of Westminster.* London: Robert Bird, 1635. STC 17783.
Anon. *Swetnam the Woman-hater Arraigned by Women.* In *Swetnam the Woman-hater: The Controversy and the Play.* Ed. Coryl Crandall. Purdue, IN: Purdue University Studies, 1969. 53–140.
Aries, Philippe. *Centuries of Childhood: A Social History of Family Life.* Trans. Robert Baldick. New York: Vintage, 1962.
Asad, Talal. *Genealogies of Religion: Discipline and Reasons of Power in Christianity and Islam.* Baltimore: Hopkins University Press, 1993.

Austern, Linda. "'Sing Againe, Syren': The Female Musician and Sexual Enchantment in Elizabethan Life and Literature." *Renaissance Quarterly* 42 (1989): 420–48.

Aylward, J. D. *The English Master of Arms from the Twelfth to the Twentieth Century.* London: Routledge, 1956.

Bacon, Francis. *The Charge of Sir Francis Bacon Knight, His Majesties Attourney Generall, touching Duells, upon an information in the Starchamber against Priest and Wright.* London: Robert Wilson, 1614.

———. "On Revenge." *Bacon's Essays.* Ed. Richard Whately. Freeport, NY: Books for Libraries, 1973.

Baker, J. H. *An Introduction to English Legal History.* 3rd ed. London: Butterworths, 1990.

Baker-Smith. "'Inglorious glory': 1513 and the Humanist Attack on Chivalry." In *Chivalry in the Renaissance.* Ed. Sydney Anglo. Woodbridge, UK: Boydell, 1990. 129–44.

Bakhtin, M. M. *The Dialogic Imagination.* Trans. Caryl Emerson and Michael Holquist. Ed. Michael Holquist. Austin: University of Texas Press, 1981.

———. *Rabelais and His World.* Trans. Helene Iswolsky. Bloomington: University of Indiana Press, 1984.

Baldick, Robert. *The Duel: A History.* New York: Barnes and Noble, 1965.

Barber, C. L. "The Family in Shakespeare's Development: Tragedy and Sacredness." In *Representing Shakespeare: New Psychoanalytic Essays.* Eds. Murray M. Schwartz and Coppelia Kahn. Baltimore: Hopkins University Press, 1980. 188–202.

———. *The Idea of Honour in the English Drama, 1591–1700.* Goteborg: Gothenburg Studies, 1957.

Barish, Jonas. *The Anti-theatrical Prejudice.* Berkeley: University of California Press, 1981.

Baron, Hans. *In Search of Florentine Civic Humanism: Essays on the Transition from Medieval to Modern Thought.* 2 vols. Princeton, NJ: Princeton University Press, 1988.

Bartlett, Robert. *Trial by Fire and Water: The Medieval Judicial Ordeal.* Oxford: Clarendon, 1986.

Barton, Anne. Introduction to *Much Ado about Nothing.* In *The Riverside Shakespeare.* Ed. G. Blakemore Evans. Boston: Houghton Mifflin, 1974. 327–31.

Bauer, Dale M., and Susan Janet McKinstry, eds. *Feminism, Bakhtin, and the Dialogic.* Albany: State University of New York Press, 1991.

Beaumanoir, Philippe de. *Coutumes de Beauvaisis.* 2 vols. Paris: A. Picard et Fils, 1970–74.

Beaumont, Francis, and John Fletcher. *Love's Cure Or, The Martial Maid.* Ed. Marea Mitchell. Nottingham, UK: Nottingham Drama Texts, 1992.

———. *The Maid's Tragedy.* Ed. Howard B. Norland. Lincoln: University of Nebraska Press, 1968.

Bement, Peter. "The Stoicism of Chapman's Clermont D'Ambois." *SEL* 12 (1972): 345–57.

Bennett, Josephine W., Oscar Cargill, and Vernon Hall, Jr., eds. *Studies in the English Renaissance Drama*. New York: New York University Press, 1959.

Bergeron, David M. *King James and Letters of Homoerotic Desire*. Iowa City: University of Iowa Press, 1999.

———, ed. *Pageantry in the Shakespearean Theater*. Athens: University of Georgia Press, 1985.

Bergson, Henri. *Laughter. Comedy*. Ed. Wylie Sypher. Baltimore: Hopkins University Press, 1980. 61–190.

Berry, Ralph. "Hamlet and the Audience: The Dynamics of a Relationship." In *Shakespeare and the Sense of Performance: Essays in the Tradition of Performance Criticism in Honor of Bernard Beckerman*. Eds. Marvin and Ruth Thompson. Newark: University of Delaware Press, 1989.

Billacois, François. *The Duel: Its Rise and Fall in Early Modern France*. Ed. and trans. Trista Selous. New Haven: Yale University Press, 1990.

Bloom, Harold. *Shakespeare: The Invention of the Human*. New York: Penguin, 1998.

Bloomfield, Morton W. "The Problem of the Hero in the later Medieval Period." In *Concepts of the Hero in the Middle Ages and the Renaissance*. Eds. Norman T. Burns and Christopher J. Reagan. Albany: State University of New York Press, 1975. 27–48.

Bolgar, R. R. "Hero or Anti-Hero? The Genesis and Development of the *Miles Christianus*." In *Concepts of the Hero in the Middle Ages and the Renaissance*. Eds. Norman T. Burns and Christopher J. Reagan. Albany: State University of New York Press, 1975. 120–45.

Bornstein, Diane. *Mirrors of Courtesy*. Hamden, CT: Archon, 1975.

Bouchet, Jean. *Epistres morales and familieres du traverseur*. Poictiers: Jacques Bouchet, 1545.

Bowers, Fredson. *Elizabethan Revenge Tragedy 1587–1642*. Princeton: Princeton University Press, 1940.

———. "Middleton's *Fair Quarrel* and the Duelling Code." *JEGP* 36 (1937): 40–65.

Bracciolini, Poggio. "On Honour." *Knowledge, Goodness, and Power: The Debate over Nobility among Quattrocento Italian Humanists*. Ed. and trans. Albert Rabil, Jr. Binghamton, NY: Medieval and Renaissance Texts, 1991.

Bracton. *Bracton De Legibus et Consuetudinibus Anglie*. Eds. G. E. Woodbine and S. E. Thorne. Cambridge: Harvard University Press, 1968–77.

Braden, Gordon. *Renaissance Tragedy and the Senecan Tradition*. New Haven: Yale University Press, 1985.

Brailsford, Dennis. *Sport and Society: Elizabeth to Anne*. London: Routledge, 1969.

Brathwait, Richard. *The English Gentleman*. London: 1630. Rpt. Norwood, NJ: Walter J. Johnson, 1975.

———. *The English Gentleman*. London: 1630. Rpt. Amsterdam: Theatrum Orbis Terrarum, 1975.

Bray, Alan. *Homosexuality in Renaissance England*. New York: Columbia University Press, 1982, rpt. 1995.

Bremmer, Jan, and Herman Readenburg, eds. *A Cultural History of Gesture*. Ithaca: Cornell University Press, 1991.

Brombert, Victor, ed. *The Hero in Literature*. Greenwich, CT: Fawcett, 1969.

———. Introduction. *The Hero in Literature*. Ed. Victor Brombert. Greenwich, CT: Fawcett, 1969. 11–21.

Brown, Steve. "The Boyhood of Shakespeare's Heroines: Notes on Gender Ambiguity in the Sixteenth Century." *SEL* 30 (1990): 243–63.

Bruni, Lionardi d'Arezzo. *Leonhardi Aretini de studiis et litteris ad illustrem dominam baptistam de Malatesta tractalus*. Liptzk, per Martinum Lantzberg, 1501. (Also 1483, 1496.)

Bruto, Giovanni Michele. *La institutione di una fanciulla nata nobilmente*. Anvers: Jehan Bellere, C. Plaintain, 1555.

Bryson, Anna. "The Rhetoric of Status: Gesture, Demeanour, and the Image of the Gentleman in Sixteenth- and Seventeenth-Century England." In *Renaissance Bodies: The Human Figure in English Culture, c. 1540–1660*. Eds. Lucy Gent and Nigel Llewellyn. London: Reaktion, 1990. 136–53.

Bryson, Frederick R. *The Point of Honor in Sixteenth-Century Italy: An Aspect of the Life of the Gentleman*. New York: Columbia University Press, 1935.

———. *The Sixteenth-Century Italian Duel: A Study in Renaissance Social History*. Chicago: The University of Chicago Press, 1938.

Bullough, Geoffrey. *Narrative and Dramatic Sources of Shakespeare*. New York: Columbia University Press, 1957–75. 8 vols.

Burnett, Mark Thornton. *Masters and Servants in English Renaissance Drama and Culture: Authority and Obedience*. New York: St. Martin's, 1997.

Burns, Norman T., and Christopher J. Reagan, eds. *Concepts of the Hero in the Middle Ages and the Renaissance*. Albany: State University of New York Press, 1975.

Bush, Douglas. *Mythology and the Renaissance Tradition in English Poetry*. Minneapolis: University of Minnesota Press, 1932. Revised ed. New York: Norton, 1963.

Butler, Judith. *Gender Trouble: Feminism and the Subversion of Identity*. New York: Routledge, 1990.

———. "Performative Acts and Gender Constitution." In *Performing Feminisms: Feminist Critical Theory and Theatre*. Ed. Sue-Ellen Case. Baltimore: Hopkins University Press, 1990. 270–82.

Calderwood, James L. *To be and not to be: Negation and Metadrama in Hamlet*. New York: Columbia University Press, 1983.

Case, Sue-Ellen, ed. *Performing Feminisms: Feminist Critical Theory and Theatre*. Baltimore: Hopkins University Press, 1990.

Cassirer, Ernst, Paul Oskar Kristeller, and John Herman Randall, Jr., eds. *The Renaissance Philosophy of Man*. Chicago: The University of Chicago Press, 1965.

Castiglione, Baldesar. *The Book of the Courtier*. Trans. Charles S. Singleton. New York: Anchor, 1959.

Castle, Egerton. *Schools and Masters of Fence, from the Middle Ages to the End of the Eighteenth Century*. London: Bell, 1893.

Chapman, George. *Bussy D'Ambois* and *The Revenge of Bussy D'Ambois*. In *The Plays of George Chapman*. Ed. Thomas Marc Parrott. New York: Russell and Russell, 1961. 1–74 and 75–148.

———. *Chapman's Homer*. Ed. Allardyce Nicoll. 2 vols. Princeton: Princeton University Press, 1967.

———. *The Revenge of Bussy D'Ambois*. Ed. Robert J. Lordi. Salzburg: Salzburg Institut, 1977.

Chartier, Roger, ed. *A History of Private Life: Vol. 3, Passions of the Renaissance*. General eds. Philippe Aries and Georges Duby. Trans. Arthur Goldhammer. Cambridge: Harvard University Press, 1989.

Clark, Ira. "Writing and Dueling in the English Renaissance." *Medieval and Renaissance Drama in England*. Ed. Leeds Barroll. Vol. 7. London: Associated University Press, 1995. 275–304.

Comensoli, Viviana. "Play-making, Domestic Conduct, and the Multiple Plot in *The Roaring Girl*." *SEL* 27 (1987): 249–66.

Cook, Carol. "'The Sign and Semblance of Her Honor': Reading Gender Difference in *Much Ado about Nothing*." *PMLA* 101 (1986): 186–202.

Correll, Barbara. "Malleable Material, Models of Power: Women in Erasmus's "Marriage Group" and *Civility in Boys*." *ELH* 57 (1990): 241–62. Rpt. in *The End of Conduct: Grobianus and the Renaissance Text of the Subject*. Ithaca: Cornell University Press, 1996.

Cox, Gerard H. "'Like a Prince Indeed': Hal's Triumph of Honor in *1 Henry IV*." In *Pageantry in the Shakespearean Theater*. Ed. David M. Bergeron. Athens: University of Georgia Press, 1985. 130–49.

Crandall, Coryl. Introduction. In *Swetnam the Woman-hater: The Controversy and the Play*. Ed. Coryl Crandall. Purdue, IN: Purdue University Studies, 1969. 1–52

Crandall, Coryl, ed. *Swetnam the Woman-hater: The Controversy and the Play*. Purdue, IN: Purdue University Studies, 1969.

Crooke, Helkiah. *Microcosmographia: A Description of the Body of Man*. London, 1615. STC 6062.

D., T. C. D. *A Discourse of Duels, shewing the Sinful Nature and Mischievous Effects of Them, and Answering the Usual Excuses mde for them by Challengers, Accepters, and Seconds*. London: Roycroft for Clavell, 1687. Wing C5462.

Davis, Natalie Zemon. "Women in Politics." In *A History of Women: Renaissance and Enlightenment Paradoxes*. Eds. Natalie Zemon Davis and Arlette Farge. General eds. Georges Duby and Michelle Perrot. Cambridge, MA: Belknap, 1993. 167–83.

Davis, Natalie Zemon, and Arlette Farge, eds. *A History of Women: Renaissance and Enlightenment Paradoxes*. General eds. Georges Duby and Michelle Perrot. Cambridge, MA: Belknap, 1993.

Davis, Natalie Zemon, and Arlette Farge. "Infractions, Transgressions, Rebellions." In *A History of Women: Renaissance and Enlightenment Paradoxes*. Eds. Natalie Zemon Davis and Arlette Farge. General eds. Georges Duby and Michelle Perrot. Cambridge, MA: Belknap, 1993. 437–43.

Dawson, Anthony. "Much Ado about Signifying." *SEL* 22:2 (1982): 211–221.

Dekker, Rudolf M., and Lotte van de Pol. *The Tradition of Female Transvestism in Early Modern Europe*. New York: St. Martin's, 1989.

D'Espagne. *Antiduello: or, a Treatise in which is discussed the lawfulnesse and unlawfulnesse of single combats*. London: Thomas Harper for Benjamin Fisher, 1632. STC 10530.

Dessen, Alan C. *Elizabethan Drama and the Viewer's Eye*. Chapel Hill: University of North Carolina Press, 1977.

———. *Elizabethan Stage Conventions and Modern Interpreters*. Cambridge: Cambridge University Press, 1984.

Di Grassi, Giacomo. *His True Arte of Defense*. London: Shaw for Jaggard, 1594. STC 12190.

Dollimore, Jonathan. "Subjectivity, Sexuality, and Transgression: The Jacobean Connection." *Renaissance Drama* 17 (1986): 53–81.

Dover, Kenneth J. *Greek Homosexuality*. Cambridge: Harvard University Press, 1978.

Dunlap, Rhodes. "James I, Bacon, Middleton, and the making of *The Peacemaker*." In *Studies in the English Renaissance Drama*. Eds. Josephine W. Bennett, Oscar Cargill, and Vernon Hall, Jr. New York: New York University Press, 1959. 82–94.

Elias, Norbert. *The Civilizing Process: The History of Manners and State Formation and Civilization*. Trans. Edmund Jephcott. Oxford: Blackwell, 1994.

Elyot, Sir Thomas. *The Book named the Governor*. 1531. Ed. S. E. Lehmberg. New York: Dutton, 1962.

Empson, William. *Some Versions of Pastoral*. Norfolk, CT: New Directions, 1960.

Epstein, Julia, and Kristina Straub, eds. *Body Guards: The Cultural Politics of Gender Ambiguity*. New York: Routledge, 1991.

Erasmus, Desiderius. *De Civilitate Morum Puerilium*. Ed. J. K. Sowards. *Literary and Educational Writings* 3 and 4. *The Collected Works of Erasmus*, Vols. 25 and 26. Toronto: University of Toronto Press, 1985.

Evans, G. Blakemore, ed. *The Riverside Shakespeare*. Boston: Houghton Mifflin, 1974.

F., G. *Duell-ease: A worde with valiant spiritts shewing the abuse of Duells that Valour, refuseth Challenges and Private Combates*. London: Ann Griffin, 1633. STC 1063.

BIBLIOGRAPHY

Feher, Michel, Ramona Naddaff, and Nadia Tazi, eds. *Fragments for a History of the Human Body, Part Two*. New York: Zone, 1989.

Ferguson, Arthur B. *The Chivalric Tradition in Renaissance England*. Washington, DC: Folger, 1986.

———. *The Indian Summer of English Chivalry: Studies in the Decline and Transformation of Chivalric Idealism*. Durham: Duke University Press, 1960.

Ferne, John. *The Blazon of Gentrie*. London: John Windet, 1586. STC 10825.

Fetrow, Fred M. "Chapman's Stoic Hero in *The Revenge of Bussy D'Ambois*." *SEL* 19 (1979): 229–37.

Findlay, Heather. "Renaissance Pederasty and Pedagogy: The 'Case' of Shakespeare's Falstaff." *Yale Journal of Criticism* 3 (1989): 229–38.

Fletcher, Anthony, and John Stevenson, eds. *Order and Disorder in Early Modern England*. Cambridge: Cambridge University Press, 1985.

Florio, John. *Second Frutes*. London, 1591. Rpt. New York: Da Capo, 1969.

Foucault, Michel. *Discipline and Punish: The Birth of the Prison*. Trans. Alan Sheridan. New York: Vintage, 1979.

Franko, Mark. *Dance as Text: Ideologies of the Baroque Body*. Cambridge: Cambridge University Press, 1993.

Friedland, M. L., ed. *Rough Justice: Essays in Crime in Literature*. Toronto: University of Toronto Press, 1991.

Frye, Northrop. *Anatomy of Criticism*. Princeton: Princeton University Press, 1957.

———. *Fools of Time: Studies in Shakespearean Tragedy*. Toronto: University of Toronto Press, 1967.

Frye, Susan. *Elizabeth I: The Competition for Representation*. Oxford: Oxford University Press, 1993.

Fuller, Thomas. *The Holy State and the Profane State*. 2 vols. New York, 1938; rpt. New York: Columbia University Press, 1966.

Furnivall, Frederick J., ed. *Early English Meals and Manners*. London: N. Trubner and Co., 1868; rpt. Detroit: Singing Tree Press, 1969.

Gaudemet, J. "Les ordalies au moyen age: Doctrine, legislation, et pratique canoniques." *La Preuve*. Vol. 17. Brussels: Recueils de la societe Jean Bodin pour l'histoire comparative des institutions, 1965.

Gent, Lucy, and Nigel Llewellyn, eds. *Renaissance Bodies: The Human Figure in English Culture, c. 1540–1660*. London: Reaktion, 1990.

Girard, René. "Hamlet's Dull Revenge." In *Literary Theory/Renaissance Texts*. Eds. Patricia Parker and David Quint. Baltimore: Hopkins University Press, 1986. 280–302.

Goffmann, Erving. *Relations in Public: Microstudies of the Public Order*. New York: Basic, 1971.

Goldberg, Jonathan. *James I and the Politics of Literature: Jonson, Shakespeare, Donne, and their Contemporaries*. Baltimore: Hopkins University Press, 1983.

———. *Sodometries: Renaissance Texts, Modern Sexualities*. Stanford, CA: Stanford University Press, 1992.

Gossett, Suzanne. "'Man-maid, Begone!': Women in Masques." *ELR* 18.1 (1988): 96–113.

Grammaticus, Saxo. *Saxo Grammaticus and the Life of Hamlet: A Translation, History, and Commentary*. Ed. and trans. William F. Hansen. Lincoln: University of Nebraska Press, 1983.

Greenblatt, Stephen. *Renaissance Self-Fashioning From More to Shakespeare*. Chicago: University of Chicago Press, 1980.

———. *Shakespearean Negotiations: The Circulation of Social Energy in Renaissance England*. Berkeley: University of California Press, 1988.

Greene, Thomas M., Peter Demetz, and Lowry Nelson, Jr., eds. *The Disciplines of Criticism: Essays in Literary Theory, Interpretation, and History*. New Haven: Yale University Press, 1968.

———. "The Flexibility of the Self in Renaissance Literature." In *The Disciplines of Criticism: Essays in Literary Theory, Interpretation, and History*. Eds Thomas M. Greene, Peter Demetz, and Lowry Nelson, Jr. New Haven: Yale University Press, 1968. 241–64.

Haber, Judith. "'My Body Bestow upon My Women': The Space of the Feminine in *The Duchess of Malfi*." *Renaissance Drama* 28 (1997): 133–59.

Hair, Paul, ed. *Before the Bawdy Court: Selections from Church Court and Other Records Relating to the Correction of Moral Offences in England, Scotland, and New England, 1300–1800*. New York: Barnes and Noble, 1972.

Hajnal, John. "Two Kinds of Preindustrial Household Formation System." *Population and Development Review* 8 (1982): 449–94.

Hall, Edward T. *The Hidden Dimension*. Garden City, NY: Doubleday, 1966.

Hallett, Charles A., and Elaine S. Hallett. *The Revenger's Madness: A Study of Revenge Tragedy Motifs*. Lincoln: University of Nebraska Press, 1980.

Hanning, Robert W., and David Rosand, eds. *Castiglione: The Ideal and the Real in Renaissance Culture*. New Haven: Yale University Press, 1983.

Hayles, Nancy. *The Ambivalent Ideal: The Concept of Androgyny in English Renaissance Literature*. Unpublished Ph.D. dissertation, University of Rochester, 1976

Hays, Janice. 'Those 'soft and delicate desires': *Much Ado* and the Distrust of Women.' *The Women's Part: Feminist Criticism of Shakespeare*. Eds. Carolyn Ruth Swift Lenz, Gayle Green, and Carol Thomas Neely. Urbana: University of Illinois Press, 1980. 79–99.

Hediger, H. *Wild Animals in Captivity*. London: Butterworth, 1950.

Heinemann, Margot. *Puritanism and Theatre: Thomas Middleton and Opposition Drama under the Early Stuarts*. Cambridge: Cambridge University Press, 1980.

Henderson, Katharine Usher, and Barbara F. McManus. *Half Humankind: Contexts and Texts of the Controversy about Women in England, 1540–1640*. Urbana: University of Illinois Press, 1985.

Hendricks, Margo, and Patricia Parker, eds. *Women, "Race," and Writing in the Early Modern Period*. New York: Routledge, 1994.

Herrick, Robert. "The Country Life, To the Honored Mr. Endymion Porter, Groom of the Bedchamber to His Majesty." In *Ben Jonson and the Cavalier Poets*. Ed. Hugh MacLean. New York: Norton, 1974. 137–9.

Heywood, Thomas. *The Fair Maid of the West, Or, A Girle worth gold*. In *Heywood's Dramatic Works*. New York: Russell and Russell, 1874, rpt. 1964. II.255–331.

———. *Gunaikeion, or, Nine Bookes of Various History Concerninge Women*. London, 1624. STC 13285.

Holinshed, Raphael. *Chronicles of England, Scotland, and Ireland*. 1587. Rpt. London: J. Johnson et al. 1808.

Holleran, James V. "Maimed Funeral Rites in *Hamlet*." *ELR* 19 (1989): 65–93.

Holmer, Joan Ozark. "'Draw, if you be men': Saviolo's Significance for *Romeo and Juliet*." *Shakespeare Quarterly* 45.2 (1994): 163–89.

———. "Shakespeare's Duello Rhetoric and Ethic: Saviolo versus Segar." *English Language Notes* 31.2 (1993): 10–22.

Howard, Jean E. "An English Lass amid the Moors: Gender, Race, Sexuality, and National Identity in Heywood's *The Fair Maid of the West*." In *Women, "Race," and Writing in the Early Modern Period*. Eds. Margo Hendricks and Patricia Parker. New York: Routledge, 1994. 101–17.

———. "Crossdressing, The Theatre, and Gender Struggle in Early Modern England." *Shakespeare Quarterly* 39.4 (1988): 418–40.

———. *Shakespeare's Art of Orchestration: Stage Technique and Audience Response*. Chicago: University of Illinois Press, 1984.

———. *The Stage and Social Struggle in Early Modern England*. New York: Routledge, 1994.

Howard, Skiles. "Hands, Feet, and Bottoms: Decentering the Cosmic Dance in *A Midsummer Night's Dream*." *Shakespeare Quarterly* 44 (1993): 325–52.

Howell, Thomas. *Devises*. London: H. Jackson, 1581. STC 13875.

Hughes, Paul L., and James F. Larkin, C. S. V., eds. *Tudor Royal Proclamations*. 2 vols. New Haven: Yale University Press, 1969.

Huizinga, Johan. *Homo Ludens: A Study of the Play-element in Culture*. Boston: Beacon, 1955.

Ide, Richard S. "Exploiting the Tradition: The Elizabethan Revenger as Chapman's 'Complete Man.'" *Medieval and Renaissance Drama in England* 1 (1984): 159–72.

———. *Possessed with Greatness: The Heroic Tragedies of Chapman and Shakespeare*. Chapel Hill: University of North Carolina Press, 1980.

Jackson, James L. Introduction. *Three Elizabethan Fencing Manuals*. Ed. James L. Jackson. Delmar, NY: Scholars' Facsimiles, 1982. v–ix.

———. ed. *Three Elizabethan Fencing Manuals*. Delmar, NY: Scholars' Facsimiles, 1982.

Jacobs, Deborah. "Critical Imperialism and Renaissance Drama: The Case of *The Roaring Girl*." In *Feminism, Bakhtin, and the Dialogic*. Eds. Dale M. Bauer and Susan Janet McKinstry. Albany: State University of New York Press, 1991. 73–84.

James I. *A Publication of His Majesty's Edict against Private Combats and Combatants.* London: Robert Barker, Printer to the King, 1613. STC 8498.

James, Mervyn. "English Politics and the Concept of Honour, 1485–1642." In *Society, Politics and Culture: Studies in Early Modern England.* Cambridge: Cambridge University Press, 1986. 308–415.

Jankowski, Theodora. *Women in Power in the Early Modern Drama.* Urbana: University of Illinois Press, 1992.

Jardine, Lisa. *Still Harping on Daughters: Women and Drama in the Age of Shakespeare.* New York: Columbia University Press, 1983.

———. "Twins and Travesties: Gender, Dependency, and Sexual Availability in *Twelfth Night*." In *Erotic Politics: Desire on the Renaissance Stage.* Ed. Susan Zimmerman. New York: Routledge, 1992. 27–38.

Javitch, Daniel. *Poetry and Courtliness in Renaissance England.* Princeton: Princeton University Press, 1978.

———. "Rival Arts of Conduct in Elizabethan England: Guazzo's *Civile Conversatione* and Castiglione's *Courtier*." *Yearbook of Italian Studies* 1 (1971): 178–98.

Jones, Ann Rosalind, and Peter Stallybrass. "Fetishizing Gender: Constructing the Hermaphrodite in Renaissance Europe." In *Body Guards: The Cultural Politics of Gender Ambiguity.* Eds. Julia Epstein and Kristina Straub. New York: Routledge, 1991, 80–111.

Jones, Ernest. *Hamlet and Oedipus.* Rev. ed. Garden City, NY: Double Day, 1949.

Jones, Richard Foster. *The Triumph of the English Language.* Stanford: Stanford University Press, 1953, rpt. 1966.

Jonson, Ben. *The Alchemist.* In *Ben Jonson.* Eds. C. H. Herford and Percy Simpson. Oxford: Clarendon, 1937. 10 vols. V: 283–408.

Jordan, Constance. *Renaissance Feminism: Literary Texts and Political Models.* Ithaca: Cornell University Press, 1990.

Jorgensen, Paul A. *Shakespeare's Military World.* Berkeley: University of California Press, 1956, rpt. 1973.

Keen, Maurice. *Chivalry.* New Haven: Yale University Press, 1984.

Kelso, Ruth. *The Doctrine of the English Gentleman in the Sixteenth Century.* Urbana: University of Illinois Press, 1929.

———. *Doctrine for the Lady of the Renaissance.* Urbana: University of Illinois Press, 1956.

Kiernan, Victor G. *The Duel in European History: Honour and the Reign of Aristocracy.* Oxford: Oxford University Press, 1988.

Kipling, Gordon. *The Triumph of Honour: Burgundian Origins of the Elizabethan Renaissance.* The Hague: University of Leiden Press, 1977.

Kistler, Suzanne F. "'Strange and Far-Removed Shores': A Reconsideration of *The Revenge of Bussy D'Ambois*." *Studies in Philology* 77 (1980): 128–44.

Kistner, A. L., and M. K. Kistner. "The Themes and Structures of *A Fair Quarrel*." *Tennessee Studies in Literature* 23 (1978): 31–46.

Knox, John. "The First Blast of the Trumpet against the Monstrous Regiment of Women." In *John Knox on Rebellion*. Ed. Roger A. Mason. Cambridge: Cambridge University Press, 1994. 3–47.

Krieger, Elliot. "Social Relations and the Social Order in *Much Ado about Nothing*." *Shakespeare Survey* 32 (1979): 49–61.

Kuchta, David. "The Semiotics of Masculinity in Renaissance England." In *Sexuality and Gender in Early Modern Europe: Institutions, Texts, Images*. Ed. James Grantham Turner. Cambridge: Cambridge University Press, 1993. 233–46.

Laqueur, Thomas. *Making Sex: Body and Gender from the Greeks to Freud*. Cambridge: Harvard University Press, 1990.

La Touche, P. "Letters patent of the King for the Establishment of the Royal Academy of Dance for the city of Paris; verified in Parliament on March 30, 1662." (Appendix 3.) Trans. Mark Franko. In Mark Franko. *Dance as Text: Ideologies of the Baroque Body*. Cambridge: Cambridge University Press, 1993. 176–80.

Lea, Henry Charles. *The Duel and the Oath*. 1866. Rpt. Philadelphia: University of Pennsylvania Press, 1974.

Leggatt, Alexander. "The Tragedy of Clermont D'Ambois." *Modern Language Review* 77:3 (1982): 524–36.

Lenz, Carolyn Ruth Swift, Gayle Greene, and Carol Thomas Neely. *The Woman's Part: Feminist Criticism of Shakespeare*. Urbana: University of Illinois Press, 1980.

Lever, J. W. *The Tragedy of State*. London: Methuen, 1971.

Levin, Richard. "The Three Quarrels of *A Fair Quarrel*." *Studies in Philology* 61 (1965): 219–31.

Levine, Laura. "Men in Women's Clothing: Anti-theatricality and Effeminization from 1579 to 1642." *Criticism* 28.2 (Spring 1986): 121–43.

———. *Men in Women's Clothing: Anti-theatricality and Effeminization, 1579–1642*. Cambridge: Cambridge University Press, 1994.

Levi-Strauss, Claude. *The Elementary Structures of Kinship*. Trans. James Harle Bell, John Richard von Sturmer, and Rodney Needham. Ed. Rodney Needham 1949. Boston: Beacon, 1969.

Lewis, C. S. "Hamlet: The Prince or the Poem?" *Proceedings of the British Academy* 28 (1942): 139–54.

Lordi, Robert J. Introduction. *The Revenge of Bussy D'Ambois*. Ed. Robert J. Lordi. Salzburg: Salzburg Institut, 1977. 1–38.

Lucas, R. Valerie. "*Hic Mulier*: The Female Transvestite in Early Modern England." *Renaissance and Reformation* 12.1 (1988): 65–84.

MacClure, Millar. *George Chapman: A Critical Study*. Toronto: University of Toronto Press, 1966.

Maclean, Ian. *The Renaissance Notion of Woman*. Cambridge: Cambridge University Press, 1980.

Maffei, Scipione. *Della Scienza Chiamata Cavalleresca*. Rome, 1710.

Marot, Jehan. "Le Doctrinal des Princesses et Nobles Dames faict et deduict en XXIIII Rondeaulx et Premierement." In *Le Lexique de Jehan Marot dans le doctrinal des princesses et nobles dames*. Ed. Giovanna Trisolini. Ravenna: Longo, 1978.

Marozzo, Achile. *Opera Nova*. Modena, 1536.

Marshall, Cynthia. "Wrestling as Play and Game in *As You Like It*." *Studies in English Literature 1500–1900* 33 (1993): 265–87.

Massinger, Philip. *The Unnatural Combat*. In *The Plays and Poems of Philip Massinger*. Eds. Philip Edwards and Colin Gibson. Oxford: Clarendon, 1976. 2: 195–272.

Maus, Katharine Eisaman. "'Playhouse Flesh and Blood': Sexual Ideology and the Restoration Actress." *ELH* 46 (1979): 595–617.

———. *Inwardness and Theater in the English Renaissance*. Chicago: University of Chicago Press, 1995.

Mauss, Marcel. "Techniques of the Body." *Economy and Society* 2 (1973): 70–88.

McCoy, Richard. *The Rites of Knighthood: The Literature and Politics of Elizabethan Chivalry*. Berkeley: University of California Press, 1989.

McMullan, Gordon, and Jonathan Hope, eds. *The Politics of Tragicomedy*. London: Routledge, 1992.

Middleton, Thomas, and William Rowley. *A Fair Quarrel*. Ed. George R. Price. Lincoln: University of Nebraska Press, 1976.

——— and Thomas Dekker. *The Roaring Girl*. In *The Works of Thomas Middleton*. Ed. A. H. Bullen. New York: AMS, 1964. 4: 1–152.

Montaigne, Michel de. *The Essayes of Montaigne*. Trans. John Florio. New York: Modern Library, 1933.

———. *Montaigne's Travel Journal*. Trans. Donald M. Frame. San Francisco: North Point Press, 1983.

Mulcaster, Richard. *Positions Concerning the Training Up of Children*. Ed. William Barker. 1581. STC 18253 Rpt. Toronto: University of Toronto Press, 1994.

Mulholland, Paul. Introduction. In *The Roaring Girl*. Thomas Middleton and Thomas Dekker. Ed. Paul Mulholland. Manchester: Manchester University Press, 1987. 1–65

Naunton, Robert. *Fragmenta Regalia, or Observations on the Queen Elizabeth, Her Times and Favorites*. 1641. Rpt. Ed. John S. Cerovski. Washington, DC: Folger, 1985.

Neilson, George. *Trial by Combat*. New York: Macmillan, 1891.

Norland, Howard B. Introduction. *The Maid's Tragedy*. By Francis Beaumont and John Fletcher. Lincoln: University of Nebraska Press, 1968.

Ong, Walter J. "Latin Language Study as a Renaissance Puberty Rite." *Studies in Philology* 56:2 (1959): 103–24.

Orgel, Stephen. *Impersonations: The Performance of Gender in Shakespeare's England*. Cambridge: Cambridge University Press, 1996.

———. "Nobody's Perfect: Or Why Did the English Stage Take Boys for Women?" *South Atlantic Quarterly* 88 (1989): 7–29. Rpt. in *Impersonations: The Performance of Gender in Shakespeare's England*. Cambridge: Cambridge University Press, 1996.

Ornstein, Robert. *The Moral Vision of Jacobean Tragedy*. Madison: University of Wisconsin Press, 1960.

Ovid. *Ovid's Metamorphoses*. Trans. Rolfe Humphries. Bloomington: Indiana University Press, 1955.

Park, Clara Claiborne. "As We Like It: How a Girl Can Be Smart and Still Popular." *The American Scholar* 42 (1973): 262–78. Rpt. in *The Woman's Part: Feminist Criticism of Shakespeare*. Eds. Carolyn Ruth Swift Lenz, Gayle Greene, and Carol Thomas Neely. Urbana: University of Illinois Press, 1980. 100–16.

Parker, Brian. "*A Fair Quarrel* (1617), the Duelling Code, and Jacobean Law." *Rough Justice: Essays on Crime in Literature*. Ed. M. L. Friedland. Toronto: University of Toronto Press, 1991. 52–75.

Parker, Patricia. *Literary Fat Ladies: Rhetoric, Gender, Property*. New York: Methuen, 1987.

——— and David Quint, eds. *Literary Theory/Renaissance Texts*. Baltimore: Hopkins University Press, 1986.

———. "Shakespeare and Rhetoric: 'Dilation' and 'delation' in *Othello*." *Shakespeare and the Question of Theory*. Eds. Patricia Parker and Geoffrey Hartman. London: Methuen, 1985. 54–74.

——— and Geoffrey Hartman, eds. *Shakespeare and the Question of Theory*. London: Methuen, 1985.

Paster, Gail Kern. "Leaky Vessels: The Incontinent Women of City Comedy." In *Renaissance Drama as Cultural History: Essays from Renaissance Drama 1977–1987*. Ed. Mary Beth Rose. Evanston: Northwestern University Press, 1990. Rpt. in *The Body Embarrassed: Drama and the Disciplines of Shame in Early Modern England*. Ithaca: Cornell University Press, 1993.

———. *The Body Embarrassed: Drama and the Disciplines of Shame in Early Modern England*. Ithaca: Cornell University Press, 1993.

Pico della Mirandola. "Oration on the Dignity of Man." In *The Renaissance Philosophy of Man*. Eds. Ernst Cassirer, Paul Oskar Kristeller, and John Herman Randall, Jr. Chicago: The University of Chicago Press, 1965.

Plato. *Cratylus*. In *The Dialogues of Plato*. Ed. and trans. B. Jowett. Oxford: Oxford University Press, 1924.

———. *Symposium*. In *The Collected Dialogues of Plato*. Eds. Edith Hamilton and Huntington Cairns. Trans. Michael Joyce. Princeton: Bollingen, 1961.

Pullin, Nicholas. Conversation at the 1999 Text and Performance Conference at the University of Florida.

Quint, David. "Bragging Rights: Honor and Courtesy in Shakespeare and Spenser." In *Creative Imitation: New Essays on Renaissance Literature in Honor of Thomas M. Greene*. Eds. David Quint, Margaret W. Ferguson, G. W. Pigman III, and Wayne A. Rebhorn. Binghamton, NY: Medical and Renaissance Text Society, 1992. 391–430.

Quintilian, Marcus Fabius. *De Institutione Oratoria*. 2 vols. Trans. W. Guthrie. London: Dutton, 1805.

Rackin, Phyllis. "Androgyny, Mimesis, and the Marriage of the Boy Heroine on the English Renaissance Stage." *PMLA* 102.1 (1987): 29–41.

———. "Foreign Country: The Place of Women and Sexuality in Shakespeare's Historical World." In *Enclosure Acts: Sexuality, Property, and Culture in Early Modern England*. Eds. Richard Burt and John Michael Archer. Ithaca: Cornell University Press, 1994. 68–95. Rpt. of "Historical Difference/Sexual Difference." In *Privileging Gender in Early Modern England*. Ed. Jean R. Brink. Kirksville, MO: Sixteenth-Century Journal Publishers, 1993. Vol. 23 of *Sixteenth-Century Essays and Studies*. 37–63.

Radcliff-Umstead, Douglas, ed. *Human Sexuality in the Middle Ages and Renaissance*. Pittsburgh: CMRS, 1978.

Rees, Ennis. *The Tragedies of George Chapman: Renaissance Ethics in Action*. Cambridge, MA: Harvard University Press, 1954.

Reiter Rayna R., ed. *Toward an Anthropology of Women*. New York Monthly Review, 1975.

Rich, Barnaby. *The Excellency of Good Women*. London: Thomas Dawson, 1613. STC 20982.

Roach, Joseph R. *The Player's Passion: Studies in the Science of Acting*. Newark: University of Delaware Press, 1985.

Roberts, Jeanne Addison. *The Shakespearean Wild: Geography, Genus, and Gender*. Lincoln: University of Nebraska Press, 1991.

Romei, Haniball. *The Courtiers Academie*. Trans. John Kepers. London: Valentine Sims, 1598.

Rose, Mary Beth, ed. *Renaissance Drama as Cultural History: Essays from Renaissance Drama 1977–1987*. Evanston, K: Northwestern University Press, 1990.

———. "Women in Men's Clothing: Apparel and Social Stability in *The Roaring Girl*." *English Literary Renaissance* 14 (1984): 367–91.

Rowe, George E., Jr. *Thomas Middleton and the New Comedy Tradition*. Lincoln: University of Nebraska Press, 1979.

Rowson, E. "The Categorization of Gender and Sexual Irregularity in Medieval Arabic Vice Lists." In *Body Guards: The Cultural Politics of Gender Ambiguity*. Eds. J. Epstein and K. Straub. New York: Routledge, 1991. 671–93.

Rubin, Gayle. "The Traffic in Women: Notes on the 'Political Economy' of Sex." *Toward an Anthropology of Women*. Ed. Rayna R. Reiter. New York: Monthly Review, 1975. 157–210.

Saccone, Eduardo. "*Grazia, Sprezzatura, Affettazione* in Castiglione's *Book of the Courtier.*" *Glyph* 5 (1979): 34–54. Rpt. as "*Grazia, Sprezzatura, Affettazione* in the *Courtier.*" In *Castiglione: The Ideal and the Real in Renaissance Culture.* Eds. Robert W. Hanning and David Rosand. New Haven: Yale University Press, 1983.

Sackvile and Bruce. Letters. In Folger MS. 1054.4. x. d. 165.

Saslow, James M. *Ganymede in the Renaissance: Homosexuality in Art and Society.* New Haven: Yale University Press, 1986.

Saviolo, Vincentio. *Vincentio Saviolo His Practise.* London: Wolfe, 1595. STC 21788.

Schein, Seth L. *The Mortal Hero: An Introduction to Homer's Iliad.* Berkeley: University of California Press, 1984.

Schiesari, Juliana. *The Gendering of Melancholia: Feminism, Psychoanalysis, and the Symbolics of Loss in Renaissance Literature.* Ithaca: Cornell University Press, 1992.

Schoell, Franck L. *Etudes sur l'Humanisme Continental en Angleterre a la Fin de la Renaissance.* Paris: Payot, 1926.

Schwartz, Jerome. "Aspects of Androgyny in the Renaissance." In *Human Sexuality in the Middle Ages and Renaissance.* Ed. Douglas Radcliff-Umstead. Pittsburgh: CMRS, 1978.

Schwartz, Murray M., and Coppelia Kahn, eds. *Representing Shakespeare: New Psychoanalytic Essays.* Baltimore: Hopkins University Press, 1980.

Seagar, F. *The Schoole of Vertue, and Booke of Good Nourture for Children.* London, William Seares, 1557. Rpt. in *Early English Meals and Manners.* Ed. Frederick J. Furnivall. London: N. Trubner and Co., 1868. Rpt. Detroit: Singing Tree Press, 1969.

Sedgewick, G. C. *Of Irony, Especially in Drama.* Toronto: University of Toronto Press, 1935.

Segar, John. *The Booke of Honour and Armes.* London: Richard Jhones, 1590.

Selden, John. *The Duello, or Single Combat.* London, 1610.

Semenza, Gregory M. Colon. "Recovering the 'Two Sorts of Sport' in Early Modern English Prose." *Prose Studies: History, Theory, Criticism* 23.3 (2001): 1–30.

Semenza, Gregory M. Colon. *Sport, Politics, and Literature in the English Renaissance.* Forthcoming.

Shakespeare, William. *The Riverside Shakespeare.* Ed. G. Blakesmore Evans. Baston: Houghton Mifflin, 1974.

Shalvi, Alice. *The Relationship of Renaissance Concepts of Honour to Shakespeare's Problem Plays.* Salzburg: Salzburg Institut, 1972.

Shepherd, Simon. *Amazons and Warrior Women: Varieties of Feminism in Seventeenth-Century Drama.* New York: St. Martin's, 1981.

Sidney, Philip. *The Countess of Pembroke's Arcadia [The New Arcadia].* Ed. Victor Skretkowicz. Oxford: Clarendon, 1987.

Silberman, Lauren. "Mythographic Transformations of Ovid's Hermaphrodite." *Sixteenth Century Journal* 19.4 (1988): 643–52.

---. *Transforming Desire: Erotic Knowledge in Books III and IV of The Faerie Queene.* Berkeley: University of California Press, 1995.
Sieveking, A. Forbes. "Fencing and Duelling." *Shakespeare's England.* Vol. 2. Oxford: Clarendon, 1966. 389–407.
Silver, George. *Paradoxes of Defence.* 1599. Rpt. London: Shakespeare Association Facsimiles, 1933.
Sloane MS. 2530, Papers of the Masters of Defence of London, Temp. Henry VIII to 1590. In *The Noble Science, A Study and Transcription of Sloane Ms. 2530.* Ed. Herbert Berry. Newark: University of Delaware Press, 1991. 41–133.
Smith, James. "George Chapman (Part I)." *Scrutiny* 3 (1934–5): 339–50.
Smith, Thomas. *The Commonwealth of England.* London: Will Stansby for I. Smethwicke, 1635.
Smythe, John. *Certain Discourses Military.* (1590) Ed. J. R. Hale. Ithaca: Cornell University Press, 1964.
Spear, Gary. "Shakespeare's 'Manly' Parts: Masculinity and Effeminacy in *Troilus and Cressida.*" *Shakespeare Quarterly* 44.4 (1993): 409–22.
Spicer, Joaneath. "The Renaissance Elbow." In *A Cultural History of Gesture.* Eds. Jan Bremmer and Herman Roodenburg. Ithaca: Cornell University Press, 1991. 84–128.
Spingarn, J. E., ed. *Critical Essays of the Seventeenth Century,* 2 vols. Oxford: Oxford University Press, 1908.
Stallybrass, Peter. "Transvestism and the 'Body Beneath': Speculating on the Boy Actor." In *Erotic Politics: Desire on the Renaissance Stage.* Ed. Susan Zimmerman. New York: Routledge, 1992.
Steadman, John. *Milton and the Renaissance Hero.* Oxford: Clarendon, 1967.
Stone, James W. "Androgynous 'Union' and the Woman in *Hamlet.*" *Shakespeare Studies* 23 (1995): 71–99.
Stone, Lawrence. *The Crisis of the Aristocracy, 1558–1641.* Oxford: Clarendon, 1965.
---. *The Family, Sex, and Marriage in England 1500–1800.* New York: Harper, 1977.
Stoye, John. *English Travellers Abroad, 1604–1667.* New Haven: Yale University Press, 1989.
Stubbes, Phillip. *The Anatomie of Abuses.* London, 1583. Rpt. Netherlands: Da Capo Press, 1972.
Taylor, Mark. "Presence and Absence in *Much Ado about Nothing.*" *The Centennial Review* 33:1 (1989): 1–12.
Tiffany, Grace. *Erotic Beasts and Social Monsters: Shakespeare, Jonson, and Comic Androgyny.* Newark: University of Delaware Press, 1995.
Thibault, Gerard. *Académie de l'espée.* Paris, 1626.
Thompson, Marvin, and Ruth Thompson, eds. *Shakespeare and the Sense of Performance: Essays in the Tradition of Performance Criticism in Honor of Bernard Beckerman.* Newark: University of Delaware Press, 1989.
Tomlinson, Sophie. "She That Plays the King: Henrietta Maria and the Threat of the Actress in Caroline Culture." In *The Politics of Tragicomedy.*

Eds. Gordon McMullan and Jonathan Hope. Routledge: London, 1992. 189–207.

Traub, Valerie. "Prince Hal's Falstaff: Positioning Psychoanalysis and the Female Reproductive Body." *Shakespeare Quarterly* 40 (1989): 456–74.

Trexler, Richard C. *Sex and Conquest: Gendered Violence, Political Order, and the European Conquest of the Americas*. Ithaca: Cornell University Press, 1995.

Tricomi, Albert. "The Revised *Bussy D'Ambois* and *The Revenge of Bussy D'Ambois*: Joint Performance in Thematic Counterpoint." *English Language Notes* 9 (1972): 253–62.

Turner, Craig, and Tony Soper. *Methods and Practice of Elizabethan Swordplay*. Carbondale: Southern Illinois University Press, 1990.

Turner, James Grantham, ed. *Sexuality and Gender in Early Modern Europe: Institutions, Texts, Images*. Cambridge: Cambridge University Press, 1993.

Underdown, D. E. "The Taming of the Scold: The Enforcement of Patriarchal Authority in Early Modern England." In *Order and Disorder in Early Modern England*. Eds. Anthony Fletcher and John Stevenson. Cambridge: Cambridge University Press, 1985. 116–36.

Vaughan, William. *The Golden-Grove, moralized in three parts*. 2 vols. London: Simon Stafford, 1600. STC 24610.

Vermeule, Emily. *Aspects of Death in Early Greek Art and Poetry*. Berkeley: University of California Press, 1979.

Vigarello, Georges. "The Upward Training of the Body from the Age of Chivalry to Courtly Civility." In *Fragments for a History of the Human Body, Part Two*. Eds. Michel Feher, Ramona Naddaff, and Nadia Tazi. New York: Zone, 1989. 148–97.

Waddington, Raymond B. "Prometheus and Hercules: The Dialectic of *Bussy D'Ambois*." *ELH* 34 (1967): 21–48.

Waith, Eugene M. *The Herculean Hero in Marlowe, Chapman, Shakespeare, and Dryden*. New York: Columbia University Press, 1962.

Walker, Obadiah. *Of Education, Especially of Young Gentlemen; in Two Parts*. Oxfordshire: The Theater, 1683. Wing W402.

Watson, Curtis Brown. *Shakespeare and the Renaissance Concept of Honor*. Princeton: Princeton University Press, 1960.

Webster, John. *The Duchess of Malfi*. Ed. Elizabeth M. Brennan. New York: Norton, 1993.

Weste, Richard. "The Booke of Demeanor." *The Schoole of Vertue*. London, 1619. Rpt. in *Early English Meals and Manners*. Ed. Frederick J. Furnivall. London: N. Trubner and Co., 1868. Rpt. Detroit: Singing Tree Press, 1969.

Whigham, Frank. *Ambition and Privilege: The Social Tropes of Elizabethan Courtesy Theory*. Berkeley: University of California Press, 1984.

Whitman, Cedric H. "The Matrix of Heroism: Ajax." In *The Hero in Literature*. Ed. Victor Brombert. Greenwich, CT: Fawcett, 1969. 61–88.

Wickham, Glynne. *Early English Stages 1300 to 1600*. 3 vols. New York: Columbia University Press, 1959.

Wieler, John William. *George Chapman: The Effects of Stoicism upon his Tragedies*. 1949. Rpt. New York: Octagon, 1969.

Wilson, Thomas. *The Art of Rhetoric.* London: John Kingston, 1560. Rpt. ed. Peter E. Medine. University Park: Pennsylvania State University Press, 1994.

Wiseman, William. *The Christian Knight.* London: John Legatt, 1619.

Woodbridge, Linda. *Women and the English Renaissance: Literature and the Nature of Womankind, 1540–1620.* Urbana: University of Illinois Press, 1984.

——— and Edward Berry. Introduction. *True Rites and Maimed Rites: Ritual and Anti-Ritual in Shakespeare and his Age.* Urbana: University of Illinois Press, 1992. 1–43.

Wroth, Lady Mary. *The Poems of Lady Mary Wroth.* Ed. Josephine Roberts, Baton Rouge: Louisiana State University Press, 1983.

Yachnin, Paul. *Stage-Wrights: Shakespeare, Jonson, Middleton, and the Making of Theatrical Value.* Philadelphia: University of Pennsylvania Press, 1997.

Ziegler, Georgianna. "My Lady's Chamber: Female Space, Female Chastity in Shakespeare." *Textual Practice* 4.1 (1990): 73–100.

Zimmerman, Susan, ed. *Erotic Politics: Desire on the Renaissance Stage.* New York: Routledge, 1992.

Zitner, S. P. "Hamlet, Duellist." *University of Toronto Quarterly* 39 (1969): 1–18.

INDEX

Adams, Robert P., 171n2
Adelman, Janet, 29, 78, 126, 194n22, 202n43
adolescents, 76–78; *See also* boy(s)
Akrigg, G. P. V., 18, 193n15
Alexander, Nigel, 202n39
Amazon, 8, 78, 136–7, 141–46, 163, 207n10, 207n13, 210n26, 210n27, 210n31
Andrewes, Lancelot, 80–81
androgyne, 8, 136–38, 145–47, 191n36, 206n5, 206n6, 207n11, 207–08n13
Anglo, Sydney, 173n6, 174n11, 180n32
Antiduello, 188n25
antitheatricalists, 60, 101, 173n8, 189n31, 197n8, 205n2
Aries, Philippe, 42, 174n10
Aristotle, 23, 58, 96, 127, 144, 180n34, 196n4, 203n47
Asad, Talal, 13
Ascham, Roger, 139
Austern, Linda, 192n9
Aylward, J. D., 19, 46, 178n24, 183n4, 187n23

Bacon, Francis, 95, 100–105, 112, 180n31, 188n24
Baker, J. H., 115
Baker-Smith, 212n1
Bakhtin, M. M., 31–32, 174n10
Baldick, Robert, 185n13
Barber, C. L., 197n12, 200n30

Barish, Jonas, 173n8, 189n31, 197n8
Baron, Hans, 171n2
Bartlett, Robert, 12–14, 175n2
Barton, Anne, 181n45, 182n54
Beaumont, Francis, and John Fletcher
  Love's Cure Or, The Martial Maid, 8, 138–40, 156–67, 211n40, 212n41
  The Maid's Tragedy, 8, 139–40, 147–50, 210n29
Bellona, 88–89
Bement, Peter, 203n46
Bennett, Alexandra G., 196n33
Bergeron, David M., 193n15
Bergson, Henri, 67
Berry, Ralph, 123, 178n24
Billacois, Francois, 21, 26, 79, 86, 118, 176n13, 178n21, 181n39, 183n4, 188n25
Bloom, Harold, 39, 182n55
Bloomfield, Morton W., 23
Blount, Charles, 18, 25
Bolgar, R. R., 24, 180n33
Bonetti, Rocco, 19, 178n24, 183n4, 191n1
Bornstein, Diane, 15, 176n12, 177n15, 180n32
Bouchet, Jean, 74
Bowers, Fredson, 198n16, 200n26, 200n29
boy(s), 6–7, 32, 61–62, 66, 68, 71–84, 92, 101–02, 105, 113,

boy(s), – *continued*
  136, 137, 157, 170, 171n2, 178n24, 191n4, 192n11, 193n15, 194n17, 194n22, 195n28, 207n8, 208n16
  adolescents 76–78
Bracton, 13
Braden, Gordon, 23, 25, 181n35
Brailsford, Dennis, 178n23, 179n25
Brathwait, Richard, 26, 58, 73
Bray, Alan, 193n15
Brombert, Victor, 23, 25
Brown, Steve, 206n5
Bruce, Lord of Kinloss, 18, 198n18
Bruni, Lionardi d'Arezzo, 74, 171n2, 192n10
Bruto, Giovanni Michele, 73
Bryson, Anna, 42, 57, 61, 189n30, 197n10
Bryson, Frederick R., 44, 97, 175n2, 177n18, 187n24
Buckingham, Duke of, 193n15
Bullough, Vern L., 86
Burnett, Mark Thornton, 181n42
Bush, Douglas, 206n5
Butler, Judith, 5, 45, 174n9

Calderwood, James L., 201n35
Castiglione, Baldesar, 20, 24–25, 29–31, 42, 58, 69, 90, 111, 172n2
Castle, Egerton, 19, 46, 51, 178n24
castration, 77, 85, 153, 195n27, 211n34
champion, 14, 35, 37, 142, 144, 148, 175n9, 197n6
Chapman, George
  Bussy D'Ambois, 8, 24, 94, 110, 126–28, 133, 202n44, 203–4n51, 204n52, 204n53, 205n60
  Homer, translation of, 202n44, 203n47, 204n51
  The Revenge of Bussy D'Ambois, 8, 24, 126–34, 203n46,
    203n49, 204n54, 204n56, 204n57, 205n58, 205n60
Chartier, Roger, 42
chivalry, 5–6, 15–17, 20–22, 24, 27–32, 37, 42, 67, 84, 86, 101, 111, 122, 174n11, 175n10, 179n30, 187n24, 212n1
Cicero, 45, 96, 100
Clark, Ira, 199n20
Comensoli, Viviana, 211n36
Cook, Carol, 30, 33, 181n40
Correll, Barbara, 73, 209n19
Cox, Gerard H., 195n30
Crandall, Coryl, 142, 145, 209n20
Crooke, Helkiah, 87
cross-dressing, 8, 136–47, 155–57, 173n8, 205n1, 206n5, 208n15, 208n16, 209n17

D., T. C. D., 187n24, 188n25
dance, 19, 29, 44, 52, 53, 90, 131, 185n15, 185n16, 186–87n22, 192n4, 192n8
Davis, Natalie Zemon, 138
Dawson, Anthony, 33
Dekker, Rudolf M., and Lotte van de Pol, 141, 208n16
Dessen, Alan C., 61, 201n36
Di Grassi, Giacomo, 7, 44, 47, 49–50, 54, 57, 59–60, 183n4, 184n10, 186n18
"A Discourse of Duels," *See* T. C. D. D.
"Le Doctrinal des Princesses et Nobles Dames faict et deduict en XXIIII Rondeaulx et Premierement," 73
Dollimore, Jonathan, 163, 165
Dover, Kenneth J., 76–77, 193n15
Duell-ease, See F., G.
Dunlap, Rhodes, 198n15

Elias, Norbert, 41–42, 105, 174n10
Elizabeth I, 5–6, 16, 25, 28, 96, 176n14, 179n24, 179n29, 185n13

Index

Elyot, Sir Thomas, 96, 171n2, 207n11
English Masters of Defense, 19, 64, 178–79n24, 189n29, 190n35, 202n38
Erasmus, Desiderius, 212n1
 De civilitate morum puerilium, 1, 41–42, 70, 139
Essex, Earl of, 18, 25, 86, 179n29, 180n33, 202n44, 204n52
Evans, G. Blakemore, 121

F., G., 1–3, 98–102, 104, 107, 115, 172n3, 188n25
fencing, 1, 3–7, 11, 17–21, 27, 41–70, 72, 75, 80, 91–94, 116, 118, 121–25, 134, 141–42, 144, 153, 155, 160, 171n1, 178n22, 178n24, 179n26, 183n4, 184n9, 184n11, 185n15, 186n17, 187n22, 187n23, 187n24, 188n25, 188n27, 189n29, 189n30, 189–90n32, 190n33, 190n34, 190n35, 191n37, 191n1, 201n36, 201–02n38, 201n39
fencing-master, 11, 51, 54, 141, 178n22, 202n38
Ferguson, Arthur B., 175n10, 180n32
Ferne, John, 172n3, 179n26
Ficino, Marsilio, 136
Findlay, Heather, 195n28
Florio, John, 179n24, 183n4
Foucault, Michel, 14, 43, 56, 182n3, 185n14, 188n26, 189n32
Franko, Mark, 44, 186–87n22
Frye, Northrop, 61, 126, 147
Frye, Susan, 36
Fuller, Thomas, 191n3

Gaudemet, J., 13
Girard, Rene, 200n27
Glanvill, 13

Goffmann, Erving, 184n8
Goldberg, Jonathan, 194n17, 195n28, 195n29, 196n32, 197n11
Gossett, Suzanne, 190n36, 205n3
Grammaticus, *See* Saxo Grammaticus
Greenblatt, Stephen, 33, 135, 181n47, 182n50, 183n5, 209n17
Greene, Thomas M., 1–2, 22, 169
Gunaikeion, or, Nine Bookes of Various History Concerninge Women, See Heywood, Thomas

Haber, Judith, 194n20
habitus, 46, 183n6
Hair, Paul, 192n7
Hajnal, John, 181n42
Hall, Edward T., 46, 48, 53, 184n8, 186n19
Hallett, Charles A., and Elaine S. Hallett, 203n46, 204–05n58
Hayles, Nancy, 207n13
Hays, Janice, 181n45
Hediger, H., 46
Heilbrun, Carolyn G., 206n5
Heinemann, Margot, 198n16
Helgerson, Richard, 4
Henderson, Katharine Usher, and Barbara F. McManus, 138, 192n6, 192n7
Henry VIII, 16
Hercules, 24
hermaphrodite, 8, 136–38, 142, 145, 162–63, 205n2, 206–07n5, 207n7, 207n11, 207–08n13, 208n14, 212n41
hero, 5–9, 11, 22–28, 32, 36–39, 61, 67, 78, 79, 84, 127–28, 133–34, 147, 169–70, 180n34, 181n37, 188n28, 195n31, 197n12, 203n47, 203n49, 203–04n50, 204n53, 205n58
Herrick, Robert, 188n29

Index

Heywood, Thomas, 51, 141
  The Fair Maid of the West, Or, A Girle worth gold, 8, 140, 150–53, 196n6, 210n31, 211n32
  Gunaikeion, or, Nine Bookes of Various History Concerninge Women, 207n9
"Hic Mulier" and "Haec Vir," 137–38, 140, 167, 209n17
Holinshed, Raphael, 195n25
Holleran, James V., 124, 134, 202n39, 202n43
Holmer, Joan Ozark, 122, 179n24, 201n38
Holmes, David, 198n16
honor, 3–5, 9, 11, 12, 16–18, 25–30, 34–39, 55, 73–76, 84, 86, 90–92, 93–141, 146, 147, 150, 154, 158–66, 172n4, 172n5, 175n1, 177n17, 177n18, 179n25, 179n30, 181n38, 183n4, 186–87n22, 187–88n24, 188n25, 190n33, 192n6, 195n27, 196n5, 196–97n6, 197n12, 198n16, 198n17, 199n19, 201n38, 205n58, 205n59, 212n1
Howard, Jean E., 137, 155, 182n54, 185n15, 190n36, 208n15, 208n16, 209n17, 210n30, 211n33, 211n34, 211n36, 211n41
Howard, Skiles, 185n15, 185n16, 186–87n22
Howell, Thomas, 32, 34
Hughes, Paul L., and James F. Larkin, 185n13
Huizinga, Johan, 176n10, 177n19, 202n40
humanism, 1–2, 18, 20, 25, 30, 33, 93, 96, 97, 119, 169, 172n2, 179n30, 192n11, 212n43, 212n1

Ide, Richard S., 202n44, 203n49, 204n52

individualism, 9, 16, 23–24, 94, 108, 119, 122, 170, 172n4, 189n32

Jacobs, Deborah, 154
James I, 1, 100, 130, 193n15, 197n11, 197n15
  A Publication of His Majesty's Edict against Private Combats and Combatants, 21, 93, 96, 102–103, 105–07, 188n25
James, Mervyn, 30, 95–99, 196n4
Jankowski, Theodora, 205n4
Jardine, Lisa, 196n3, 212n43
Javitch, Daniel, 178n22, 179n28
Jeronimo, 178–79n24, 183n4
Jones, Ann Rosalind and Peter Stallybrass, 208n14
Jones, Ernest, 200n33
Jones, Richard Foster, 56, 188n29
Jonson, Ben, 177n14
  The Alchemist, 7, 62–70, 191n39
  Discoveries, 197n14
  Epicoene, Or, The Silent Woman, 124
  Volpone, Or, The Fox, 124, 188n29
Jordan, Constance, 137–38
Jorgenson, Paul A., 181n44
joust, 5, 15–19, 175–76n10, 176n11, 176n14, 177n19, 178n23, 187n24, 201n38
judicial duel, *See* trial by combat

Keen, Maurice, 15–16, 175n10, 180n32
Kelso, Ruth, 72–74, 172n2, 172n4, 177n17, 178n20, 192n8, 196–97n6
Kepers, John, 171n1, 187n24
Kiernan, Victor G., 175n3, 176n11, 179n30
Kipling, Gordon, 186n22
Kistler, Suzanne F., 203n45, 204n58, 205n60

Kistner, A. L., and M. K. Kistner, 198n16, 200n24
knighthood, 5, 15–16, 21, 23–28, 30, 31, 36–37, 65, 90, 98–100, 107, 172n3, 172n5, 174n11, 174n12, 176n14, 177n18, 180n33, 188n25, 210n28
Knox, John, 207n10
Krieger, Elliot, 182n54
Kuchta, David, 179n27

Laqueur, Thomas, 75–76, 79, 92, 137, 173n8, 183n5, 193n16, 207n12
La Touche, P., 186n22
Lea, Henry Charles, 13, 175n2
Leggatt, Alexander, 204n57
"Letters patent of the King for the Establishment of the Royal Academy of Dance for the city of Paris; verified in Parliament on March 30, 1662," 186n22
Lever, J. W., 204n53, 204n57
Levin, Richard, 115, 199n19, 200n26
Levine, Laura, 4, 173n8, 183n5, 190n36, 197n8
Levi-Strauss, Claude, 200n26
Lewis, C. S., 200–01n33
The Life of Long Meg of Westminster, 211n39, 212n44
Lllull, Ramon, 5, 97, 174n11
Lordi, Robert J., 126, 204n56, 205n58, 205n59. *See also* Chapman.
Low, Jennifer, 175n7, 202n41
Lucas, R. Valerie, 207n13, 209n17, 212n44
Lucifer, 1–2

MacClure, Millar, 203n47, 203n48
Maclean, Ian, 173n8
Maffei, Scipione, 97
Marot, Jehan, 73
Marotti, Arthur F., 4

Marozzo, Achile, 177n18
Mars, 88–89
Marshall, Cynthia, 125
Massinger, Philip
 The Unnatural Combat, 7, 71, 81–84, 92, 107
Maus, Katharine Eisaman, 33, 182n50, 183n6, 190n36, 200n31, 201n33
Mauss, Marcel, 46, 183n6
McCoy, Richard, 176n13
Middleton, Thomas, 198n16
 and William Rowley, *A Fair Quarrel*, 94, 109–18, 120, 197n13
 The Phoenix, 199n21
 and Thomas Dekker, *The Roaring Girl*, 8, 139–40, 147, 150–51, 153–56, 157–58, 188n24, 210n31, 211n35
middling sort, the, 7, 20–22, 94, 97–98, 103, 116
misogynists, 80, 140–47, 155, 209n22, 212n42
Miss Julie, *See* Strindberg, August
Montaigne, Michel de, 44, 197n9, 209n17
Mulcaster, Richard, 192n11
Mulholland, Paul, 211n37, 211n39

Naunton, Robert, 18, 25–26, 113, 181n41
Neilson, George, 12, 174n12, 175n4
Norland, Howard B., 148

Ong, Walter J., 171n2
ordeal, 12, 14, 122, 175n4
Orgel, Stephen, 79, 173n8, 183n5, 190n35, 191n36, 194n17
Ornstein, Robert, 126, 203n45
Ovid, 136, 207n7, 208n13, 209n21

Park, Clara Claiborne, 141, 181n48
Parker, Brian, 21, 198n16, 199n19, 199n22, 200n25

Parker, Patricia, 32, 126
Paster, Gail Kern, 41, 46, 72, 74–76, 78, 81, 87, 92, 173n8, 182n52, 183n6, 200n32
penetration, 7, 44, 47–48, 75–82, 89, 92, 194n20
Pico della Mirandola, 1, 22, 32, 136
Plato, 109, 136–37
Plautus, 64
Price, George R., 113
proxemics, 44, 60–75, 92, 184n8, 185n15
Pullin, Nicolas, 202n41

Quint, David, 42, 44
Quintilian, Marcus Fabius, 121, 191n38, 197n14

Rackin, Phyllis, 87, 98, 135–36, 138–39, 183n5, 188n28, 191n36, 195n27, 196n1, 201n35, 206n6
Rees, Ennis, 203n47
Rich, Barnaby, 72
Roach, Joseph R., 51, 61, 191n38
roaring boy(s), 6, 32, 58, 61, 66, 101, 102, 105, 110, 114, 117, 199n19
Roberts, Jeanne Addison, 210n26
Roberts, Josephine, 208n14
Rocco, *See* Bonetti
Romei, Haniball, 96–97, 105, 113, 116, 164, 187n24, 199n23. *See also* Kepers, John
Rose, Mary Beth, 211n36
Rowe, George E., Jr., 198n16
Rowson, E., 193n12
Royal Academy of Dance for the City of Paris, 186n22
Rubin, Gayle, 200n26

Saccone, Eduardo, 58
Sackvile, Edward, 18, 198n18
Saslow, James M., 206n5
Saviolo, Vincentio, 11, 19–20, 44, 46–54, 57, 59–60, 75–76, 116, 122, 175n1, 177n18, 178–79n24, 183n4, 184n10, 186n17, 186n18, 186n21, 187n24, 189n30, 190n34, 198n16, 199n18
Saxo Grammaticus, 201n34
Schein, Seth L., 181n37
Schiesari, Juliana, 20
Schoell, Franck L., 203n46
Schwartz, Jerome, 136–37, 206n6
Seagar, F., 73
Sedgewick, G. C., 195n30
Segar, John, 171n1, 187n24, 198n17
Selden, John, 12, 187n24
Semenza, Gregory M. Colon, 192–93n11
Senchus Mor, 175n2
Shakespeare, William, 25, 98, 133–34, 160, 177n14, 181n43, 191n36, 201n35
 As You Like It, 113, 125, 145, 194n17, 209n17
 Coriolanus, 78, 81, 194n22
 Hamlet, 8, 12, 94, 110, 118–127, 134, 184n11, 200n27, 200–01n33, 202n38
 1 Henry IV, 7, 12, 62, 71, 81, 84–92, 103, 175n7
 Henry V, 194n24
 Julius Caesar, 200n30
 King Lear, 126
 Macbeth, 126, 200n30
 The Merchant of Venice, 145
 Much Ado about Nothing, 6, 27–39, 117, 182n51
 Othello, 111, 126
 "The Rape of Lucrece," 74, 192n6
 Richard II, 13–14, 175n7
 Romeo and Juliet, 179n24
 Twelfth Night, 138
Shalvi, Alice, 196n5

Index

Shepherd, Simon, 137, 163, 210n27, 210n31
Sidney, Philip, 16, 24–25, 176n14, 177–78n20, 179n29, 210n28
Sieveking, A. Forbes, 174n13
Silberman, Lauren, 136, 206n5, 207n7,
Silver, George, 6, 19, 44, 49–50, 59, 178n24, 183n4, 187n24, 188–89n29, 191n1
Singer, June, 206n5
Sloane MS. 2530, Papers of the Masters of Defence of London, 190n35
Smith, James, 203n46
Smith, Thomas, 172n5
Smythe, John, 185n13
soldier(s), 26, 28–36, 79, 82, 87, 90–91, 109–116, 129, 130, 133, 158, 161–62, 172n2, 185n14, 190n33, 199n23, 201n37, 202n44, 208n16, 212n42
spatiality, 7, 41–92
Spear, Gary, 78, 81, 193n13
Spenser, Edmund, 136, 157, 206n5, 207n11
Spicer, Joaneath, 42, 44, 182n1, 192n5
Spingarn, J. E., 23
sprezzatura, 58–59, 89–90, 111
Stallybrass, Peter, 174n10, 191n36. *See also* Jones, Ann Rosalind, and
Steadman, John, 23, 36, 180n34
Stone, James W., 202n42
Stone, Lawrence, 3, 19, 21–22, 25–26, 28–29, 46, 95, 112, 172–73n5, 178n22, 187n23, 188n25, 192n6, 196n1, 197n7
Stoye, John, 19, 178n22
Strindberg, August, 64
Stubbes, Phillip, 205n2
subjectivity, 45–46, 183n6, 184n8, 194n24
suicide, 125, 126, 148–49, 165

Swetnam, Joseph, 210n24
Swetnam the Woman-hater Arraigned by Women, 8, 71, 80, 140–147, 150, 166, 194n19

Taylor, Mark, 182n51
Tiffany, Grace, 206n6, 208n13
Thibault, Gerard, 60
Tomlinson, Sophie, 191n36
tournament, 15–16, 176n10, 176n11, 176n12, 176–77n14, 187n24
Traub, Valerie, 91, 194n23, 195n31
Trexler, Richard C., 74, 77–78, 85, 193n14
trial by combat, 4–5, 12–22, 27, 37, 38, 103, 113, 122, 130, 139, 150–51, 174n12, 175n2, 175n4, 175n7, 175n8, 175n9, 176n10, 181n39, 187n24, 201n35
Tricomi, Albert, 203n48
Tudor, 3, 5, 8, 16, 20–21, 29, 55, 95, 97, 134, 173n5, 176n12, 176n14
Turner, Craig, and Tony Soper, 6, 46, 174n12, 184n12, 185n13, 186n20

Underdown, D. E., 192n7, 212n43

Vaughan, Robert, 209n23
Vaughan, William, 42
Vermeule, Emily, 79, 194n18
Vigarello, Georges, 42–44, 54–56, 60, 182n3, 186–87n22, 188n26, 190n33
Vives, Juan Luis, 74, 192n8

Waddington, Raymond B., 24, 203n51
Waith, Eugene M., 24, 127, 202n44, 203n51
Walker, Obadiah, 45, 58, 61, 183n7, 192n4

ward, 7, 44, 46–52, 54, 57, 59, 80, 144, 174n14, 184n10, 186n18
Watson, Curtis Brown, 196n6
Webster, John, 194n20
Wells, Robin Headlam, 171n2
Weste, Richard, 191n4
Whigham, Frank, 16, 169, 173n7
Whitman, Cedric H., 181n37
Wickham, Glynne, 15, 176–77n14
Wieler, John William, 203n46
Willoughby, Lord, 26, 159
Wilson, Thomas, 45
Wiseman, William, 23, 98–105, 107, 188n24
woman, 3, 7–8, 21, 27, 32, 33, 41, 44, 65–66, 72–84, 85–89, 92, 94, 98, 101, 108, 115, 117–18, 120, 132–33, 135–167, 170, 173n8, 175n9, 176n14, 181–82n48, 182n49, 182n52, 182n1, 187n22, 190–91n36, 191n2, 192n5, 192n7, 192n10, 192n11, 194n17, 194n18, 194n19, 195n25, 195n26, 196–97n6, 197n7, 197n9, 200n26, 205n1, 205n2, 205n3, 205n4, 206n5, 207n9, 207n10, 208n16, 208–09n17, 209n20, 209n21, 209n22, 209n23, 210n24, 210n25, 210n27, 210n31, 211n34, 211–12n41, 212n42, 212n43
Woodbridge, Linda, 197n6, 205n1, 209n22, 210n25, 210n31, 212n42
Wroth, Lady Mary, 137. *See also* Roberts, Josephine

Yachnin, Paul, 4

Ziegler, Georgianna, 73–74, 192n6
Zitner, S. P., 121–22